BRITAIN AND THE CINEMA IN THE SECOND WORLD WAR

Also by Philip M. Taylor

THE PROJECTION OF BRITAIN: British Overseas Publicity and Propaganda, 1919–39

BRITISH PROPAGANDA IN THE FIRST WORLD WAR (*with Michael Sanders*)

Britain and the Cinema in the Second World War

Edited by
Philip M. Taylor

Lecturer in International History
University of Leeds

St. Martin's Press   New York

© Philip M. Taylor 1988

All rights reserved. For information, write:
Scholarly and Reference Division,
St. Martin's Press, Inc., 175 Fifth Avenue, New York, NY 10010

First published in the United States of America in 1988

Printed in Hong Kong

ISBN 0-312-01605-0

Library of Congress Cataloging-in-Publication Data
Britain and the cinema in the Second World War / edited by Philip M.
  Taylor.
    p. cm.
Based on a conference held in London in May 1985, and organized by
the InterUniversity History Film Consortium in conjunction with the
Imperial War Museum.
Bibliography: p.
Includes index.
ISBN 0-312-01605-0 : $30.00 (est.)
1. World War, 1939-1945—Motion pictures and the war.   2. Moving-
pictures—Great Britain—History.   I. Taylor, Philip M.
II. InterUniversity History Film Consortium.   III. Imperial War
Museum (Great Britain)
D743.23.B74   1988
302.2'343'0941—dc19   87-27017
                                                                CIP

Contents

Contents

v

Preface

The essays which appear in this volume for the most part originated as papers delivered at a conference on 'Britain and the Cinema in the Second World War' held in London in May 1985 and organised by the InterUniversity History Film Consortium, in conjunction with the Imperial War Museum and with the help of the British Universities Film and Video Council. The Consortium was founded in the late 1960s and proceedings of earlier conferences organised by it have been edited by Nicholas Pronay and D. W. Spring in *Propaganda, Politics and Film 1918–45* (Macmillan, 1982) and by Nicholas Pronay and Keith Wilson in *The Political Re-education of Germany and her Allies after the Second World War* (Croom-Helm, 1985). For this volume, the chapter by Sue Harper was subsequently commissioned to provide an additional dimension not covered specifically by the conference, while Tony Aldgate's contribution was changed in view of the material that since appeared in his joint work with Jeffrey Richards, *Britain Can Take It: The British Cinema in the Second World War* (Blackwell, 1986). The other contributions have been revised for this volume, which aims to give an indication of the 'state of the art' of current historical research into the area of film and history.

At the time of writing, the InterUniversity History Film Consortium comprises the Universities of Leeds, Nottingham, Birmingham, Wales and Liverpool, Queen Mary College, London, the London School of Economics and Political Science, together with Westminster College, Oxford, and the Colleges of St Mark and St John, Plymouth, and of Ripon and York St John. The aims of the Consortium, apart from its considerable involvement in the production of educational historical compilation films, include the promotion of the study of film and the mass media from a historical perspective. Although its conferences attract the attention and attendance of film historians, both nationally and internationally, the contributors to this volume are historians with an interest in films rather than film historians *per se*. The approach and methodology of these essays is, therefore, the same as that employed by most historians, even though here the authors are dealing with a source of historical evidence that has only recently come to be fully appreciated, yet which continues to present problems of evaluation not yet wholly overcome. The films under scrutiny, for example, are not examined in isolation; they are studied in a wider context employing written records of production, government and reception. In other words, although films are regarded as texts in their own right, all the contributors recognise that film is an inherently persuasive medium, the significance of which can only be fully understood if examined in the wider context of the personalities, studios and society which produced the final product. Contextual rather than purely textual analysis is here the order of the day.

Philip M. Taylor

Notes on the Contributors

Anthony Aldgate is Lecturer in History at the Open University. He edited and co-directed *The Spanish Civil War* (British Universities Historical Studies in Film, No. 3) for the InterUniversity History Film Consortium and he is the author of *Cinema and History: British Newsreels in the Spanish Civil War* and co-author of *Best of British: Cinema and Society, 1930–70* and *Britain Can Take It: The British Cinema in the Second World War*.

Clive Coultass is Keeper of Audio-Visual Records at the Imperial War Museum in London. He is the author of several articles about archives, film and history and has organised various film historical conferences, notably *Film and World War Two*, as well as exhibitions, such as *The Screen Goes to War*. He was Vice-President of IAMHIST (the International Association for Audio-Visual Media in Historical Research and Education) from 1978 to 1985.

Sue Harper is Senior Lecturer in Literary Studies and Cultural Studies at Portsmouth Polytechnic. She has published widely in the fields of nineteenth-century literature and 1940s film, particularly on the Gainsborough Studio. She also publishes poetry and is an advisor and external examiner for the Open University.

Nigel Mace is Senior Lecturer in History and Film and Television Studies at the College of St Mark and St John, Plymouth and was Visiting Professor at Dartmouth College, New Hampshire, in 1983. He teaches courses on film history, film criticism and television.

Robert Murphy has written widely on British cinema. He is currently based at the University of Kent at Canterbury, where he is researching the final volumes of the *History of the British Film* series begun by Roger Manvell and Rachel Low. He is also finishing his doctorate on the economic history of the British film industry in the 1930s.

John Ramsden is Reader in Modern History at Queen Mary College, London University. He has produced the film *Stanley Baldwin* in the

InterUniversity History Film Consortium's Archive Series and he is the author of *The Age of Balfour and Baldwin, 1902–40* and *The Making of Conservative Party Policy*. His most recent publication is *Real Old Tory Politics*.

Jeffrey Richards is Reader in History at Lancaster University. He is the author of *Visions of Yesterday, Swordsmen of the Screen* and *The Popes and the Papacy in the Early Middle Ages*. His most recent books are *Best of British: Cinema and Society, 1930–70* (co-author), *The Age of the Dream Palace: Cinema and Society in Britain, 1930–39* and *Britain Can Take It: British Cinema in the Second World War* (co-author).

K. R. M. Short is Senior Lecturer in History at Westminster College, Oxford. He is the author of *The Dynamite War* and editor of *The Historical Journal of Film, Radio and Television*. He has also edited *Feature Films as History, Film and Radio Propaganda in World War Two* and *Broadcasting Over the Iron Curtain*.

Peter Stead is Lecturer in History at the University College of Swansea and has been Visiting Lecturer and Scholar-in-Residence at Wellesley College, Massachusetts. A former Executive Secretary of the InterUniversity History Film Consortium, for which he wrote and directed *The Great Depression* (British Universities Historical Studies in Film, No. 5), he has written articles in the areas of working-class and film history. He is currently completing a book on *The Working Class in American and British Feature Films*.

Philip M. Taylor is Lecturer in International History at the University of Leeds and was visiting Professor of Political Science and History at Vanderbilt University from 1983 to 1984. He is currently Executive Secretary of The InterUniversity History Film Consortium, for which he wrote and directed *A Call to Arms: Propaganda and Rearmament in the 1930s* (British Universities Historical Studies in Film, No. 7). He is the author of *The Projection of Britain, 1919–39* and co-author of *British Propaganda in the First World War*.

Introduction:
Film, the Historian
and the Second World War

Philip M. Taylor

For a particular generation that was too young to remember the second world war, or for those who were born in the decade or so after it, film has remained a vital source of 'evidence' for providing substance to the oral history on which they were weaned. For such people, in their formative years, moving pictures provided direct access to the past, the nearest they could get to the experience which had done so much to shape the world into which they were born. Churchill was the hero; Hitler the villain. The Italians were cowards; the Japanese were inexplicable. Dunkirk was a victory; Dresden was necessary. The Germans may have been formidable opponents, but their defeat made the Allied victory seem all the greater. Douglas Bader looked like Kenneth More, Rommel looked like James Mason and every RAF pilot should have looked like David Niven. And for the most part films of the second world war, together with post-war films about the war, confirmed the stereotypes. Perhaps such stereotyping was the inevitable consequence of victory. However, set against the backdrop of cold war, the traumas of decolonisation and the threat of atomic annihilation, culminating in a Cuban missile crisis that scared just about everyone out of their wits, the second world war became the object of what may be described as a cinematic historiography that often said more about the post-war period than it did about the war itself.[1]

The last of the habitual cinema-going generations was also the first true television generation. For them the second world war was ever-present, its glorification unprecedented due to the role which film and television played in post-war British society. When we were not playing on bombsites pretending to 'kill' our reluctant schoolmates who had the misfortune to be nominated as 'Germans' between Saturday morning matinees on how the *Bismarck* had been sunk by courageous little British biplanes or how British officers had

1

escaped from Colditz in a home-made glider, we watched the new magic box in the corner of the parlour instilling in us the merits of 'All Our Yesterdays' and 'Victory at Sea'. On school playgrounds throughout the country the great battles of the second world war were re-enacted, while growing numbers of German tourists sat horrified in British hotel rooms mesmerised by our continued war consciousness. And when, in 1966, the World Cup final was played between England and West Germany, did not one wag comment when asked for his views before the match: 'Well, we've beaten them twice at their national sport; I don't see why we shouldn't defeat them once at ours'?

How common was the experience of this generation when, in the 1950s and early 1960s, they returned home from school full of excitement at the latest history lesson which revealed what had actually happened during the war, only to be told by their parents that they had it all wrong because, after all, their elders and betters had actually been there! They had seen the war with their own eyes, heard it with their own ears and, for most of them, the experience was the single most important episode in their entire life, when they had actually been a part of history. True, many fathers had suffered the reality of war with all its horrors at various fighting fronts across the globe. Closer to home, mothers, grandparents and elder brothers and sisters had suffered also, whether at the hands of German airmen or as a result of wartime exigencies. But none – unless one had been very lucky – had been in the Cabinet Room with Mr Churchill when policy and military decisions of momentous historical significance had been made. They had, however, read newspapers or, even more commonly, listened to the radio or been to the cinema. It was from such sources that most ordinary people had gained their views of what was actually happening, developed their ideas about why they were fighting and why they were suffering. It was, after all, *their* war, The People's War, the first in which enfranchised men *and women* could help to determine the final outcome. And the values and attitudes thus developed were subsequently instilled into the 'baby-boom' generation. Not that those values *per se* were questionable; indeed, even most thoughtful eighteen-year-olds today would feel the war against Nazism was a 'just war'. But what was not appreciated fully by contemporaries, or by their offspring, at least until comparatively recently, was the degree to which those attitudes and values were being shaped by a British government whose control over the wartime media was near enough total and the object of admiration from no less a figure than Joseph Goebbels himself.

Propaganda has never been an activity with which the British have felt comfortable; it is felt to be the sort of thing which foreigners go in for and, in this period, it was inextricably associated with the work of Joseph Goebbels. But as the Nazi Propaganda Minister himself recognised, and just as his Führer did before him, the British have proved that they have a peculiar talent for propaganda, particularly in wartime. Hitler devoted two chapters in *Mein Kampf* to praising the role of British propaganda in helping to defeat Germany in 1918, and tributes to its continued skill permeate the second world war Goebbels diaries. In America also, British propaganda was felt to have been a major factor in 'duping' the United States into the first world war on the Allied side in 1917. Even today one is repeatedly struck by the somewhat antiquated images which still survive abroad of 'England' as a pastoral society and of the 'English Gentleman' as its guardian. But in Britain itself the myth that the government did little or nothing to promote such images, at least in peacetime, has persisted. In war, admittedly, it was necessary to employ certain 'un-British' techniques: to bolster morale; to prevent valuable information from reaching the enemy; to demoralise the opposition. Propaganda, Censorship and Psychological Warfare. But even then, whereas the Nazis had a Ministry of Propaganda which told lies, the British had a Ministry of Information which told the truth. The wartime reputation of the BBC appeared to symbolise the integrity of a democratic government at war. However, 'a common cultural conceit in liberal democracies is the belief that the amount of censorship at any given time is decreasing and that speech is becoming increasingly free, while quite the opposite situation obtains'.[2] The very fact that most people in Britain do not believe that the British normally go in for that sort of thing is, in itself, good propaganda.

Film is of course an excellent source of propaganda. But it is also a rich source of historical evidence unique to the twentieth century. If handled carefully, it can tell us much about the immediate past. Yet in Britain, despite the efforts of a few pioneers,[3] its significance was largely overlooked by many twentieth-century historians until the 1960s, when at last the influence of European and North American academic trends began to penetrate the inherent conservatism of the British historical profession. Progress, in absolute terms, was rapid, but compared with other areas of expansion within higher education it was far less impressive. For example, at a time when historians were scouring the somehow more 'respectable' official documents newly released at the Public Records Office under the thirty-year rule to produce a massive literature on the origins of the second world war, research into film was being dominated by new academic disciplines which tried to claim it as their own special preserve – often without reference to its historical significance. That particular strand of scholasticism has continued to grow, complete with its own language, to the point where historians infrequently understand the semantics and methodology employed. Film became an intellectual plaything at a time when the medium itself could no longer command the mass appeal it once enjoyed in the 1930s and 1940s.

By 1980 some film historians and film-makers had had enough. Kevin Brownlow launched a blistering attack in the *New Statesman* on semiotic film criticism, in which he argued that teachers of film in higher education (mostly, it must be added, in fine art or English, rather than in history departments, where film courses were still a rarity) were 'blind *and* perverse when it comes to Semiology and Related Jargon'. Brownlow saw semiology as a 'disease', a form of arrogant intellectual élitism dominated by Marxists who belied the purpose of both film and teaching as means of communication.[4] Paul Rotha agreed, stating that 'these "semiologists" so-called are a menace to serious well-informed film critics and a real hindrance to young film students whose number steadily grows'.[5] Brownlow's critics felt he had gone too far, maintaining, as did Stuart Hood, that he did not have 'the patience to penetrate beneath the jargon to the important issues the semioticians have raised'.[6] Perhaps so. But whereas many valid points have undoubtedly been raised by such scholars, they have not always been of particular use to the historian. This may well be the historical profession's own fault. As one basic textbook noted in 1976 (in a footnote!) 'of the three areas – theory, criticism, and history – film history is the one most neglected here. Not out of any bias, but simply because there does not seem to be as much activity, or at least innovative activity, in this area as there is in theory and criticism.' And the author added, 'I hope this situation will soon change.' Ten years on, much has in fact changed. Since the appearance in 1976 of Paul Smith's volume, *The Historian and Film*, many scholarly historical monographs and compilations have appeared,[8] while an academic journal devoted specifically to the area has been founded[9] and more and more history courses and conferences on the subject are taking place. Such activities apply the rigours of historical methodology to this vitally important instrument of social engineering in order to understand the past, to understand why people behaved as they did, why they believed what they believed and how their values were passed down to a generation which reacted as it did in the 1960s and early 1970s. Most historians now recognise that film is indeed too serious a business to be left purely to the semioticians.

Of the three principal types of film – feature films, documentaries and newsreels – historians initially concentrated on the latter two, partly perhaps out of caution, since features were invariably works of fiction (even 'historical' feature films tended to subordinate accuracy to entertainment) and they had anyway become the object of structuralist or auteurist attention, which at that time intimidated all but the most committed. But given the natural preoccupation of the historian with sources, non-fiction film offered a more familiar entrée into the brave new world of film as evidence. The initial work on documentary demonstrated that even these sources were not simply windows on the past. Although they used actuality footage, they did not provide us with unbiased records. John Grierson, the effective founder of the British documentary film movement at the onset of the sound era, saw his task as 'the *creative* treatment of actuality', while newsreels were also shown to be capable of being far more than simple recorders of events as though they were merely visual newspapers.[10] With an increasingly sophisticated appreciation of film as an inherently persuasive medium, and of the fact that fictional forms were just as effective communicators of ideas and values as any other, historians felt that the time had come to tackle feature films.[11] They quickly learned that there was 'no intrinsic difference between "fiction" and "factual" films as records of mass communication and that there were no distinctions in terms of importance made between them by the politicians, civil servants and others whose business it was to deal with what was then a new factor in national life'.[12] They also came to realise that the power of film as communicator rested on its repetitive and cumulative ability to emphasise stereotypes: the impact of a single film was limited compared to the constant repetition of certain themes over a period of time to a mass audience. Hence the rationale for the present volume which, despite the absence of any essay relating to the newsreels, concentrates on thematic treatments of British production by using wartime films as texts within the broader political, social and cultural context of 'Britain at war'.

During the second world war 'going to the pictures' remained, as it had been in the 1930s, an 'essential social habit'[13] and 'far and away the most popular entertainment',[14] particularly for working-class people between the ages of fifteen and thirty-five.[15] Indeed, following the short-lived and short-sighted policy of the government, which closed all cinemas on the outbreak of war, its popularity steadily increased. By 1945 30 million people were attending the cinema in Britain every week, a figure which had risen from 19 million in 1939. After November 1939 there were no fewer than 4000 cinemas in operation at any given time. Although the long-established dominance of Hollywood films was never seriously challenged by the British film industry during the war, British cinema nonetheless enjoyed something of a 'golden age' between 1939 and 1945, both in terms of popularity and creativity. Whereas the American motion picture industry produced an average of about 400 feature films per year during the war years, the British output was only about 15 per cent of that figure. Most of these films, it must also be remembered, were escapist, with comedy films being particularly popular. Even so, contemporary testimony was unanimous that the quality of British films had improved markedly, and they often competed successfully at the box office with the American product, both at home and abroad, to the point where (for what it was worth) some were even awarded 'Oscars' by the American Academy of Motion Pictures: *In Which We Serve* (1941) and *Henry V* (1944) were awarded Special Academy Awards while *Desert Victory* (1943) won the 'Oscar' for Best Documentary, even beating one of the now legendary *Why We Fight* series of films (*The Battle of Russia*) into second place. By the end of the war, when 80 per cent of the screen fare was still imported from Hollywood, the film trade 'discovered that whereas large sections of the public stayed away from the cinema 15 years ago rather than see a British film, in 1945 they went to a picture for the reason that it was British'.[16]

The admiration of the American film industry for what the British had achieved during the war was one thing, but the fact that this was achieved under the type of wartime conditions which the British government had enforced upon the native film industry made the achievement even more extraordinary. On the outbreak of war, studio space was requisitioned for storage purposes (resulting in a drop in the number of operational film studios from 22 to 9), technicians were called up, taxes affecting the industry were increased, as were seat prices as a result, film stock (i.e. celluloid, classified as a strategic war material) was in short supply and rigorously controlled by the Board of Trade, while wartime conditions inevitably required the introduction of a whole host of new regulations and arrangements for the control of morale. The simple fact of the matter was that any film which appeared on British cinema screens during the war could only do so if it had secured the approval of the British government, and in so far as the specific official body responsible was concerned, this meant the Ministry of Information (MoI).

Although the public profile of the MoI throughout the war was – with notable and well publicised exceptions – relatively low-key, its influence on all the various media of communication, on the means by which civilians gained their view of what was happening beyond their own immediate experience, was all-pervasive. Itself the producer of 1887 'official' films, the MoI was also responsible for approving (or otherwise) over 3000 newsreel issues and nearly 400 feature films. In other words, its influence was invariably more real than apparent. This was largely due to the highly effective system of censorship which the MoI was able to implement after its disastrous start to the war. In effect no newspaper article, radio broadcast or clip of film was allowed to reach the public unless the British government, operating through the MoI, allowed it to do so. This is not to say that mistakes did not happen; indeed, particularly during the early war years, examples of official displeasure at what was believed to be adverse publicity, or attempts to censor the media, did occur. The case of the news of the despatch of the British Expeditionary Force to France, when newspapers containing the information were actually seized from early morning commuters by policemen, was one well-known example of post-censorship (that is, closing the stable door after the horse had bolted).[17] Churchill's attempt in 1942 to prevent the film *The Life and Death of Colonel Blimp* from being made was another example, this time of pre-censorship (preventing the horse from ever being sired).[18] But what is striking about the overall record of wartime censorship in Britain is not the number of press articles or broadcasts or films that were banned, but rather the number that were not. By 1942 the MoI was operating such an effective system of censorship that even the majority of those 20 to 30 million weekly cinema-goers were unaware of the extent to which the images before them were being controlled by the government – despite that certificate which

appeared before every film and declared that 'This is to certify that
this film has been passed by the British Board of Film Censors'.

This may well have been conditioning. The certificate had
prefaced every film released commercially in Britain since the
founding of the British Board of Film Censors (BBFC) in 1912. For a
misguided period in September and October 1939 it had even stated
'and complies with the requirements of the Ministry of Information'. This type of naïvety reflected the general inadequacies of the
MoI when it came into being on the outbreak of war. Despite the fact
that planning for propaganda in war had begun as early as 1935,[19]
the process had been hampered by the policy of appeasement – the
aim of which was to avoid, not initiate, war – by uncertainty and
inter-departmental rivalry, by personality clashes and by philo-
sophical reluctance. By September 1939 the role which the two most
significant mass media, radio and film, would play in wartime was
still, astonishingly, undecided. Even where there had been concentration, namely on censorship, the preparations were inadequate,
resulting in those early farces, mounting press and parliamentary
criticism of the MoI and the physical separation of this negative
aspect of opinion-forming from the positive work of propaganda in
the establishment of the Press and Censorship Board between
October 1939 and April 1940. Gradually the BBC was able to develop
a relationship with the government which enabled it to retain a high
degree of autonomy and independence from MoI control, while still
functioning as an effective propaganda agency. As for the British
film industry, however, once the cinemas had fully reopened in
November 1939, there was to be far less room for manoeuvre.

In 1937 the President of the BBFC, Lord Tyrrell, could state quite
confidently that there was not 'a single film shown today in the
public cinemas of this country which dealt with any of the burning
questions of the day'.[20] This remarkable admission reflected the
existence, pre-war, of an already highly effective system of social
control. There had been no need to bring the productions of the five
newsreel companies (Universal, Pathé, British Movietone,
Gaumont British and Paramount) under BBFC regulations; for the
most part they had supported the government. During the war,
however, they were subjected to official censorship, both before and
after production. Indeed, as Nicholas Pronay's research has shown,
between 1939 and 1945 'the newsreels bore the brunt of the
propaganda war in Britain'[21] and they were certainly the most
stridently aggressive form of film propaganda. Given the emphasis

which the government placed on newsreel propaganda, nothing – not even the proven loyalty and patriotism of the companies themselves – could be left to chance.

In other areas of film production, particularly feature films, the BBFC paradoxically actually relaxed some of its more stringent regulations. Once there was no longer any need for cinematic appeasement with the declaration of war, banned pre-war political films such as *I Was a Captive of Nazi Germany* and *Professor Mamlock*, together with such anti-Nazi American productions as *Confessions of a Nazi Spy* and *The Great Dictator*, could now be shown. As one of the censors stated in October 1939, 'during wartime our rule against the representation of living persons does not extend to enemy aliens'.[22] But other regulations relating to non-political issues were also relaxed. Since a major theme of British domestic propaganda was that this was to be a 'people's war', films depicting the working classes in a serious rather than comical light were now allowed, as in the well-known case of *Love On The Dole* (1940). The working classes were, after all, not only the very people who thrived on the cinema, but also the very members of the community who would now be called upon actually to fight the war. In effect such changes constituted a revolution in British cinema history, and the skills developed pre-war by the documentary film-makers, for example, were now eagerly sought after by wartime studios eager to capitalise on the new sense of realism (or perhaps 'authenticity' would be a more appropriate word) which cinema audiences began to demand, the government came to promote and which post-war British television was to exploit.

That the British film industry was able to respond so effectively to the changed conditions brought about by war was due largely to the latitude which the MoI was eventually able to extend to it. The BBFC, that guardian of the establishment's conscience before the war, was ill-equipped (largely because of the staff it employed) to deal with the new circumstances, and its role in fact declined as the war progressed.[23] Not that the MoI was initially suited either. Film-makers may soon have learned that they could operate more effectively if they dealt directly with the MoI rather than with the BBFC, but they did so at first at their own risk. Alexander Korda had in many respects established the pattern by quickly producing (out of his own money) *The Lion Has Wings*, which reached the screen by November 1939, the first wartime propaganda feature film and one for which the MoI was grateful, though not responsible. While the

MoI went through its early teething pains and through four director generals (Lee, Pick, Monckton and Radcliffe) and four ministers (Macmillan, Reith, Duff Cooper and finally, until the end of the war, Bracken) between September 1939 and July 1941, its Films Division under the initial directorship of Sir Joseph Ball was also forced to ride a storm of criticism. One problem was that the MoI had not been designed as a film production outfit; rather, it was to commission films from the private sector. Ball's pre-war involvement in Conservative Party propaganda, together with his decision to rely upon the more commercial section of the British film industry (newsreel companies, advertising agencies and the like) meant that well-meaning artists 'were bound to say the right things the wrong way and to barge unwittingly into all sorts of political intricacies'.[24] The result was that the success of *The Lion Has Wings*, released with MoI approval, must not disguise the fact that two-thirds of the films produced for the MoI during the first six months of war 'were either immediately withdrawn or never released; those which were shown ran the gauntlet of pungent and increasingly hostile criticism in the press, and produced constant complaints in and out of Parliament'.[25]

Although much of this criticism originated from sectors of the industry excluded at first by Ball, namely the documentary film movement, cinema audiences did feel the same. Ball was abruptly replaced in December 1939 by Kenneth Clark, who knew nothing of films but who succumbed to public pressure. In the spring of 1940 the GPO Film Unit[26] was fully incorporated into the MoI to serve as a production outfit, renamed the Crown Film Unit and housed at the requisitioned Pinewood Studio. But it was only in April 1940 when Clark was promoted and replaced as head of the Films Division by Jack Beddington (who remained in the post to the end of the war) that the official machinery was to be put on a lasting footing – a system which incorporated the documentarists. Beddington, himself a former director of publicity for the Shell Group with its record of promoting documentary films, brought in as his chief adviser Sidney Bernstein, an ally of the movement, and as his films supervisor Arthur Elton, a prominent member of the movement itself. Another important appointment was Thomas Baird, an expert on non-theatrical distribution, who took over that particular aspect of the MoI's activities, which now appeared to be the area most favoured by the Films Division. The danger, however, that the new personnel would go over completely to non-theatrical production –

and perhaps alienate the mass audience still further – was checked by the report of the Thirteenth Select Committee on National Expenditure in August 1940, which recommended priority being given to theatrical mass distribution. And as an internal MoI document pointed out, for the film to be good propaganda, it must also be good entertainment.[27] Although the attempted documentary takeover of the Films Division was to affect official film policy for the remainder of the war, enabling the production *inter alia* of short films which were frequently critical of government policy,[28] the cross-fertilisation which resulted from the reforms of 1940 was a major reason for the second world war being a golden age of British cinema, an era which produced such highly acclaimed feature-length documentaries as *Target for Tonight*, *Desert Victory* and *Western Approaches*.

One significant result of this new phenomenon was the rewriting, cinematographically as in other popular forms of popular communication (notably the *Daily Mirror*), of the history of the inter-war years in the light of the advent of war, and particularly in the light of the wartime advent as Prime Minister of British political history's greatest film fan, Winston Churchill. 'Appeasement', a genuinely popular policy pre-war, suddenly became a dirty word, while its protagonists became 'guilty men'. Britain at war suddenly discovered, through the mass media but especially at the cinema, that what had been regarded as a noble policy whereby justifiable German grievances against the Treaty of Versailles had been rectified through negotiation had now somehow been disreputable. 'Munich', which Churchill had described in 1938 as a 'total and unmitigated defeat' for Britain's interests, was no longer the triumph represented by every British newspaper bar one at the time or by Gaumont British's famous eulogy to 'Chamberlain the Peacemaker'. Rearmament, presented between 1935 and 1939 as a policy designed to safeguard the peace so dearly won in 1918, was now seen – just as Churchill in his 'wilderness years' had maintained all along – as being 'too little, too late'. According to the British film industry, in other words, the war demonstrated what every sensible person had always known, namely that dictators could not be appeased, no matter what the price, and that armaments deterred rather than provoked aggression. The popular image of Chamberlain has never been the same since.

Because such issues were presented during the war as being inextricably related to a Conservative-dominated National Government in the 1930s, they unwittingly provided, as it turned out, a perspective which in 1945 was not only to prove self-defeating personally for Churchill, while serving the Labour Party well, but which also proved extremely valuable to British foreign policy during the cold war era. During the second world war itself, however, the now redefined ills of the past served to provide a justification for 'why we fight'. After a great war, a general strike and a great depression, the newly enfranchised British working classes may well have wondered why, a mere generation after the war to end all war, they were once again fighting German aggression. To find an answer they need have walked no further than the nearest cinema. Historians have at last begun to profit by emulating that example.

Notes and References

1.   No work dealing specifically with this topic has been written, but see R. Manvell, *Films and the Second World War* (London, 1974), from which substance to this claim can be gleaned.
2.   G. N. Gordon, *Persuasion: the theory and practice of manipulative communication* (New York, 1971) p. 502.
3.   Notably George Kitson Clark, who was involved in the founding of the British Universities Film [now: and Video] Council in 1948, and the founders of the InterUniversity History Film Consortium in 1968. For a history of the latter, see the introduction by Nicholas Pronay in N. Pronay and D. W. Spring, *Propaganda, Politics and Film, 1918–45* (London, 1982).
4.   *New Statesman*, 25 January 1980.
5.   Ibid., 8 February 1980.
6.   Ibid.
7.   Bill Nichols (ed.), *Movies and methods* (Berkeley, 1976) p. 3.
8.   Notably N. Reeves, *British film propaganda in the first world war* (London, 1986); A. Aldgate, *Cinema and history: British newsreels in the Spanish Civil War* (London, 1979); J. Richards, *Visions of Yesterday* (London, 1973) and *The Age of the Dream Palace: cinema and society in Britain, 1930–39* (London, 1984); P. Sorlin, *The Film in History: restaging the past* (Oxford, 1980); K. R. M. Short (ed.), *Film and radio propaganda in World War Two* (London, 1983) and *Feature Films as history* (London, 1981); James Curran and Vincent Porter (eds), *British cinema history* (London, 1983); J. C. Robertson, *The British Board of Film Censors* (London, 1985); M. Dickinson and Sarah Street, *Cinema and State* (London, 1985); A. Aldgate and J. Richards, *Britain Can Take It: the British cinema in the Second World War* (Oxford, 1986).
9.   *The Historical Journal of Film, Radio and Television*, founded in 1981

under the editorship of K. R. M. Short. In 1984 the *Journal of Contemporary History* ran a special double issue on 'Historians and Movies: the state of the art'.

10. On British newsreels see Aldgate, *Cinema and history* (op. cit.); N. Pronay, 'British newsreels in the 1930s: 1. audience and producers' and '2. their policies and impact', in *History* 56 (1971) 411–8 and 57 (1972) 63–72; Pronay, 'The newsmedia at war', in Pronay and Spring, *Propaganda, Politics and Film* (op. cit.), 173–208. On American newsreels see R. Fielding, *The March of Time, 1935–51* (New York, 1978); on British documentaries see Roy Armes, *Film and reality: an historical survey* (London, 1974); Eric Barnouw, *Documentary, a history of the non-fiction film* (New York, 1974); R. M. Barsam, *Non-fiction film: a critical history* (London, 1974); Rachel Low, *Documentary and educational films of the 1930s* (London, 1979), *Films of comment and persuasion in the 1930s* (London, 1979) and *Film making in 1930s Britain* (London, 1985); E. Sussex, *The rise and fall of British documentary* (London, 1975). On American documentaries see R. D. MacCann, *The People's Films* (New York, 1973).

11. The two most significant works following Richards' pioneering *Visions of Yesterday* (op. cit. 1973) were Sorlin's *The Film in History* (op. cit. 1980) and Short's edited collection, *Feature Films as history* (op. cit. 1981).

12. N. Pronay, 'The Moving Picture and historical research', in *Journal of Contemporary History*, 18 (1983) 3, 369–70.

13. A. J. P. Taylor, *English history, 1914–45* (London, 1965) p. 313.

14. Angus Calder, *The People's War* (London, 1971) p. 423.

15. Wartime Social Survey, *The Cinema Audience* (London, 1943).

16. M. Epstein (ed.), *The Annual Register, 1945* (London, 1946) p. 341.

17. For the full story see I. McLaine, *Ministry of Morale: home front morale and the Ministry of Information in World War II* (London, 1979) p. 38. This important book does not, however, cover the film propaganda activities of the MoI – a curious omission!

18. I. Christie (ed.), *Powell, Pressburger and Others* (London, 1978).

19. Philip M. Taylor, '"If war should come": preparing the fifth arm for total war, 1935–39', in *Journal of Contemporary History* 16 (1981) 27–51.

20. N. Pronay, 'The first reality: film censorship in liberal England' in Short, *Feature Films as history* (op. cit.) p. 124.

21. N. Pronay, 'The newsmedia at war', in Pronay and Spring, *Propaganda, Politics and Film, 1918–45* (op. cit.) p. 203.

22. J. Richards, 'The British Board of Film Censors and content control in the 1930s', in *Historical Journal of Film, Radio and Television*, 1 (1981) 95–116 and 2 (1982) 38–48.

23. J. Robertson, *British Board of Film Censors* (op. cit.).

24. F. Thorpe and N. Pronay, *British Official Films in the Second World War* (Oxford, 1980) p. 21.

25. Ibid.

26. P. Swann, 'John Grierson and the GPO Film Unit, 1933–39', in *Historical Journal of Film, Radio and Television*, 3 (1983) 1.

27. 'Programme for film propaganda' (Public Record Office (PRO), London, 1940: INF 1/867).
28. N. Pronay, '"The Land of Promise": the projection of peace aims in Britain', in Short, *Film and radio propaganda in World War Two* (op. cit.) pp. 61–77.

1

British Society in the Second World War

John Ramsden

Between 1939 and 1945 the British were *at* war – not just in a country that was technically going through a period of hostilities; not at war merely in some distant land familiar only from cigarette and picture postcards; not just at war with the honour of the nation at stake as in South Africa in 1899; not even at war as when the rolling boom of distant gunfire could be heard from the South Downs in 1915, or as when civilians scanned ever-lengthening casualty lists and dreaded the arrival of telegrams in 1917. From 1939 to 1945 the British were *at* war, as a people and as a nation, as they had never been before.

The physical face and sound of Britain changed within hours of the ultimatum that expired on 3 September 1939. The sound of the sirens that came so quickly after Chamberlain's broadcast on that Sunday morning was to be a constant feature of British life for almost six years. So also were the silence of the church bells, to last until they could ring out a message either of victory or invasion, the sounds of fire engine bells, ARP wardens' whistles and actual explosions of bombs and landmines alongside the sharper rattle of the ack-ack, and eventually the most frightening of all sounds – the engine cutout that heralded the approach of the doodlebug.

Eyes told the same story as ears. The British people became accustomed to the presence of a large uniformed contingent in their midst, and not only the servicemen of all the Allied countries that gradually turned a garrison fortress into a jumping-off point for the re-invasion of Europe: uniforms were omnipresent not only for the armed forces, but for many civilians too, for the massively expanded fire service, for the wardens, for special constables, for observers and fire watchers, for the land army and, of course, for the Home Guard. Even for those outside these semi-militarised ranks, the ubiquitous gas masks of 1939–40 were a common uniform of the new front line, a constant reminder of the universality of war, with Mickey Mouse gas masks a reminder of the vulnerability of children. Similarly the sight of familiar buildings sandbagged, their windows cross-taped against the effects of explosion, quite apart from bomb damage as such, was a constant reminder of an ever-present threat. Posters, whether directly aimed at public morale by the government and local authorities or, more inventively, aimed at sales by astute firms like Bovril or Heinz, all shrieked 'War' from every hoarding. What was not visible made the point just as effectively: no signposts; names painted over even on the notice boards of parish churches and post offices lest they inadvertently aid an invader; and at night practically nothing visible at all because of the universal blackout.[1]

Millions of people were directly affected by war in the most direct way possible – by conscription, by evacuation, by voluntarily leaving the dangerous zones for safer places, by the immediate experience of death and destruction. The effects of government policy occasioned by war – controls, taxation and above all rationing – ensured that war remained an ever-present feature of every family's normal life. The war itself as *the* fixed conversational point is perhaps slightly easier to grasp in the 1980s than before: for a generation that suddenly became aware of a place called Goose Green, of the relative fighting merits of Harriers and Pucaras, and of the urgency of getting home in time to hear the evening news bulletins in 1982, it is very much easier to imagine (or recall) the sudden emergence at the forefront of mind and conversation of Tobruk or Cassino or Bastogne, to understand excitement about the Spitfire's victory over the Messerschmidt, and to grasp the enormous significance of the BBC in wartime. Anyone who, in 1982, saw Vera Lynn leading the finale of the Falklands victory concert at the London Coliseum, watched by a vast audience on the BBC, may even have felt how uncomfortably close the parallels were getting. And 1982 even gave some glimpse of the consternation felt in 1938 and 1939 by a generation encouraged since 1918 to believe that war was a thing gone for ever along with a more uncivilised past. De Tocqueville reminds us that history is a picture gallery in which there are few originals and many copies.

The first and, on the face of it, most surprising thing to say about the British at war is how united they were. Surprising in view of earlier expectations for, at the time of the East Fulham by-election, of the Oxford Union debate and of the Peace Ballot in 1935, very few would have predicted the possibility of a nation that was united through an extended and gruelling conflict only a few years later.[2] Very few expected it and certainly not the government: much of its planning for a future war had assumed a far worse military situation on the home front than ever actually occurred – gas bombs, hundreds of thousands of civilian casualties, paper coffins and mass graves – but it had also assumed a cracking of morale and a consequent destruction of the social fabric. Hence the misguided plans made by the MoI for the first months of the war, a spirit of exhortation that entirely misjudged the public's mood; hence also the equally misguided reluctance of the service departments to release bad news and so take people into their confidence, even when the MoI itself realised the error and urged greater trust in the people.[3] But, as Churchill himself said on the outbreak of war, a democracy can only be effective in its war effort if it is united, and in all important aspects Britain was – and remained – united on the main issue. The cause of this, albeit coincidentally, was the failure of appeasement: when asked by his parliamentary private secretary at Munich what was the purpose of getting such an untrustworthy character as Hitler to sign that bit of paper, Chamberlain had replied that if he signed and kept his word, then well and good, but if he signed and broke his word, 'it will show the Americans what sort of man he is'.[4]

Not only the Americans, of course, but the British people too. Quintin Hogg, who fought the Oxford by-election of 1938 as a defender of the Munich settlement, switched over to the war party as soon as Hitler occupied Prague in the following March, declaring his own personal war on Hitler to the surprised guests at the Oxford Railwaymen's Dinner.[5] When Chamberlain announced the expiry of Britain's ultimatum he told his listeners that 'it will be evil things that we are fighting against' and, in a subsequent list of those evil things, the main charge was 'bad faith'. A few months later Hugh Dalton for the Labour Party wrote that 1939 was in every way different from 1914: then the nations had blundered into a war for which the diplomats of all countries should share the blame, but:

> this second time, just twenty-five years later, the diplomatic documents are very clear. This is Hitler's war. He was egged on no doubt by Ribbentrop and others, and some around him may have tried to hold him back. But Hitler knew what he wanted and had the power to take it . . . . Almost alone among men he had the power to choose, and he chose war.[6]

There is no sign that any significant number of people in Britain disagreed with this view, or with Labour's official statement of war aims, that it regarded 'this war as a lesser evil than the slavery which finally would be the only alternative'.[7] The later discoveries of just how evil the Nazi régime was – far more evil than Chamberlain knew in 1939 or the Labour Party were capable of imagining in 1940 – served only to reinforce unity on the issue of war.

There were certainly conscientious objectors (some 60 000 in all; a far higher number than in 1914–18), which is hardly surprising, given what Baldwin had called the 'wild flood of pacifism' in Britain less than ten years earlier. But what was striking was not how many there were but, given the attitude of the vast majority of the population in 1933–5, how few. George Orwell noted in 1941:

> At the moment when it seemed likely that England might be invaded, Anthony Eden appealed over the radio for Local Defence Volunteers. He got a quarter of a million men in the first twenty-four hours, and another million in the subsequent month. One has only to compare these figures with, for instance, the number of conscientious objectors to see how vast is the strength of traditional loyalties compared with new ones.[6]

Hitler did more than any man to reinstate the 'just war' response to religious pacifism. A nation whose government had pursued a policy of appeasement and whose rearmament had been both belated and defensive could go to war without any need to reproach itself about who was to blame, a principle that remained largely intact until the publication of a great many diplomatic documents after 1945 and the evolution of entirely different theories about the diplomacy of the 1930s by A. J. P. Taylor, Martin Gilbert and others. Britain therefore went to war united and with a sober, almost fatalistic, determination quite unlike the heady excitement of 1914 – as the novels of Evelyn Waugh or Anthony Powell indicate – and unlike the seething and discontented state of France so effectively captured in Sartre's *Roads to Freedom*.

It is generally agreed that the actual experience of war when it really hit Britain in 1940 accentuated that feeling of unity and acted in a number of ways to bring the parts of the nation together. As in 1914–18, casualty figures helped to unite a community sharing a common grief, if never quite in the simplistic manner portrayed in the 1942 film *Mrs Miniver*. The early heroes of the war in Fighter

Command were an élite force from a fairly narrow social background, much like the officer corps between Mons and the Battle of
the Somme, but they were soon joined in the casualty lists by
bomber aircrews of a greater social diversity, by thousands of
working-class seamen in the Royal and Merchant Navies, and by
about 60 000 civilians of all classes and ranks. Mass Observation
found almost a sense of relief in some southern towns when they
had their first heavy air raids, raids that enabled the local population
to feel that they too could suffer and endure something of what
London and Coventry had been through.[9] And when Buckingham
Palace was bombed nobody was more pleased than the king and
queen, who at last felt able 'to look the East End in the face'. Indeed
the monarchy continued to play an important unifying role, as it had
increasingly done since the 1935 Jubilee and despite the embarrassment of the Abdication in 1936. The king made important broadcasts, especially at Christmas; Princesses Elizabeth and Margaret
were heard on 'Children's Hour' while the Battle of Britain was
being fought; Elizabeth even had a well-publicised Royal Command
performance of ITMA on her birthday in 1942;[10] and the family had a
timely national war hero in Lord Louis Mounbatten, significant also
in the contrast his career made with his own father's naval eclipse in
1914.[11]

Mass evacuation and the life of the shelters provided eye-openers
for members of all classes. There were three waves of evacuation – in
1939, during the blitz of 1940 and during the flying bomb scares of
1944 – with over a million evacuees in official billets and many more
removed to the care of relatives or simply migrant refugees. The
condition of slum children came as a revelation to the middle-class
and rural families on whom they were billeted, and their social
habits a source both of amusement and of horror. Giles could draw a
Daily Express cartoon in 1940 in which a lord of the manor received a
dozen grubby urchins into his ancestral hall, they with catapults
hidden behind their backs, he with a shotgun behind his. Another
observer could write wryly of ladies who 'Inspired by Britain's
glorious cause/With seven maids to do the chores/Gather round at
country teas/And grouse about evacuees'. But the reality was that
many were truly shocked by what they saw and never forgot their
shock; *The Economist* claimed that evacuation was 'the most important subject in the social history of the war because it revealed to the
whole people the black spots in its social life'. It is, after all, one thing
to read about conditions in Jarrow or to see films about malnutrition

in poor families, but quite another to have the children concerned in your own home. For the evacuated children, the sight of the country and of more comfortable life-styles may well have been just as important, though the political and social impact necessarily came rather later.[12]

Similarly the shared experience of sheltering from a common danger in air raids was another social leveller, whether it be in the underground stations or in the basements of West End stores, to which so many East Enders trekked night after night in 1940. These underground shelters were overcrowded, impossibly noisy and insanitary, but Mass Observation found thousands still making their nightly move to the tube stations in 1943, months after the last serious raid on London. Shelter life had by then become a social norm in its own right and people were saying that they found it impossible to sleep normally in a bed. Even when all due allowance is made for the golden glow of nostalgia, it *is* clear that the life of the shelters appealed to many precisely because it was a communal life, a life of interdependence where sharing could reinforce a sense of security.[13]

Rationing and food control could have the same impact. Profiteering and conspicuous consumption, which had stirred up such strong feeling in the first world war, were far less important in the second. The points system of rationing produced a sensible compromise between fairness and choice and, while a black market selling goods to the rich inevitably developed and a so-called grey market of bargaining became widespread in some goods, they did not seriously undermine the rationing system as a whole. Rationing, on the other hand, had a beneficial effect in levelling up the diet of the poorest, especially children. The need for this had been clear enough to doctors and social investigators for many years before the war, but its fairly rapid achievement was one of the incidental by-products of the controls which were generally acceptable in wartime, yet so difficult to bring about before 1939. Much the same can be said for other areas of the economy. There was a sharp rise in the standard of living of men in work, reflected both by rises in wage rates and by the availability of almost limitless overtime in a war economy, but assisted too by price controls. The shortage of manpower that explains this improvement also goes a long way towards explaining the burgeoning powers of the trade unions: membership rose by a third during the war, even with millions of men away in the forces, and the movement as a whole made up in six years all the membership loss that had occurred during the bleak 1920s and 1930s. With Ernest Bevin at the Ministry of Labour there was also no danger that the unions would be kept at arm's length by the government machine.[14] Unions grew in confidence and authority as well as in membership.

All of this was a natural consequence of the slow but steady removal of the phenomenon of high unemployment which had characterised Britain continuously since 1921; even when Britain had been at war for a year, there were still a million unemployed in the summer of 1940, but the gradual gearing-up of the war economy whittled this away to a negligible figure by 1942, and to an all-time low at the end of 1943 when less than a hundred thousand men were registered as unemployed. The all-party government which committed itself in a 1944 White Paper to the maintenance of full employment was thus committing itself to the *maintenance*, rather than the changing, of the status quo. In this field, as in so many others, the coalition government was offering a policy that would be common to all the parties' manifestos in the post-war general election when it came in 1945. All parties committed themselves to carrying through a pattern of proposals that had been collectively agreed and, in some cases like education or employment policy, to maintaining that which already existed.[15] In that sense the 1945 result can be seen to be at least partially a vote for the status quo – for the status quo of 1945, that is, not the status quo of 1939 – rather than as a vote for change. Or, as Anthony Howard put it somewhat more controversially, 1945 can be seen as 'the greatest restoration of traditional social values since 1660'.[16] In one sense, of course, the popular achievement of – and commitment to – full employment marked a vital change from the political past: those mainly Conservative politicians who had maintained throughout the inter-war years that unemployment was as uncontrollable as the winds or the weather found that their credibility was shattered when full employment could be not only promised but actually achieved by 1945. The gaps between rich and poor remained very wide in 1945, especially in housing, despite wartime levels of taxation, but the division into two nations of the employed and unemployed was no more.

Employment could also mean working *together*, both directly for the war and in work of a more normal sort that contributed to the war effort. A host of good causes rooted in the war again fostered a sense of unity and of the individual's obligation to society: the requisitioning of railings for munitions (even a former Prime Minister's ornamental gates), saving of surplus rubber and paper, war savings movements, the Spitfire Fund and a hundred more such causes were essentially demonstrations of a voluntarist commitment to the war that went beyond such compulsory methods as taxation or rationing. The villain of such good causes, the 'squanderbug', was the symbol of greed and individualism run riot at society's expense. The common core of all such causes was a view of common ownership of wealth and the obligations of wealth that went far beyond anything that had been widespread before 1939. The experience of war work in factories or in uniformed organisations also levelled social barriers, especially for women: it may be said to have done for women something of what the shared trench experience of 1914–18 had done for men. The film *Millions Like Us* (1943) can be seen as the tip of that particular iceberg. The cinema fed this sense of the importance of women's war work with a new sense of realism, as one worker recalled:

> We wanted reality now, we wanted to be recognised. We wanted everyone who saw the film to see what we were really doing. And in these films, that is how it was, and we were really thrilled. We used to sit there and think, 'Look at that actress, she's working on a machine like I do.'[17]

Unity was also fostered in the advance towards a common culture that was a feature of the BBC's own contribution to the war effort. Often derided before 1939 as a remote educational medium for the middle classes, the BBC unquestionably broke through to a mass working-class audience during the war years: the increased production of radio sets (though never matched by the increased number of receiving licences) and big increases in the circulations of the *Radio Times* and the *Listener* all point to this breakthrough. The listening figures for such programmes as ITMA, Music While You Work and Forces' Favourites showed the BBC moving into a new down-market area of broadcasting for the masses, without ever quite losing its more didactic role – as the enormous success of the Brains Trust showed.[18] When Shakespeare failed, film producers could always turn to the phrases of news bulletins for their titles: *One of Our Aircraft is Missing* or *Fires Were Started*. Unity was, then, maintained and in many ways enhanced as the war progressed: a spirit of mutual interdependence that originated from the war crisis and contributed to the nation's survival through it. As J. B. Priestley told his radio audience in the last of his Sunday night 'Postscripts' in 1940, 'when so many of you wrote to say that I gave you courage and hope, I wanted to explain that it was you who gave me courage and hope, the truth being I suppose that we all gave each other courage and hope, like members of a sensible, affectionate family'.[19]

The British at war were also perhaps unusually conscious of their nationality – of what it was they had in common in Priestley's image of the nation as a large family. There was of course a major source for this national identity in the events that could be observed in the summer of 1940 and in the following winter: Dunkirk could be seen as a peculiarly 'British' sort of triumph, a success for improvisation and for private citizens in small boats; the Battle of Britain could be seen as an exciting gladiatorial contest, one open to spectators in the south-east, with newspaper vendors occasionally giving on their placards the numbers of German and British planes shot down in the cricket-score form of '128 for 33'. The fighter pilots of 1940 could indeed be portrayed plausibly as heroic young men with a rebellious and high-spirited nature as well as a taste for the calculated understatement, which was just what pre-war literature and films had led the British to expect from their heroes. The stoical endurance of London and other cities under blitz conditions was another source of national pride. Serious research indicates how nearly both morale and local administration broke down in Coventry, Portsmouth and Southampton, and how rumours of rioting and martial law spread in Merseyside. But these *are* isolated examples, and when set against the general pre-war expectation that bombing would create panic, disorder and looting, the endurance of British civilians under fire was a legitimate source of national pride. It was underlined by the opinion of foreigners like Ed Murrow and Quentin ('I am a neutral') Reynolds, whose pro-British reports to the United States no doubt helped enormously to reinforce the British people's high opinion of their own fortitude in their 'finest hour'. They were also fortified greatly in this by Churchill, whose sense of the epic and the heroic came into its own perhaps more in 1940–1 than ever before or later: his contribution through radio speeches was probably as important as anything done in cabinet or with the generals and air marshals, and in this he was uncharacteristically modest, at least in retrospect, when he said of 1940 that 'the British people were the lions. I only provided the roar.'

Churchill's sense of the historic (and of history itself) gave him the background for such a role, but he was by no means the only British historian to place the struggle in its longer-term context even while the battle raged. In 1940 Oxford University Press managed, despite paper restrictions, to reissue the collected war speeches of William Pitt the Younger (last printed, significantly, in 1915 and 1916), in due course no doubt cashing in on Robert Donat's success in the film role of *The Young Mr Pitt* (1942).[20] Meanwhile the weathercock of British popular historians was making the same connection to rather better effect. Arthur Bryant had in the 1920s written adulatory biographies of Baldwin and a book on modern Conservatism. He moved on to explicit criticism of appeasement and to become an advocate of rearmament via his three-volume biography of Pepys in the 1930s. Moved by the nation's finest hour in 1940, he wrote *English Saga*, which placed the contemporary national struggle for survival in the context of the previous three hundred years of British policy. Influenced, perhaps, by Charles Petrie's book *How Britain Saved Europe* (1941), Bryant went on to publish his greatest work, a trilogy on the Napoleonic wars: appropriately he published *The Years of Endurance* in 1942 and *The Years of Victory* in 1944, both books that sold widely and were widely read. (Here the analogy begins to break down because it can hardly be thought that there was much appropriate about the timing of the third volume, *The Age of Elegance*, in 1950.) It is no coincidence, however, that historians and publishers, let alone film companies, should be looking back to earlier wars for inspiration, looking though not to the painful memories of 1914–18 but to earlier epic (and unambiguously successful) struggles. It was perhaps equally significant that the historian who was to the (just) left of centre what Bryant was to the right, G. M. Trevelyan, was also hard at work. He had finished his trilogy on the wars of Winston Churchill's great ancestor long before 1939 and his interests now shifted far from that sort of history. In 1944 he too published his best – and certainly his best-selling – book, *English Social History*, probably more suitable than Bryant's work for the British people at that stage of the war, the apparently emerging age of the common man.

The extent to which 1940 reawakened interest in British history as a source of inspiration can also be seen in an increased awareness of the arts, both during the war and even *through* the war itself. Expectations aroused by the first world war and by the Spanish civil war as to the connection of war and poetry were hardly justified in the event, and the question 'where are the war poets?' became a lively topic of intellectual debate. Robert Graves pointed out in reply that mechanised warfare did not accord well with the needs of poetic rhythm (Vaughan Williams, though, like Shostakovich, had shown that mechanisation fitted very well with the needs of dramatic classical music). Now that the entire nation was in the front line, there was no public to 'warn' of the horrors of war as Wilfrid Owen had sought to do; the public could all see it for themselves. In fact, in the second world war as in the first, some of the greater poets were not recognised until some time after the event, as was the case with Keith Douglas. Others like John Pudney were not only known at the time but were often quoted on the cinema screen.[21]

Other arts flourished more obviously and with positive government encouragement, the theory being that literature and music were expressions of the human spirit that symbolised what the nation was fighting for. Hence, perhaps, the rather belated use of English classic literature by the British film industry where Hollywood had been plundering it for years. Such films as Carol Reed's *Kipps* (1941) or Laurence Olivier's *Henry V* (1944) were obvious examples, both in their way important vehicles of propaganda as well as being quintessentially English. Hence too the revival of the Old Vic company for touring purposes and the inauguration at the New Theatre in the last year of the war of one of the highest-ever pinnacles of British classic drama.[22] Government aid, channelled through the Council for the Encouragement of Music and the Arts (forerunner of the Arts Council) also kept alive a number of orchestras both in London and the provinces, celebrated in the film *Battle for Music* in which Malcolm Sargent conducted Beethoven's Fifth while bombs rained down. It led on too to the première of Benjamin Britten's opera *Peter Grimes* in 1945, another quintessentially English work and one by a pacifist. There was also obvious propaganda value in films of Myra Hess playing Bach or Mozart to a lunchtime audience including the queen in a darkened National Gallery from which the paintings had been removed, concerts that began in 1941. The fact that she was playing German music, as did other performers and orchestras, fitted well with the then official policy of distinguishing between Nazism on the one hand and Germany on the other. Mendelssohn, as a German composer banned by the Nazis, was a favourite but, perhaps with memories of *Triumph of the Will*, few orchestras included Wagner in their programmes. Visual art could flourish too, though many of the most memorable examples are not of conventional battlefield scenes but of the home front at war: Stanley Spencer's 'Shipbuilding on the Clyde' or Felix Topolski's 'Night in Dockland 1940' (both in the Imperial War Museum) are typical of the war artists' attempts to portray the whole nation at war. In 1943 *Picture Post* included a major feature on Stanley Spencer's work as a war artist, and a film about his work for the war effort was made in the same year.[23]

Some unlikely writers also contributed to the sense of national pride and national identity that the war was shaping, including such diverse personalities as George Orwell and Noël Coward, both of whom had in their different ways sought to debunk the prestige of the British Empire in the 1930s. Orwell seems to have been greatly surprised by his own sense of Englishness when it was put to the test in 1940, but *The Lion and the Unicorn* was an important contribution to the debate about national identity, the existence of which he not only found undeniable but also the most powerful of all emotions and loyalties.[24] Coward, as might have been expected from the side of his character that had produced the play *Cavalcade* in 1931 and had made his unashamedly patriotic speech at its opening night, now became a sort of super-patriot. His play and film *This Happy Breed* provided both a sly dig at pre-war governments and a celebration of ordinary English virtues, while *In Which We Serve* celebrated history, royalty, heroism and national unity all in one 1941 box-office crowd-puller. A song like 'London Pride' could encapsulate in one popular hit many of the cluster of interrelated emotions that the war evoked. The first two verses about the range of London life and London's past merely set the scene for the last verse, which begins:

> In our city darkened now, street and square and crescent,
> We can feel our living past in our shadowed present,
> Ghosts beside the starlit Thames
> Who lived and loved and died
> Keep throughout the ages London Pride

And so to the final chorus, which ends with the words:

> Grey City/Stubbornly implanted
> Taken so for granted/For a thousand years,
> Stay, stay/Smokily enchanted
> Cradle of our memories and hopes and fears.
> Every blitz/Your resistance toughening,
> From the Ritz to the Anchor and Crown,
> Nothing ever could override the pride of London Town.

Pride, history, class unity, the sense that this is an historic period and, above all, indomitable endurance: many of the popular themes of the war in one verse.[25]

In one sense this drive to a national identity and increased unity implied a wholly different approach to authority, the implications of which ranged from national events like the fall of Chamberlain in 1940 and the election of the first majority Labour government in 1945, through to local changes in areas, firms and other institutions. At the national level there began in 1940 a systematic destruction of the reputations of the ruling group that had governed Britain in the past generation. Their domestic policy was retrospectively invalidated when the war domonstrated that it was possible to achieve much of what they had said was impossible, and their foreign policy was in any case largely undermined by the actual outbreak of war. With the publication of *Guilty Men* in 1940 and its mass sale to a public anxious to find scapegoats for national humiliation, the hunt was on. *Guilty Men* was written by Beaverbrook journalists with the proprietor's connivance, and neither Beaverbrook nor Churchill himself did much to stop the witch-hunt which ensued; indeed, Churchill eventually put an official seal of approval on it in his own war memoirs published in 1948. From 1940 onwards the country was governed by a combination of the Labour Party and a section of the Conservative Party that owed its allegiance to the Prime Minister rather than to the party. This enabled Labour to make a smooth and painless transition to be the major part of the political establishment as the war went on, not least because Churchill and his cronies preferred to hold ministries where the actual war was being fought, leaving to Labour the more visible posts on the home front, the posts that had rather more to do with the post-war world than had, say, Harold Macmillan, stuck in North Africa.[26] Having hijacked his party and co-operated in the ruination of its traditional leadership, Churchill found that he had no credible team to lead the country for a peacetime government. Meanwhile, as Herbert Morrison told the king in 1945, the Labour ministers had learned from their Conservative colleagues how to run a government department.[27]

A similar challenge to old authority was to be found at local level and in the government machine when tested by war. Under the stress of heavy bombing much of the local civic leadership of Portsmouth simply boarded early afternoon trains and left for the countryside, leaving the city to its fate, a response that did much to weaken local morale and to destroy their own position as local leaders. In Plymouth, by contrast, Lord and Lady Astor were everywhere to be seen, Nancy dancing with sailors on the Hoe and doing cartwheels to entertain people in the shelters, and an efficient local government machine was staying at its post and keeping the emergency services going. Portsmouth, unfortunately, was more typical than Plymouth. As local government cracked under the strain of war, local leaders lost considerable prestige, and the regional offices of government ministries moved in to fill a vacuum.[28] Centrally, too, old methods and procedures were tested by war and found wanting: even a case like the Ministry of Information, a department which did not even exist until war broke out, turned out to be unfitted in both its organisation and its personnel for the tasks given to it.

Experience in the 1940 campaigns led to new methods for the selection of officers for the army, methods that went beyond the old informal interviewing panels to a more systematic evaluation of a candidate's potential with the assistance of psychologists. The same techniques were adapted by a radical secretary of the Civil Service Commission, Percival Waterfield, on the grounds that they would be needed for candidates who wanted to transfer from army to civil service when the war ended. The civil service proved a far more difficult beast to change than even the army, and Waterfield's methods struggled unavailingly against the force of inertia for the next generation, making little impact on the home civil service and none at all on the Foreign Office.[29] The old guard's resistance could be seen in other ways too, in the censoring of 'Cassandra' of the *Daily Mirror*, in the removal of a government subsidy from *Picture Post* so that its subversive message could not get through to the troops abroad, in the ultimate banning of J. B. Priestley from the BBC as 'too political', and in Churchill's attempts – in the end unavailing – to ban the film *The Life and Death of Colonel Blimp*.[30]

For all that, there did emerge as the war went on a new and more radical climate of opinion, as Paul Addison, Arthur Marwick and many others have shown. It was in many ways a non-party force, epitomised by the 1941 Committee, by the contribution of such thinkers as Keynes and Beveridge from a Liberal Party that was itself largely moribund, and by such non-political forces as the Church, the Teachers' Union, the doctors and the Town and Country Planning Association. Almost imperceptibly the emphasis shifted to these moulders of middle opinion, already an important influence before 1939, though never a dominating one. Now they had the field left open to them by a Conservative Party wrecked by Churchill and the war and by a Labour Party that knew it wanted social progress but had no very clear idea of how to get it.[31] Hence the war that began with a remarkable degree of national unity in the national cause of survival ended with a general election which, though characterised by a lot of party bickering of a rather nasty sort, had all parties essentially committed to the same programme. It was a programme which only Labour was well fitted to carry out in the circumstances of 1945, but it was a common programme which was already shaping the political positions of Harold Macmillan, Rab Butler and Quintin Hogg as well as of Hugh Gaitskell and Aneurin Bevan. Thus the war helped to set the scene for the consensus known as Butskellism, when for a generation, as A. J. Balfour remarked of an earlier age, the parties 'had enough in common to enable them to bicker about inessentials'.[32]

Notes and References

1. See, for example, Angus Calder, *The People's War* (London, 1969), Susan Briggs, *Keep Smiling Through* (London, 1975), and Charles Whiting, *Britain Under Fire* (London, 1986).
2. Martin Ceadel, *Pacifism in Britain, 1914–45* (Oxford, 1980).
3. Ian McLaine, *Ministry of Morale* (London, 1979) pp. 12–108; Tom Harrisson, *Living Through the Blitz* (London, 1976) pp. 22–4.
4. Ian Colvin, *Vansittart in Office* (London, 1965) p. 276.
5. Lord Hailsham, *The door wherein I went* (London, 1975) p. 116.
6. Hugh Dalton, *Hitler's War* (London, 1940) p. 10.
7. Ibid., p. 183.
8. George Orwell, *Collected Essays, Letters and Journalism* (London, 1970) II, p. 84.
9. Harrisson, *Living Through the Blitz* (op. cit.) p. 143.
10. Asa Briggs, *The BBC: the first fifty years* (London, 1985) pp. 176–237.
11. Philip Ziegler, *Mountbatten* (London, 1985).
12. Susan Briggs, *Keep Smiling Through* (op. cit.) pp. 19–36; Arthur Marwick, *Britain in a Century of Total War* (London, 1970) pp. 266–8; C. Jackson, *Who will take our children?* (London, 1985).
13. Angus Calder and Dorothy Sheridan, *Speak for yourself* (London, 1984) pp. 101–6.
14. Calder, *The People's War* (op. cit.) pp. 393–400.
15. Marwick, *Britain in a Century of Total War* (op. cit.) p. 317.
16. Anthony Howard, 'We are the masters now', in M. Sissons and P. French (eds), *The Age of Austerity* (London, 1964) p. 33.
17. Joanna Mack and Steve Humphreys, *London at war* (London, 1985) p. 120.

18.   Asa Briggs, *The BBC: the first fifty years* (op. cit.) p. 211.
19.   J. B. Priestley, *All England Listened* (London, 1967) p. 142.
20.   R. Coupland (ed.), *The war speeches of William Pitt the Younger* (London, 1940).
21.   Calder, *The People's War* (op. cit.) pp. 516–23. John Pudney was quoted in *The Way to the Stars*.
22.   Robert Hewison, *Under Fire* (London, 1979) pp. 154–5.
23.   Tom Hopkinson, *Picture Post* (London, 1984) p. 141.
24.   Orwell, op. cit., II, 74–133.
25.   Noël Coward, *The Lyrics of Noël Coward* (London, 1978) pp. 269–70.
26.   Paul Addison, *The Road to 1945* (London, 1975).
27.   J. Wheeler-Bennett, *King George VI* (London, 1958) p. 653.
28.   Harrisson, *Living Through the Blitz* (op. cit.) pp. 142–234.
29.   R. A. Chapman, *Leadership in the British civil service* (London, 1984).
30.   Ian Christie (ed.) *Powell, Pressburger and Others* (London, 1978) pp. 105–21.
31.   Addison, *The Road to 1945* (op. cit.).
32.   Introduction to Walter Bagehot's *The English Constitution* (London, 1928).

2

The British Film Industry: Audiences and Producers

Robert Murphy

Between 1933 and 1937 the average output of the British film industry was approximately 150 feature films (films of 60 minutes or longer) a year; during the war years it was only 42. The industry had suffered a serious slump in 1937, resulting in numerous bankruptcies, severe cutbacks and a considerable reduction in the number of films made. But there was another reason for the decline in output. The 1927 Films Act had imposed on the American companies which dominated the British market an obligation to supply a percentage of British films. By 1933, of the 168 British feature films released, 97 were commissioned by American companies. They included a handful of bigger-budget films, such as Alexander Korda's *The Private Life of Henry VIII* (1933), but the great majority were 'quota quickies' – very low-budget films with little entertainment value. The 1938 Films Act killed the 'quota quickie' by introducing a minimum cost provision and by allowing a double or triple quota qualification for films which cost more than the minimum. This made it possible for American companies to carry out their obligations by making fewer, but more expensive, films. Metro-Goldwyn-Mayer (MGM), for example, which had been responsible for some of the worst of the 'quota quickies', redeemed its reputation with a series of big-budget quality productions such as *A Yank at Oxford* (1938), *The Citadel* (1938) and *Goodbye, Mr Chips* (1939). This was part of a general realignment. The industry was no longer polarised between low-budget 'quickies' on the one hand and epics made with an eye to the American market on the other. And with films like *Vessel of Wrath* (1937), *South Riding* (1938), *Bank Holiday* (1938), *The Lady Vanishes* (1938) and *Pygmalion* (1938) the British film industry began to produce films that were as popular and as well made as their American counterparts.

31

A glance at the trade journals for the summer of 1939 reveals a confident and expanding industry. Odeon took over the American Paramount-Astoria circuit; Associated British announced record profits; a new distribution company, Grand National, launched itself successfully with *The Stars Look Down*; and Gaumont British announced the reopening of its Shepherds Bush studio, closed since the 1937 slump.[1] Indecisive, unenlightened government policy effectively punctured the industry's optimism. The closure of cinemas ordered by the government on the outbreak of war hardly encouraged film producers to carry on as normal, while *Kine Weekly* protested: 'Our immediate duty is to offer some outlet for the intelligence; to present in pleasant, harmless form, relief from the very ugly world in which we are living today. Can one think of a safer anodyne to the disturbed public mind than the screenplay?'[2] Although, in the immediate absence of aerial bombardment, the government was forced to agree, its films policy nonetheless remained confused and arbitrary. Studios at Elstree, Shepperton, Pinewood, Wembley, Walton-on-Thames, Beaconsfield, Isleworth and Twickenham and several of the stages at Denham were requisitioned. Film technicians, who were paradoxically accorded reserved status, were thrown into unemployment. By the end of 1939 frustration permeated the entire industry, as *Kine Weekly* expressed it: 'So what has happened? Film production has almost completely ceased. The Films Act would have gone within a week or two of the outbreak of war but for the violent protests of producers and labour, and British film production today has never been in a more parlous state at a time when its strength and vitality is all important.'[3]

The uncertainties of government policy left most producers chary of embarking upon any particularly ambitious production programme. Gaumont British did proceed with the opening of its Shepherds Bush studio, having agreed to supply the quota needs of MGM and Twentieth Century Fox (both of which had abandoned their own production activities in Britain). Michael Balcon at Ealing was in the middle of shooting *The Proud Valley* when war was declared and vowed to continue production whatever the obstacles. With his co-directors Reg Baker and Stephen Courtauld he submitted a plan to the MoI to subsidise production through the entertainment tax. Unsurprisingly, it fell on deaf ears. Associated British lost its main studios at Elstree, but Pathé, which was part of the same group, had a studio at Welwyn which supplied the ABC cinema circuit with a regular diet of macabre thrillers which included *Dead Men Are Dangerous* (1939) and *The Dark Eyes of London* (1939). *Traitor Spy* (1939), a melodramatic spy thriller, was also being made there when war broke out, and production at the studio continued on a small scale throughout the conflict. Korda's London Films, the other major production company, managed to produce the first real war film, *The Lion Has Wings* (1939), but Korda had already lost control of his studio and he seems to have reached agreement with his friends at the Conservative Party that he would be of more use to the war effort making pro-British films in Hollywood.

Of the American companies making films in Britain, Warner Brothers was the only one with an unrequisitioned studio, at Teddington. They closed it voluntarily on the outbreak of war but, once it became evident that the cinemas were attracting their normal number of patrons, resumed production and continued to make films there until the autumn of 1944, when the studio suffered a direct hit by a flying bomb. The quota remained in force until October 1942 – after America had entered the war – when it was suspended until 1947. It appears to have exercised little influence on the number of American films made in Britain. Most of the American companies made two or three films a year, generally of sufficient quality to ensure their distribution in the United States as well as in Britain. Columbia, for example, managed to steal George Formby from Ealing and cannily brought 'forces sweetheart' Vera Lynn to the screen. According to Joe Friedman, Columbia's managing director, 'it will be our policy to offer them [cinema exhibitors] British entertainment of the kind they can conscientiously screen, and which are not just so many legislative spools of celluloid'.[4]

But the most remarkable contribution to film production in the early days of the war came from British National, a small company founded by J. Arthur Rank and Lady Yule back in 1933. It had a critical but hardly a commercial success with its first film, *Turn of the Tide* (1935), after which Rank left the company to involve himself in more ambitious projects such as Pinewood Studios and C. M. Woolf's General Film Distributors. British National continued as 'a second-rate production concern with a casual output of pictures'[5] until the outbreak of war. Earlier in 1939 they had been joined by John Baxter, a young director who had been responsible for a number of interesting and low-budget populist films such as *Doss House* (1933), *Song of the Plough* (1933), *Music Hall* (1934), *Flood Tide* (1934), *The Small Man* (1935) and *Hearts of Humanity* (1936). Baxter's presence, combined with the outbreak of war, seems to have galvanised British National into action. While others cut back, the company announced an ambitious production programme and kept Denham studios open with the Powell and Pressburger film *Contraband* (1940).

Not surprisingly in view of pre-war Anglo-German relations, and particularly after the Munich crisis, a number of anti-German films were made before September 1939, though like *The Spy in Black* (1939), which was the most successful of them, they tended to employ a first world war setting. Others fell foul of the British Board of Film Censors until open hostilities made the need for cinematic appeasement less appropriate.[6] Even so, during the period of the 'phoney war', from September 1939 to April 1940, there is a noticeable light-headed 'we're going to hang out the washing on the Siegfried line' quality about many of the films made. Of the 50 feature films released in 1940 nineteen were comedies, and of these fourteen had a war theme. They can broadly be categorised as follows: (1) a number of semi-comic spy thrillers, such as John Paddy Carstairs' *Meet Maxwell Anderson*, Tim Whelan's *Ten Days in Paris* and Mario Zampi's *Spy for a Day*, which were all made for American companies (respectively RKO, Columbia and Paramount); (2) a substantial number of comedies which deal with life in the services, such as John Baxter's *Laugh It Off* (with Tommy Trinder), Ian Dalrymple's *Old Bill and Son* (John Mills and Morland Graham), *Pack Up Your Troubles*, *Garrison Follies* and *Somewhere in England* (the last three of which were made by Butchers, a 'B' movie company which rapidly adapted its pre-war output of musicals, thrillers and farces to wartime conditions); (3) a large group of comedies dealing with the unmasking of spies, saboteurs, fifth columnists and other undesirable elements, such as *All At Sea*, where aging music-hall comic Sandy Powell becomes a sailor on 'HMS Terrific' and comes into conflict with a gang of spies. Also in this third category falls *Under Your Hat*, where Jack Hulbert and Cicely Cortneidge go off to the French Riviera to recover a secret carburettor stolen by enemy agents, as well as George Formby in *Spare a Copper* and *Let George Do It*, Arthur Askey in *Bandwaggon*, Tommy Trinder, Claude Hulbert and Michael Wilding in *Sailors Three*, and Basil Radford and Naunton Wayne in *Crooks Tour*.

Around half the films released during 1940 ignored the war, many of them having been made or scheduled before war broke out, films like Ealing's *Return to Yesterday* and *Saloon Bar*, Gainsborough's

Charlie's Big-Hearted Aunt, and Warner Brothers' 'B' movies such as *Doctor O'Dowd* and *The Midas Touch*. The remainder, the serious war films, dealt either with the war at sea – Gainsborough's *For Freedom* (about the pursuit of the Graf Spee) and Ealing's *Convoy*, both of which were critical and popular successes – or with spying and/or resistance to the Nazis: Powell and Pressburger's *Contraband* is about naval warfare and German spies; the Boultings' *Pastor Hall* shows ordinary, decent Germans trying to stand up to Nazi bullies; *Night Train to Munich* combines elements of *The Lady Vanishes* with the story of a Czech professor and his daughter stoutly resisting Nazi tyranny.

Two other 1940 pictures are worthy of mention: Warner Brothers' *The Briggs Family* (with Edward Chapman), the first of the home front family sagas which culminated four years later in Noël Coward's *This Happy Breed*; and Ealing's *The Proud Valley* which, like a number of the films made in the late 1930s such as *South Riding* and *The Stars Look Down*, offered a moderate critique of society. With *The Proud Valley*, though, an ending which was to have pointed to the iniquities of the coal owners was changed to accommodate the 'everybody pulling together' ethos of wartime.

In the absence of statistical returns, any assessment of box-office popularity is inevitably subjective and imprecise. *Kine Weekly*'s Josh Billings explained in 1946:

> This is the ninth year in which we have compiled box-office returns, but although we have been frequently quoted and just as frequently condemned, we are still offered no voluntary aid and information from renters through their publicity departments. True, we get from some a list of their releases, but this contains no indication of individual successes. The information contained in these pages comes from executive co-operation – the renters sales departments and the circuit chiefs are always most helpful – and from our own, not inexperienced observations and system of check ups.[7]

Once a year Billings picked out around a hundred films, on a month-by-month basis, which appeared to have been particularly success-ful. Using this as a guide, British films seem to have been much less successful in 1940 than they had been in 1939, when a British film, *The Citadel* (albeit backed by MGM and directed by the American King Vidor), was considered the top film of the year, and when 25

British films were mentioned as successful. In 1940 the two top films were *Rebecca* and *Foreign Correspondent* – both, ironically, directed by Alfred Hitchcock in America – and only thirteen British films were mentioned as successful. However, most of these thirteen came from the studios which had made most effort to come to terms with the war. Five were produced at Gainsborough (*Bandwaggon*, *Charlie's Big-Hearted Aunt*, *Gasbags*, *For Freedom* and *Night Train to Munich*), four at Ealing (*Proud Valley*, *Let George Do It*, *Convoy* and *Spare a Copper*) and two at British National (*Gaslight* and *Contraband*).

The following year things began to look up. There was a slight decrease in the number of British films released, but the best film of the year – *The 49th Parallel* – was British and the number of British films mentioned as successful went up to eighteen. There were still a great many comedies, despite Dunkirk and the Battle of Britain; both Gainsborough and Ealing produced more comedies than serious films, and Butchers' topical 'B' movies again did well. Francis Baker, managing director of Butchers, explained the appeal of the 'Gert and Daisy' pictures which – along with the 'Somewhere' series – can be regarded as typical of Butchers' output:

> Gert and Daisy pictures are topical as well as funny. In the first one [*Gert and Daisy's Weekend* (1941)] the public is now exercising its laughing faculties for the good of wartime morale over the comediennes' adventures with mischievous evacuee children; in the second one [*Gert and Daisy Clean Up* (1942)], the lively pair will be hilariously implicated in affairs of the Merchant Navy, the black market, a salvage drive and a wartime Christmas party.[8]

Although about half of the films released during 1941 did not deal directly with the war, there was a definite break with the pre-war period. George King, for example, an independent producer responsible for large numbers of 'quota quickies' in the 1930s, was on the outbreak of war still making traditional melodramas such as *The Chinese Bungalow* and *Crimes at the Dark House*. But in the middle of 1940 he decided to form a production company with Leslie Howard, British Aviation, specifically to make war films. Their début was a lavish film biography of R. J. Mitchell, designer of the Spitfire, *The First of the Few* (1941).

A similar change occurred at Teddington, where Warner Brothers switched from low-budget thrillers and farces to a much smaller number of quality productions. In 1941 they released Thorold Dickinson's celebration of British democracy, *The Prime Minister*, as well as *Atlantic Ferry*, a romance set against a background of early transatlantic steam ferries, with topical references to the benefits of Anglo-American friendship. As to serious war films, Ealing enjoyed some success with the stagey, old-fashioned *Ships With Wings*, and the glamour attached to the RAF was exploited – in very different ways – by RKO with *Dangerous Moonlight* (1941) and by the Crown Film Unit with *Target for Tonight* (1941). However, the war films that proved to be the biggest critical and commercial successes – Powell and Pressburger's *The 49th Parallel* (an independent production backed by, among others, J. Arthur Rank, Oscar Deutsch and the MoI) and *Pimpernel Smith* – dealt with moral issues rather than with violent action: both concentrated on depicting the moral superiority of the quietly decent Englishman and his allies by contrast to the cold, ruthless Nazi fanaticism. Both share a thematic similarity with those films which celebrate Britishness either in terms of history (Warner Brothers' *The Prime Minister* and *Atlantic Ferry*, Gainsborough's *Kipps* and British National's *This England*) or in terms of contemporary society (Humphrey Jennings' *Listen to Britain*, Anthony Asquith's *Quiet Wedding* and, at the lower end of the market, pastorals such as *Sheepdog of the Hills* and *The Farmer's Wife*).

In some of these patriotic films, particularly those made by British National, there is an undercurrent of radicalism, a determination that the end of the war should also mean the beginning of a new and better society. For example, with unemployment no longer such a problem, the BBFC at last allowed Walter Greenwood's best-seller *Love On The Dole* (1940) to be filmed. Under John Baxter's direction this seemingly 'safe' subject was turned into a passionate denunciation of the misery and waste of the 1930s. The film was warmly received, as was Baxter's remake of *Doss House*, *The Common Touch* (1941), which combines his sentimental regard for down-and-outs with a powerful plea for a new society where the Rich help the Poor and property development is for the benefit of the people. Baxter was quite open about the propagandist aims of his films, though he was concerned that many of the films dealing with the war were alienating audiences by 'neglecting the dramatic possibilities for the propaganda potentialities'. British National, he promised, would deliver:

pictures with a promise of the better times that are to come, pictures that will show them just what we are fighting for, pictures with a glimpse of the better world we all envisage after these sacrifices and hardships are through, pictures that will spur them on to fresh effort and endeavour because they hold out hope and compensation for all they could have suffered – and what better propaganda could you have than that?[9]

Baxter's concern with the new post-war society enabled British National to operate beyond the confines of another debate: whether or not the public was satiated with war films.

Michael Balcon, enamoured of documentary realism since recruiting Cavalcanti and Harry Watt to his Ealing team, stoutly asserted the need 'to reflect each phase of the war'; despite the misgivings of some other studio heads, nearly half the films released in 1942 dealt seriously with the war, and there were another 10 comedies with a war background. The most successful were British National's *One of Our Aircraft is Missing*, Ealing's *The Foreman went to France*, British Aviation's *The First of the Few*, and Two Cities' *In Which We Serve* – undoubtedly the most successful British film of the war years. The popularity of war films was boosted by the emergence of an exciting new theme: the resistance to the Nazis in occupied countries. Powell and Pressburger featured the Dutch resistance in *One of Our Aircraft is Missing* and Asquith the Belgians in *Uncensored*. *Secret Mission* and *Tomorrow We Live* dealt with the French resistance, *The Day Will Dawn* with Norway. Apart from such films dealing directly with the war, Gainsborough's *The Young Mr Pitt* proved there was still mileage in regurgitating historical parallels, while British National attempted a home front saga with *Salute John Citizen* (directed by Maurice Elvey). Contrary to expectations, the suspension of the quota had little effect and American companies in Britain each continued to turn out two or three films a year, most of which enjoyed a degree of commercial success.

In 1943 the success of British war films continued. There was, after all, a bit more to show in terms of military action. The first of the documentary compilation films, *Desert Victory*, appeared and a couple of films, *Fires Were Started* and *The Bells Go Down*, looked back with equanimity, if not nostalgia, at the blitz. Fewer films dealt directly with the war but there was now a very definite war culture – populist, strident, sentimental, with an insistence on having immediate answers to the big questions of life tempered by an awareness of the absurdity of sudden death. The popular heroes of this new world – Tommy Handley and the ITMA team, Vera Lynn, even the Brains Trust – were duly recruited by the film industry. The example of *In Which We Serve* encouraged a trend towards ambitious big-budget film production. Powell and Pressburger made their first film, *The Life and Death of Colonel Blimp* (1943), under the umbrella of the Rank-backed Independent Producers Company. Two Cities joined forces with Leslie Howard and Derek de Marney's Concanen company to produce another four films in 1943: *The Gentle Sex*, *The Lamp Still Burns*, *The Flemish Farm* and *The Demi-Paradise*, all of which were successful. Two Cities also had backing from J. Arthur Rank, who was emerging as the most powerful force in the industry. Controlling two of the three major circuits (Odeon and Gaumont-British), Rank reaped the benefits of the boom in cinema-going, and money which would have been creamed off in excess profits tax was instead channelled into film production. As costs rose, the complaints about the lack of American 'reciprocity' over the distribution of British films in the United States grew louder and Rank made plans for a new international distribution company, Eagle-Lion, in preparation for a serious assault on the American market.

In 1944 only 35 British films were released, though this was largely the fault of the American companies, which managed only four mediocre films between them (*Bell-Bottom George*, *He Snoops to Conquer*, *One Exciting Night* and *Hotel Reserve*). The most striking development of the year was the intrusion of what might broadly be termed fantasy films. The success of *The Man in Grey* the previous year had indicated the public's desire for 'escapist' entertainment, and Gainsborough, the studio responsible, followed it up with another costume picture, *Fanny by Gaslight*, and two contemporary melodramas, *Madonna of the Seven Moons* and *Love Story*, which offended the critics but were highly successful at the box office and confirmed Margaret Lockwood, James Mason, Phyllis Calvert and Stewart Granger as genuinely glamorous British stars in the Hollywood mould.

It was not just a matter of the emergence of the Gainsborough cycle of melodramas. Comedies also abandoned wartime conditions for a variety of exotic locales. *Bees in Paradise* (1944) saw Arthur Askey stranded on a desert island ruled by beautiful women; *Time Flies* (1943) transported Tommy Handley to the court of Queen Elizabeth I; *Fiddlers Three* (1944) cast Tommy Trinder and his pals back even further to Ancient Rome; Clive Brook's *On Approval* (1943) begins with a montage sequence of wartime events before whisking us away to the never-never land of drawing-room comedy. Ealing, hitherto the bastion of war realism, released in 1944 *Champagne Charlie*, a celebration of the good old days of the English music hall, as well as Priestley's utopian fantasy *They Came to a City* and *Half-Way House*, one of a series of films exploiting the contemporary interest in mysticism and the supernatural. British National persevered with showing the faults of the old society (*The Shipbuilders*) and the problems to be faced in the brave new world of the future (*Heaven is Round the Corner* and *Medal for the General*) but occasionally drifted off into fantasy, particularly with Paul Stein's *Twilight Hour* and John Baxter's *Dreaming*.

By 1944 Two Cities had become the most important production company in Britain. With a lofty concern for quality production, it ignored the trend towards escapist fantasy and provided additions to cycles which had seemed at an end: Noël Coward's *This Happy Breed*, the most successful British film of the year; Olivier's *Henry V*, with its celebration of British heroism; and *The Way Ahead*, showing a cross-section of British society being welded into an efficient, homogeneous fighting force. Two Cities also attempted new developments with Bernard Miles' *Tawny Pipit* and Jeffrey Dell's *Don't Take It To Heart*, both of them whimsical comedies featuring a gallery of eccentric rural characters. Neither were particularly successful (although *Tawny Pipit* later picked up a cult following in the United States) but the formula was taken up with great success by Ealing later in the decade.

Despite the successes of the Two Cities films and the Gainsborough melodramas, 1944 was not a very good year at the box office for British films; 1945 was much better. Sydney Box's *The Seventh Veil* was the top film of the year and 20 of the 39 films released were mentioned by Billings as successful. The trend towards serious fantasy intensified. Ealing offered a superb collection of ghost stories, *Dead of Night*, and the costume drama *Pink String and Sealing Wax*. Gainsborough provided *They Were Sisters* and *A Place of One's Own*. (*The Wicked Lady*, released at the end of the year, was the top box-office film of 1946.) British National, while expressing concern for the problems of post-war society in *The Agitator*, also began to pick up on the cinematic possibilities of wartime spivvery and black-marketeering in *Murder in Reverse* and *Don Chicago* (though less effectively than Sidney Gilliat's *Waterloo*

Road of 1945, a key film linking war realism with the post-war spiv cycle). There was also a marked shift in the type of comedies made. The Flanagan and Allen, George Formby, Frank Randle and Old Mother Riley cycles drew to a close and there emerged a new type of sophisticated comedy – *29 Acacia Avenue, Perfect Strangers, Blithe Spirit* – which now attracted the audiences. With an end in sight, there was no longer such an aversion to war subjects. Documentary compilation films such as *The True Glory* and *Burma Victory* proved popular and, in the first flush of victory, there was a marked tendency to pay tribute to Anglo-American co-operation: *Great Day, Journey Together* and two of the most popular films of the year, Asquith's *The Way to the Stars* (Two Cities) and Herbert Wilcox's *I Live in Grosvenor Square* (for ABPC, which had been virtually dormant for most of the war).

It is debatable whether the British film industry would have acquired the sort of critical and commercial success which it did between 1939 and 1945 without the second world war. Though severely limited by wartime restrictions, the upsurge of patriotism and of interest in Britain's heritage meant that audiences wanted to see British films about British subjects. And there is no doubt that British film-makers did grasp the opportunities, both in terms of exciting subject matter and as a common frame of reference, offered by the war. But it was not just a matter of British film-makers turning to realism to deal with the war and then being enticed back to 'escapism' by commercial pressures. The war provided opportunities for film-makers to explore new subjects and to use new techniques, and it was an experience they were not to forget so easily.

Notes and References

1. *Kine Weekly*, 3 August 1939, pp. 3–9.
2. Ibid., 7 September 1939, p. 4.
3. Ibid., 11 January 1940, p. 2.
4. Ibid., 14 January 1943, p. 108.
5. Ibid., 8 January 1942, p. 56.
6. J. C. Robertson, *The British Board of Film Censors* (London, 1985).
7. *Kine Weekly*, 19 December 1946, p. 47.
8. Ibid., 8 January 1942, p. 42.
9. Ibid., 14 January 1943, p. 103.

3

National Identity in British Wartime Films

Jeffrey Richards

Joan Rockwell has written:

My basic premise is that literature neither 'reflects' nor 'arises from' society, but rather is an integral part of it and should be recognised as being as much so as any institution, the Family for instance or the State . . . Fiction is a social product, but it also 'produces' society . . . Fiction is not only a representation of social reality, but also a necessary functional part of social control, and also paradoxically an important element in social change. It plays a large part in the socialization of infants, . . . in the conduct of politics, and in general gives symbols and modes of life to the population, particularly in those less easily defined areas such as norms, values and personal and inter-personal behaviour. The implications of this are that fiction can give us two types of information about society: first, in a descriptive way, facts about the state of technology, laws, customs, social structure and institutions. Second, more subtle and less easily obtained information about values and attitudes.[1]

I would suggest that this is also true of films, which have functioned continuously as an agent of instruction and social control, not in isolation but as part of the wider national culture. Cinema is, in the Gramscian sense, one of the structures that transmits and promotes the dominant national ideology and creates and preserves for it a consensus of support. The status quo is not, of course, static: it can – and does – change, and the consensus with it. It did so classically during world war two when, as Paul Addison has so persuasively argued, a new political consensus emerged to replace that of the 1930s.[2] That new consensus, transcending class and party, was based on a belief in the welfare state, full employment and Keynesian economics. A similar consensus emerged about the national character though, in this case, it was not a new consensus but merely an intensification and an affirmation of an existing view. Indeed, the projection of an approved view of the national character was on the agenda for wartime film-makers, as the Ministry of Information's memorandum which outlined the desired propaganda themes for cinematic dramatisation indicated by specifically pointing to the value of the feature film in conveying 'British life and character' (showing 'our independence, toughness of fibre, sympathy with the underdog etc.').[3]

In fact one of the most valuable tasks which the cinema could perform in wartime was to project an image of the national character and the national identity that would promote support for the war effort and attract the sympathy and support of overseas allies. It has been unfashionable in academic circles in recent years to talk of national character because of its nineteenth-century overtones of race, class and empire. But the study of a nation's self-image seems to me to be a crucial element in understanding its actions, both internal and external. In these matters I share the view articulated by Sir Ernest Barker in 1927 when he pointed out that national character or identity is essentially a cultural product:

> Not only is national character made; it continues to be made and re-made. It is not made once and for all; it always remains, in its measure, modifiable. A nation may alter its character in the course of its history to suit new conditions or to fit new purposes.[4]

There can be alternative views of the national character, but there will always be a dominant one, and it will be the dominant one which will be enshrined in, transmitted by and promoted through popular culture, and in particular by the cinema.

Shakespeare was quoted regularly in British wartime propaganda. His most frequently used speech was that of John of Gaunt on his deathbed ('. . . this earth, this realm, this England') from *Richard II*. It turned up regularly on the wireless, in patriotic anthologies and in morale-boosting stage presentations. It gave the cinema no fewer than three film titles: *This England* (1941), *The Demi-Paradise* (1943) and *This Happy Breed* (1944), and I want to examine in some detail their 'blessed plots' in search of the cinematic projection of the national identity. The first factor that should be noted is that despite the almost obligatory presence of Gordon Jackson or John Laurie as the token Scotsman in films which depicted the national effort in microcosm (*The Foreman Went to France* (1942); *Millions Like Us* (1943); *The Way Ahead* (1944)) and despite the occasional nods in the direction of Wales (*The Proud Valley* (1940); *The Silent Village* (1942)), the national identity derived almost entirely from England, which was often used interchangeably with Britain to describe the nation. I shall perforce do the same with apologies to the Celtic fringe.

The film *This England* (tactfully retitled *Our Heritage* for its Scottish release) typifies the tendency of wartime propagandists to draw on the rural myth to define the nation. The celebration of the countryside as a source of national strength has been brilliantly expounded and indeed indicted by Martin Wiener.[5] Wiener sees the glorification of the countryside and all things rural as a deliberate rejection of the urban and industrial reality of Britain by a non-industrial, non-innovative and anti-materialist patrician culture. It was endorsed by a gentrified bourgeoisie which, having made its money, sought to turn itself into country gentlemen and distance itself from the 'dark satanic mills' where its 'brass' had been made. The rural myth, pumped out in novels, poems, paintings and advertisements from the 1880s onwards, had a direct effect on evocations of the national character. The Englishman was said to be at heart a countryman, and his character – thanks to his rural roots – to be based upon the principles of balance, peacefulness, traditionalism and spirituality.

The widespread dissemination of the rural myth is to be explained in part by its appeal both to the Romantic Right and to the Romantic Left. For the right the country meant the country house and the country church, the squire and the parson, and a deferential, hierarchical society. For the left it meant folk music, the village community, rural crafts and honest peasantry. Over the years the rural myth would count amongst its proponents such disparate figures as Rudyard Kipling and William Morris, Stanley Baldwin and F. R. Leavis. What united them was a distaste for modern industrial society which drove them to look back to some Arcadian golden age before the industrial revolution.

The attitude is typically embodied in a collection of essays, extracts and poems edited by J. B. Priestley under the title *Our Nation's Heritage*, first published in 1939 and reprinted in 1940. It concentrated exclusively on the countryside and contained a piece written in 1927 by H. V. Morton, the prolific travel writer and rural mythographer, who declared:

The village that symbolises England sleeps in the subconscious-
ness of many a townsman. A little London factory hand whom I
met during the war confessed to me when pressed and after great
mental difficulty that he visualised the England he was fighting
for . . . not as London, nor as his own street, but as Epping Forest,
the green place where he had spent bank holidays. And I think
most of us did. The village and the English countryside are the
germs of all that we are and all that we have become: our
manufacturing cities belong to the last century and a half; our
villages stand with their roots in the Heptarchy.[6]

Morton was talking of world war one, but the same theme recurred
in world war two. One of the most popular songs of the second war
was 'There'll always be an England'. And what sort of England?

> There'll always be an England while there's a country lane,
> As long as there's a cottage small beside a field of grain.

When Ivor Novello composed a special wartime song, it ran:

> We'll remember the meadows and the fields of weaving corn
> We'll remember the music of the land where we were born
> We'll remember the laughter and the sunshine after rain
> And we'll grin, grin, grin till we win, win, win
> And they come back again.

It did not, however, achieve the same success as his world war one
anthem, 'Keep the Home Fires Burning'.

Latterday commentators have had fun with such conceits. Angus
Calder, not unjustly, noted:

> Georgian poets and their associated cricket correspondents had
> dwelled nostalgically on the beauties of the English countryside
> and the virtues of the English yokel, while the former had
> decayed and the latter, if they had much enterprise, had fled to
> the towns. Even during the war, many writers who should have
> known better implied that the soldiers and airmen were dying to
> preserve an essentially rural Britain . . . In fact, as evacuated
> schoolteachers found, the more picturesque parts of Britain were
> inhabited by increasingly demoralised, and often remarkably
> incestuous, communities of near paupers.[7]

Even during the war itself the rural fallacy was exposed by Sir Denis Brogan in his book *The English People* (1943):

> To believe that a people who have for generations lived in towns, of whom only a small proportion has any direct connection with the land, has in some mystical way evaded the consequences of this state of affairs, is to believe in miracles . . . This illusion . . . that England is full of workers anxious to return to the land which their great grandfathers left . . . is widely spread in England because two different things are confused, the love of flowers, gardens, open spaces and the holiday delights of rural life, with the less picturesque, less common, less literary passion for the utilisation of the land that marks the true farmer or the true peasant . . . A nation of flower-growers like the English is a nation of shop-keepers, not a nation of farmers.[8]

Whereas Wiener regards the rural myth as a powerful factor in Britain's industrial decline, promoting hostility to progress, innovation, enterprise and industrialisation, the myth nonetheless served an important role during the war. For while cities could be blitzed and bombed, the countryside remained – eternal, timeless, self-renewing and indestructible: a fitting symbol for Britain at bay. It is significant that in *The Way Ahead*, Carol Reed's 1944 film about a unit of conscripts, when the soldiers gather round a wireless in North Africa it is a talk about the countryside at harvest – a moment that plunges them into instant nostalgia for their homeland.

The complex of images and ideas embodied in the rural myth was dramatised in *This England*. It was prefaced by a poem:

> The earth of England is an old, old earth,
> Her autumn mists, her brambleberry flame,
> Her tangled, rain-soaked grass, were still the same
> Time out of mind before the Romans came,
> Though from the skies men hurl their slaughter down
> Still there will be the bracken turning brown.

The opening narration sets the tone for a film in which industrialisation is seen as an aberration, and rural life and work on the land the ideal: 'This England, among whose hills and valleys since the beginning of time have stood old farms and villages. The story of Rookeby's farm and the village of Clevely is the story of them all.' In view of this it is perhaps not inappropriate that the film should have about it the air of a glorified village pageant. The action centres on four episodes from Britain's past, all designed to stress her heroic spirit in times of adversity: the Norman conquest, the Spanish Armada, the Napoleonic wars and the first world war. The film stresses the timelessness and eternity of England and the English by having the same actors play the same symbolic roles in each episode: vicar, doctor, blacksmith, publican and – in particular – yeoman farmer Rookeby (John Clements) and farm labourer Appleyard (Emlyn Williams). It shows that they are prepared to fight and kill to defend the land, and it ends with the characters once more involved in a war and John Clements reciting the 'This England' speech.

In locating the nation's source of strength as an alliance of country gentry and rural working class against foreign aggression in order to defend the land, the film provides the necessary consensual message for a national effort in wartime. But in coupling this national resistance with local resistance in 1086, 1588 and 1804 against oppressive, corrupt or neglectful landlords, the film adds a distinctly radical element which mirrors the shift to the left in the national mood and the desire for a fairer, more just and humane post-war society which led to the election of the Labour government in 1945. It is significant that it is Appleyard – the working class 'hodge' figure – who is the perpetual conscience of gentleman farmer Rookeby, reminding him of his duty to the land in 1588 and 1804 when he is tempted to abandon the farm for a different way of life. It is perhaps equally significant that Appleyard remains the servant and Rookeby the master. Revolution, after all, must not be carried too far.

But *This England* was not a terribly good film and three later, and much better, films express the rural myth more convincingly.[9] The enchanting *Tawny Pipit* (1944) was written and directed by Bernard Miles and Charles Saunders. Taking full advantage of the glorious rural location shooting, it tells how the local squire and the local vicar mobilise the village of Lipsbury Lea to protect the breeding ground of the rare tawny pipit birds. The defence of the pipits is the difference between the forces of democracy and the Hun. It is why we fight, as the squire Colonel Barton-Barrington (Bernard Miles) declares: 'Love of animals and nature is part and parcel of the British way of life.' The story, however, has an even wider symbolic significance. The village is Britain, electing to fight under its traditional leaders by democratic decision. They have to fight the forces of the Military (the army wants to use the breeding area for tank manoeuvres), of Bureaucracy (the Ministry of Agriculture wants to plough it up) and of Fifth Columnists (villainous egg-stealers infiltrate the village to appropriate the pipits' eggs). They also have a gallant ally in the person of a Russian sniper, Lieutenant Bokolova, who is saluted by the village children with a spirited rendition of the *Internationale*. The war brings to the countryside erstwhile nightclubbers as land girls and cockney kids as evacuees. They are all made better, both physically and spiritually, by their contact with the countryside and the pipits. A convalescing RAF pilot and his nurse play a prominent part in the struggle for the pipits, an equation of their work in the actual war effort with this symbolic struggle for Britain's national heritage. At the end the pilot, now recovered, flies his plane, renamed *Anthus Campestris* (tawny pipit), over the village, dipping his wings in honour of the birds. The symbolism has become a fighting truth.

There is a radical tinge to another rural drama: Cavalcanti's *Went the Day Well?* (1942), a powerful and at times chilling account of the occupation of the English village of Bramley End by German paratroopers. 'There'll always be an England' is heard on the wireless at the manor house and the film lays the usual stress on the beauty and tranquillity of the Chiltern countryside, an idyllic setting which makes the intrusion of Nazi brutality and violence all the more horrific. But the village is also characterised by those elements of Englishness seen to be derived from the countryside: peaceful-ness, traditionalism and spirituality. The peacefulness is clear from the outset. Bramley End is a society that is warmly communal, devout and cheerfully deferential to its 'natural' leaders of the upper and upper-middle class. The chief focal points of village life are the pub (where the community celebrates its communality), the church (where it consummates its spirituality) and the manor house (home of the autocratic local chatelaine, Mrs Fraser).

Obedient to the concept of the 'people's war', a central theme of wartime propaganda, the whole village community unites: the publican and his sailor son, the land girl, the sexton, the postmis-tress, the policeman – all play their part, and some lose their lives, to regain their freedom from the Germans. But there is radicalism in the suggestion of the unsoundness of the old ruling class. The local squire, Oliver Wilsford (Leslie Banks), turns out to be a fifth columnist and the snobbish though likable Mrs Fraser complacently disregards evidence of German infiltration. The German officers,

Ortler and Jung, posing as Englishmen, move easily amongst the ruling circles of the village because they 'speak the same language' (Jung, for example, had stroked the Jesus boat at Cambridge). This depiction accords well with the widespread feeling that elements of the upper class were pro-fascist. Sir Oswald Mosley, the British fascist leader, was after all a baronet and married to one of the Mitford girls. Admiral Sir Barry Domvile, Lord Tavistock and others actively sought to promote peace with Germany in 1940 because of their sympathy with Nazi Germany.[10] There were rumours current in 1942 that five dukes were seeking a negotiated peace with Germany.[11] It is also the case that two of the humblest and least considered figures in the village alert the outside world to the plight of Bramley End: poacher Bill Purves, who is killed, and cockney evacuee George Truscott, whom Bill has taught the country skills. Against this it should be noted that Mrs Fraser, who has filled her house with evacuees, dies heroically saving the children from a hand grenade, and it is the vicar's daughter who disposes of the treacherous Wilsford. Perhaps most telling of all is the fact that the manor house (symbol of England, history and tradition) is taken over by the people and defended by them as the last bastion of freedom against the Germans. It is a struggle of the whole people, of all classes: a united effort.

But perhaps the most notable rural paean is *A Canterbury Tale* (1944), a rich and complex fable by Michael Powell and Emeric Pressburger which perplexed critics and public alike at the time of its release. Powell subsequently described the film as his version of 'Why We Fight': 'a crusade against materialism', an exploration of the spiritual values that England embodies and the belief that the roots of the nation lie in the pastoral. The film, ravishingly photographed in Powell's native Kent, rejoices in the sense of the living past, in country crafts, rural beauty, the intimacy of man and nature. The England evoked by *A Canterbury Tale* is the rural England of Chaucer and Shakespeare, and its spirit resides in Thomas Colpeper, gentleman farmer, magistrate, historian and archaeologist, a man who understands England's nature and seeks to communicate its values, a part played with chilling charismatic power by Eric Portman. The film recreates the Canterbury pilgrimage for a trio of latterday visitors who discover spiritual peace and revitalisation on the Pilgrims' Way.

The final sequence of the film, in which all the characters are gathered uplifted and transfigured in the cathedral as bells ring,

'Onward Christian Soldiers' is sung and troops move off to war, prefigures the just and inevitable victory of those qualities for which Britain fights and which the countryside enshrines: freedom, stability, tradition, peacefulness and spirituality. The intention of the film was made clear by its press book, which declared:

> *A Canterbury Tale* is a new story about Britain, her unchanging beauty and traditions, and of the Old Pilgrims and the New. As the last scene of the picture fades away, to those who see it and are British, there will come a feeling – just for a moment – of wishing to be silent, as the thoughts flash through one's mind: 'These things I have just seen and heard are all my parents taught me. That is Britain, that is me.'

Alas, in general, the public seems not to have thought this. Instead, they seem to have thought, 'What on earth is this all about?' The film was not a box-office success.[12]

The Demi-Paradise (1943) was directed by Anthony Asquith and written and produced by the Anglophile White Russian émigré Anatole de Grunwald. It was the British cinema's main contribution to Anglo-Russian friendship, with Laurence Olivier giving a brilliant performance as the bemused Russian engineer whose preconceptions about England are gradually dispelled and who comes to appreciate the secret of Britain's survival and success. In fact it emerges far more as a celebration of England and Englishness than it is of Russia. Ivan Kouznetsoff visits England first in 1939 to negotiate for the building of an ice-breaker. He arrives believing that the English are humourless, arrogant, narrow-minded, hypocritical, warlike, the embodiment of capitalist and imperialist tyranny. He finds the country complacent, easy-going and old-fashioned, and goes to stay with the upper class Tisdall family, who are both country gentry and industrial managers, in the composite market town and seaport with the resonant name of Barchester. Each of the members of the family has a distinct ideological role to play in enlightening Ivan over the falseness of the various myths about 'perfidious Albion'.

The father, Herbert Tisdall, a cricket-loving gentleman, tells Ivan that, far from being warlike, Britain will do all she can to avoid trouble. But when it comes to the crunch she will fight. When Ivan taxes his wife with the English being narrow-minded, she disarmingly agrees. Daughter Ann gives a resounding defence of the

British Empire when he talks of the English setting out to conquer the world. She claims that it was acquired by private adventure rather than state expansion, the work of explorers, romantics, individualists and, since acquisition, well governed. Most surprising of all for Ivan is his encounter with Ann's grandfather, Runalow, the acceptable face of Victorian values. Runalow is a gentle, wise and cultivated eccentric in wing collar and pince-nez, an engineering genius who has learned Bradshaw by heart (thus demonstrating the true Englishman's love of railways), a millionaire not interested in money but in playing the piano and reading poetry. He built up his firm from nothing by his own efforts, not for financial gain but so that he could afford the things he wanted: a piano, a garden and books. He did not stop work once he had got these things because he had responsibilities towards his employees. The motto of his firm is 'Duty and Service'. But Ivan is finally exasperated by the local pageant – a convincingly awful recreation, complete with Women's Institute choir and doggerel verse of great moments from Britain's past such as the Armada and Waterloo. 'You are living in the past', Ivan tells them accusingly, little realising that tradition and the past are sources of Britain's strength.

When he returns, a year later, the war has started. England is galvanised into action; Ann has joined the WRNS; the Tisdalls are entertaining cockney evacuees, but still find time to listen to Miss Beatrice Harrison playing her cello to the nightingales on the terrace for a BBC broadcast (a recreation of an actual wartime occurrence). Ivan tells Runalow that Britain is finished. Runalow says Britain will fight on. With what? The strength of her traditions and the belief in duty and service. With Hitler's invasion of Russia, Ivan suddenly finds himself an ally of the British. The annual pageant is held, exactly the same as last year except for a tableau for victory. It raises £1000 for Ivan's home town and he finds himself applauding the pageant, at last having understood its meaning. The workers agree to overtime to complete the Russian ice-breaker, which is duly launched amidst a chorus of 'For he's a jolly good fellow' in honour of Ivan. The Russian then makes a speech explaining how he first arrived in England full of misconceptions but now realised that the English are a 'grand, great people'. Much of the world thinks that they care only about money; in fact they care about cricket, nightingales and a good job well done. Much of the world thinks they are perfidious and hypocritical; in fact they are warm and kindly, but it amuses them to let the world think they are not because of their sense of humour. Their sense of humour is the key: if you can laugh, you can be tolerant and freedom-loving, for there is no laughter where there is no freedom. The Russians can laugh and the British can laugh and together they will win the battle against violence, selfishness and greed.

Ivan's final speech brings together the ideas that have run through the film defining the national identity: a sense of duty, a sense of tradition, a sense of tolerance, a sense of humour, a sense of service, a heroic individualism which at its most potent can invent, explore and conquer and at its most pronounced can blossom as a benign and lovable eccentricity, seen in *The Demi-Paradise* in the presence at the pageant of those most beloved of British eccentrics, Margaret Rutherford and Joyce Grenfell.

If in *This England* the downland village of Clevely is England and the countrymen are its heart, and if in *The Demi-Paradise* it is the seaport town of Barchester and the upper-middle class, in *This Happy Breed* (1944) England is No. 17 Sycamore Road, Clapham, and its heart is the lower-middle class. *This Happy Breed* was the play by Noël Coward filmed by the team he had assembled to make *In Which We Serve* in 1941: David Lean, Ronald Neame and Anthony Havelock-Allan. If *In Which We Serve* was a film about the present (fighting the war), *This Happy Breed* was its analogue and counterpart, a film about the past and future which avoided the war altogether, something which by 1944 filmgoers were anxious to do. It evokes the imminent end of the war, in fact, with narrator Laurence Olivier declaring that with the return of the troops, 'hundreds and hundreds of houses are becoming homes again'. But it also presents a selective view of the events of 1919–39 in such a way as to assuage any guilt feelings the lower-middle class may have entertained about their endorsement of the National Government and its appeasement policy. This Clapham Cavalcade intermingles the joys and sorrows of the Gibbonses, Frank and Ethel (Robert Newton and Celia Johnson) and their three children (marriages, births, deaths, quarrels and reconciliations), with the great events of the age (British Empire Exhibition, general strike, Abdication, Munich). It does so in such a way as to endorse the role of the lower-middle class as the backbone of the nation. For although, like the nation, the younger members of the Gibbons family can flirt with innovation, they settle in the end for the tried and the true. Son Reg and son-in-law Sam become involved in radical politics but both end up being tamed and neutralised by marriage. Daughter Queenie rejects her background as 'common' and runs away in search of the bright lights, but she too eventually settles down with faithful Bob from next door and shows every sign of becoming the archetypal supportive wife and mother that Ethel has been to Frank.

The film does, however, also make the resounding statement about the British political process which is essentially a plea for continuity and a return to 'normality' after the war. This involves Frank and/or Ethel during the course of the film rejecting communism and fascism, filing reverently past the coffin of King George V, visiting the Empire Exhibition at Wembley, breaking the general strike and passionately rejecting appeasement. In discounting what Ethel calls 'that Bolshie business', Frank expounds his (and Coward's) evolutionary philosophy:

> Oh, there's something to be said for it; there's always something to be said for everything. Where they go wrong is trying to get things done too quickly. We don't like doing things quickly in this country. It's like gardening. Someone once said we was a nation of gardeners, and they weren't far out. We're used to planning things and watching them grow and looking out for changes in the weather . . . What works in other countries doesn't always work here. We've got our own way of settling things. It may be slow and it may be a bit dull, but it suits us alright and it always will.

In fact, only a year later, Labour took Clapham from the Conservatives at the general election and swept to power to initiate their peaceful revolution. But it *was* a peaceful revolution, and it was one which grew out of trends and developments initiated by the war. It called for no great change in the national character or self-image. Indeed, as Paul Addison has pointed out, reserved, terse, pipe-smoking, cricket-loving ex-army officer Clem Attlee was rather closer to the traditional English archetype than Winston Churchill, the flamboyant maverick, the Romantic man-child with his Puckish sense of humour, his unique command of the language and his highly developed sense of destiny. The strength of the nation was that it was able to produce, to accommodate and to profit from both of them.

In real life the 'happy breed' turned to the Labour Party for their 'brave new world'. But they recognised in the Gibbonses fellow souls. For the film provoked a remarkable reaction. It struck a chord of recognition and sympathy. It was perhaps the first time that the suburban middle class had been portrayed in the round; the sort of incarnation they were used to previously was in Ivor Novello's hilarious satire on Clapham manners and mores, *I Lived With You* (1933). In *This Happy Breed* they were being taken seriously and treated with respect. The *Manchester Guardian* called the film 'an essential photo for John Bull's family album'.[13] William Whitebait of the *New Statesman*, who had not liked *In Which We Serve* and admitted to being no fan of Coward, was completely overwhelmed by the film: 'It would be hard to overpraise the skill, the feeling and the enhanced fidelity of the film'.[14] More important than the critics, the public liked it. C. A. Lejeune wrote in the *Observer*, 'No film in my memory has brought in more letters of appreciation', and the film became the top money-maker of 1944.[15]

It touched people's hearts because Coward was writing from the heart, as he was when he broadcast to the Australian people in 1940 and said:

There is one thing I do know, not only with my mind and experience but with my roots and my instincts and my heart, and that is the spirit of the ordinary people of England: steadfast humour in the face of continual strain and horror, courage, determination and a quality of endurance that is beyond praise and almost beyond belief.[16]

It is these qualities that are to be seen in the Gibbonses, albeit in a peacetime setting, and the Gibbonses can also be seen to possess what Coward in another broadcast called the assets of the British character: 'our individual honesty, our horse-sense, our irrepressible humour and our strange power of adjustment to new circumstances'.[17]

The picture, then, which emerges from all three films is more or less consistent. It is applied equally to the countryman, to the upper-middle class and to the suburban lower-middle class. But how does it relate to non-cinematic evocations of England and the English character? The war had brought into sharp focus the meaning of England and Englishness. The result was a spate of books and articles analysing the nature of England and the English, and I want to look now at the views of six contrasting commentators.

In 1940 the British Council commissioned a series of eleven essays on various aspects of British life which were published as a collected volume under the title *British Life and Thought* in 1941. The author of 'the Englishman' was Earl Baldwin of Bewdley who, during the 1930s as plain Stanley Baldwin, had been projected as an archetypal Englishman, a conservative John Bull, bluff, honest and common-sensical, a pipe-smoking, cricket-loving, detective-story-reading combination of country squire and paternalist managing director of an old-established family firm. He began his study with the fact that Britain was an island, from which he traced insularity, a measure of complacency and a sense of superiority to 'foreigners'. But along-side these qualities he saw tolerance and compromise, a strong sense of duty, a mistrust of logic and pervasive anti-intellectualism, a spirit of 'dauntless decency' and a broad and good-hearted sense of humour. The Englishman, he believed, was above all an individual-ist, given to grumbling but in the main considerate and easy-going, sentimental, a lover of home and garden, animals and sport. But 'he will not be interfered with by his employer, by his neighbour or on a greater scale by another nation. He is apt to resist at a point and when his mind is made up and his tenacity . . . is . . . acknowledged even by his enemies. You can lead him a long way; you cannot drive him an inch. He will neither cringe nor be bullied.'[18]

At perhaps the other end of the political spectrum was George Orwell, the Old Etonian, who consciously recreated himself as a socialist John Bull. Orwell had hobbies and hobby-horses, was given to praising such English institutions as suet pudding, red pillar boxes and comic seaside postcards, and was given to vituper-ating against what he called 'the pansy left', most notably for their lack of patriotism. In his memorable essays *The Lion and the Unicorn* (1942) and *The English People* (1944) Orwell saw the common people of England as law-abiding, considerate, gentle, decent, patriotic, insular, private, anti-intellectual, sentimental, given to compro-mise, class-ridden, lovers of home and garden, sport and animals. It is a picture, in other words, that is almost identical to the one painted by Baldwin, with the notable and characteristic addition of 'class-ridden'. J. B. Priestley was another socialist John Bull and in his 1939 novel *Let the People Sing*, filmed in 1942, he put into the mouth of his Czech professor Krolak a similar definition of the English:

The great traditions of this country . . . are these. First, the liberty of the individual. So long as they do no harm to others, men must be allowed to develop in their own way. Second, that which goes with liberty – toleration. Third, voluntary public service. Fourth, a very deep love, a poetical love, rooted deep down in the unconscious, of England and the English way of life, of the fields and the woods, flowers and birds, of pastimes, of the poets and storytellers. Fifth, which you find everywhere among the common people, humour and irony and along with these a profound depth of sentiment.[19]

Between the essentially twin positions of left and right lay the liberal centre preaching the same view. The Liberal philosopher and historian Sir Ernest Barker, who wrote regularly on the national character in books like *National Character* (1927), *Britain and the British People* (1942) and *The Character of England* (1947), saw it as comprising tolerance, individualism, balance, compromise, a sense of humour, equanimity, social homogeneity, amateurism, eccentricity, class consciousness, a tradition of voluntary work. Occupying a similar place on the political spectrum was Leslie Howard – not just a film star but, after J. B. Priestley, the most popular and important broadcaster on the overseas service of the BBC. In his regular broadcasts to the USA he highlighted the qualities which had emerged in the English during the war, 'qualities which seem to me to represent the best there is in human nature: the qualities of courage, devotion to duty, kindliness, humour, coolheadedness, balance, common sense, singleness of purpose . . . and idealism'.[20] In a later broadcast he added: 'the one thing we have contributed to the civilisation of the world which is new and our own, something which the Germans have never known the meaning of, something called tolerance'.[21]

All the commentators so far mentioned are English. But what of a view from abroad? Leland DeWitt Baldwin (no relation to Stanley) was an Anglophile American who, in *God's Englishman* (1943), wrote a history of Britain to explain the emergence of the English character, in the course of which he distilled the views of a host of British and foreign commentators from the previous half-century, including Wilhelm Dibelius, George Santayana, Esmé Wingfield-Stratford, W. M. Dixon, Price Collier and Rebecca West. Leland Baldwin detected that the Englishman was distinguished by insularity and a sense of superiority, a distrust of logic, a facility for tolerance and compromise, a capacity for moral indignation, a sense of humour ('never more apparent than when he is confronting a terrible crisis, particularly a war') and an 'unparalleled reverence for the law'. The English, he concluded, were hopelessly sentimental, class-ridden, sports-loving, anti-intellectual, courteous, endowed with a gift for understatement, respect for privacy and an indomitable sense of fair play. At the root of the English character is 'respect for the individual'.

These were essentially impressionistic accounts, of course, but they achieve a remarkable unanimity from both domestic and foreign commentators, whether on the left or the right politically. By the very nature of the concept there can be no scientific analysis of national character, but we can compare such impressions with a report not intended for publication which is probably as near to being objective as it is possible to get. It was by Dr Stephen Taylor on the first year's work of the Home Intelligence Unit, set up to monitor national morale. It made various generalisations and drew some conclusions about the national character:

> The British public as a whole shows a very high degree of common sense . . . The British public are pragmatic. They are little influenced by immaterial, ethical or theoretical considerations. There are three main exceptions: i) a determination not to be 'put upon' or 'messed about' except by their own consent; ii) a determination not to allow others to be 'put upon'; iii) a sense of fair play.
>
> The British public has a basic stability of temperament with a slightly gloomy tinge. Arising from this: i) a tendency . . . to voice grumbles loudly; ii) a delight in 'knowing the worst'; iii) a tendency to doubt rather than believe any new information and particularly a suspicion of 'newspaper talk'. The public has a great capacity for righteous indignation when things go wrong. Gratitude is rarely exhibited. A fundamental tenet of the British public creed is that all in authority, above all 'officials', are inefficient. The public is unimaginative . . . [and] basically lazy with, in consequence, a very large reserve and capacity for effort on the rare occasions when it considers this vitally necessary . . . This innate laziness leads secondarily to a high degree of tolerance.[22]

With but a few differences of emphasis and omissions, and containing a few less flattering home truths, this conforms remarkably with the picture painted both in books and films about the national character.

Three qualities in particular run through almost every wartime British film and together provide central strands in the national character. First – and vital – is the sense of humour. This showed itself in the national penchant for comedy films, with George Formby being the top British box-office attraction from 1938 to 1943. Humour was also a strong component even of serious war films and with it went automatically a sense of balance and proportion. The sense of humour is singled out in Ivan Kouznetsoff's analysis of the national character in *The Demi-Paradise*. In *Pimpernel Smith* the Gestapo chief General von Graum, solemnly proclaiming the sense of humour to be the English secret weapon, proceeds to search for it, ploughing through *Punch* and Edward Lear, P. G. Wodehouse and Lewis Carroll, reading extracts to his bemused assistants without raising a smile. Eventually he declares it to be a myth. But the point of this sequence is in a sense the justification of the film, for the action of Pimpernel Smith, with Leslie Howard ridiculing and outwitting the Gestapo, demonstrates unequivocally that a sense of humour *is* the English secret weapon: the essential quality which separates a civilised society from a barbaric one.[23]

The second quality is tolerance. This may proceed, as Stephen Taylor suggested, from laziness or it may proceed from the recognition that, in a nation with more than its fair share of individualists and eccentrics, tolerance is the only feasible policy to adopt. George Santayana said of England that it 'is a paradise of individuality, eccentricity, heresy, anomalies, hobbies and humours'.[24] The task of the authorities in wartime was to reconcile this paramount individualism with the need for corporate effort. As F. C. Bartlett wrote, domestic propaganda must recognise 'that men act where their affections, sentiments and emotions are engaged, but that these must and can be led by intelligence without losing their strength. It knows that the stability of the social order does not depend upon everybody saying the same thing, holding the same opinions, feeling the same feelings, but upon a freely achieved unity which with many sectional and individual differences is neverthe-less able to maintain an expanding and consistent pattern of life.'[25] It is this which inspired the making of those films about mixed groups of people from different backgrounds and classes who are success-fully welded together for the war effort whilst retaining their individuality – films like *Millions Like Us, The Gentle Sex, Fires Were Started, The Bells Go Down* and *The Way Ahead*. The keynote of these films was people learning tolerance of each other and building co-operation and comradeship through it. Mutual tolerance as the basis of political consensus was to remain a cardinal principle of British public life until 1979, when it was summarily abolished.

Stoicism or emotional restraint is the third quality, the essence of the much-parodied British fondness for understatement, reserve and the stiff upper lip. This was seen as a central and indeed admirable national characteristic. The last great film of the war, for example, *The Way to the Stars* (1945), a film by Anthony Asquith, Terence Rattigan and Anatole de Grunwald about life on an RAF base during the period 1940–4, was warmly welcomed by critics and public alike. *Daily Mail* readers voted it the best film of the war years. The critics mirrored the public mood well: their reviews right across the spectrum, from the *Observer* to the *Daily Sketch*, stressed its essential qualities: its Englishness, its realism, its emotional restraint. In a sense they were equating all three.[26]

It is a truism that the war saw a change in the nature of British films, what can perhaps be described as democratisation and documentarisation. Critics called for realism and what they meant was realism of setting, content and character. This led to the lower-middle class and, within limits, the working class being treated seriously for the first time in the mainstream cinema. But I do not believe that this signalled any change in the depiction of the national identity. In the early war films like *Night Train to Munich* and *Ships with Wings*, for instance, the qualities perceived as being national appeared to be largely confined to the upper classes, who played the dominant part in the action. But as the other classes got their cinematic meed, they were seen to share the same characteristics.

Sue Harper has suggested that the national character 'may well have been revealed in the Gainsborough melodramas as feckless, pleasure-loving and flamboyant'.[27] But I would suggest that the significance of the Gainsborough melodramas was that they took account of the release of sexuality, the desire for instant gratification triggered by the war which threatened to erode 'the national character'. Hence a series of highly-coloured dramas in which in every case the exponents of this creed were punished by death and where the representatives of national qualities triumphed. The Gainsborough melodramas are indeed important evidence of the responsiveness of popular cinema to ideas and movements in society.

How did the dominant image work upon the mass audience? George Orwell, that most perceptive of social observers, noted that

Myths which are believed in tend to become true, because they set up a type or persona which the average person will do his best to resemble. During the bad period of 1940 it became clear that in Britain national solidarity is stronger than class antagonism. If it were really true that 'the proletarian has no country', 1940 was the time to show it. It was exactly then, however, that class feeling slipped into the background, only reappearing when the immediate danger had passed. Moreover it is probable that the stolid behaviour of the British town populations under the bombing was partly due to the existence of the national 'persona' – that is, to their preconceived idea of themselves. Traditionally the Englishman is phlegmatic, unimaginative, not easily rattled, and since that is what he thinks he ought to be, that is what he tends to become. Dislike of hysteria and 'fuss', admiration for stubbornness, are all but universal in England, being shared by everyone except the intelligentsia. Millions of English people willingly accept as their national emblem the bulldog, an animal noted for its obstinacy, ugliness and impenetrable stupidity. They have a remarkable readiness to admit that foreigners are more 'clever' than themselves, and yet they feel that it would be an outrage against the laws of God and Nature for England to be ruled by foreigners.[28]

This 'persona' was one of the reasons that the Home Intelligence Unit could conclude in 1941 that 'there is at present no evidence that it is possible to defeat the people of Britain by any means other than extermination'. The cinema played a vital role in promoting and sustaining that 'persona' throughout the war.

Notes and References

1. Joan Rockwell, *Fact in Fiction: the use of literature in the systematic study of society* (London, 1974) pp. vii–viii, 4.
2. Paul Addison, *The Road to 1945* (London, 1977).
3. PRO INF 1/867, also published in I. Christie (ed.), *Powell, Pressburger and Others* (London, 1978) pp. 121–4.
4. Sir Ernest Barker, *National Character* (London, 1927) p. 8.
5. Martin Wiener, *English Culture and the Decline of the Industrial Spirit* (Cambridge, 1981).
6. J. B. Priestley (ed.), *Our Nation's Heritage* (London, 1940) p. 158.
7. Angus Calder, *The People's War* (London, 1971) p. 483.

8.   Sir Denis Brogan, *The English People* (London, 1943) pp. 235–6.
9.   Leslie Halliwell recalls being taken as a boy with a school party to see *This England*: 'Even the history master roared with derisive laughter at the inept and boring goings-on'. The history master left immediately after the film, leaving his delighted charges to glory in the supporting feature, *The Mummy's Hand*. Leslie Halliwell, *Seats in all Parts* (London, 1985) p. 93.
10. Richard Griffiths, *Fellow Travellers of the Right* (London, 1980) pp. 368–74.
11. J. L. Hodson, *Home Front* (London, 1944) p. 181.
12. For a full discussion of *A Canterbury Tale* see J. Richards and A. Aldgate, *Best of British* (Oxford, 1983) pp. 43–59.
13. *Manchester Guardian*, 29 May 1944.
14. *New Statesman*, 27 May 1944.
15. C. A. Lejeune, *Chestnuts in Her Lap* (London, 1947) p. 117.
16. Noël Coward, *Australia Revisited – 1940* (London, 1941) p. 7.
17. Ibid., p. 23.
18. British Council, *British Life and Thought* (London, 1941) p. 458.
19. J. B. Priestley, *Let the People Sing* (London, 1939) p. 384.
20. Leslie Howard, 'Shopkeepers and Poets', broadcast 14/15 October 1940 (BBC Written Archives, Caversham, Talks script microfilm 234).
21. Leslie Howard, 'New Order in Europe', 23/4 December 1940 (ibid.).
22. Dr Stephen Taylor, *A Review of some conclusions arising out of a year of Home Intelligence Reports*, October 1941 (INF 1/292).
23. For a full discussion of *Pimpernel Smith* see A. Aldgate and J. Richards, *Britain Can Take It* (Oxford, 1986) pp. 44–75.
24. George Santayana, *Soliloquies in England* (London, 1922) p. 30.
25. F. C. Bartlett, *Political Propaganda* (Cambridge, 1940) p. 152.
26. For a discussion of *The Way to the Stars* see Aldgate and Richards, *Britain Can Take It* (op. cit.) pp. 277–98.
27. *Historical Journal of Film, Radio and Television*, 5 (1985) p. 220.
28. George Orwell, *Collected Essays, Journalism and Letters* (Harmondsworth, 1982) III, p. 21.

4

The People as Stars:
Feature Films as National
Expression

Peter Stead

Although the inevitability of war aroused many fears and anxieties, it also prompted a few hopes. There were perceptive film-makers and critics, for example, who sincerely hoped and believed that war would finally push British cinema through some final barriers by inspiring the writing of better stories and the production of sharper, tougher and, above all, more realistic films. The twelve months before the actual outbreak of hostilities gave ample evidence of a new maturity in British films: production standards seemed higher and many critics detected a new sureness of touch in matters social. There was certainly a new pride and a new sense of anticipation in the British film industry but, in order fully to appreciate the situation when war began, we need to remind ourselves of the terms in which British films hitherto had generally been discussed.

The 1930s had been the decade in which critics and journalists had first begun to take seriously the mass entertainment feature film. Writers in Britain always retained a suspicion of and even a contempt for Hollywood, but slowly they were beginning to identify those qualities which the film-going masses had long detected in American films. The upshot of their analysis was that American films seemed to feed off a vitality inherent in American life, and this realisation was accompanied by a growing feeling that British films, by comparison, were rather lifeless. As early as 1927 one journalist spoke of how America 'had found in the motion picture a definite medium of national expression', whereas 'the British spirit has not yet found national expression on the screen'. For the next ten years the majority of London critics were to make the same observation.[1] There were varied explanations for this contrast in national cinemas, but perhaps the most fundamental came from J. B. Priestley, who asserted that English working-class life did not provide 'as good film material' as did American society.[2]

Priestley was always asking interesting questions about popular culture, in both Britain and in America, but in general the critical debate on film tended to be repetitive and restricted.[3] No one was too disposed to take up Priestley's point about the formality of life in Britain, and only rarely would any critic suggest that censorship had precluded a social cinema. The extremely limited terms of the debate suggest a degree of disingenuousness – but equally it reveals the extent to which Hollywood was setting the standards, defining the idiom and determining the levels of expectation of the feature film. The full measure of Hollywood's cultural triumph can be seen in the way in which British critics attached very little significance to what had been achieved in establishing indigenous film genres. They had little time for the arty world of documentary: Arthur Vesselo, for example, disliked the mix of art and propaganda, while Priestley disputed the documentarists' claim that they had come to terms with reality, his verdict being that 'they have not been more nakedly truthful than the rest of us'.[4] The critics showed even less respect for a brand of indigenous comedy that was proving highly successful amongst certain working-class audiences. The British film industry was almost certainly a little ashamed of the Gracie Fields and George Formby films of the period and, realising that they could never become the basis of an internationally successful cinema, took steps to ensure that the London critics never saw them. However, all the evidence suggests that metropolitan writers were quite happy to ignore what they considered to be provincial and rather silly films; even John Grierson preferred Hollywood's version of reality to the music-hall antics of Fields and Formby or even the embarrassing sentimentality of John Baxter's social dramas.[5] Such attempts at a native cinema were dismissed as a cultural cul-de-sac.

What critics wanted to see was British studios competing directly with Hollywood and for this to be achieved it was felt that the fuller technical expertise which some studios at least had acquired ought now to be put at the disposal of better written and more realistic stories. Again it was Priestley who most tellingly summed up the debate when he urged commercial studios and documentary film-makers to pool their talents. His view was that 'only the faintest drabble of real English life is allowed to trickle into most of our films' and he argued that the 'strengthening and thickening' of British films could only be achieved by combining commercial expertise with documentary flair. His prescription was precise, geographical and prescient, since he concluded that 'If these Arabian Nights caliphs could have left the Savoy Grill and those earnest young experiments could have been marched out of Soho Square and both parties could have met somewhere near Haymarket, then British films might have entered a new glamorous life.'[6] Such a meeting was not to come in the Haymarket, but was to form the very basis of British feature films during the second world war.

Meanwhile something along these lines was already happening. In 1938 the encouraging reactions to *South Riding* and *Pygmalion* suggested that the time was ripe for the melodramatic handling of social issues in the American style. British producers had carefully noted the success of Hollywood's social problem films in both America and Britain and, following the 1938 Quota Act, there was in any case even more American money, advice and talent pouring into London. Aubrey Flanagan's comment was that in some studios it was 'as easy to purchase an Old Fashioned as it was a mild and bitter'.[7] In effect Hollywood had come to England, and there was now every incentive to give British stories the full Hollywood treatment.

The last months of peace brought a clutch of films that had the critics searching for new superlatives. There was tremendous acclaim for *The Citadel*, but such critics as P. L. Mannock did not even try to disguise the fact that it was essentially an American achievement.[8] All the Hollywood hallmarks were there: the melodrama, the dismissal of trade unionism and the emphasis on individual fulfilment, but, more especially, now there was the quality of dialogue and camerawork, the authenticity of the medical details and a thrilling sense of life in South Wales and London. Just as King Vidor had successfully taught the British how not to be afraid of social themes, so also had he reminded them of the cinematic mileage that could be extracted from respectable middle-brow novels. As MGM were filming A. J. Cronin's *The Citadel*, Isadore Goldschmidt was setting up the same author's *The Stars Look Down*. Yet it was Hollywood production values which now ensured that a crew was sent to Cumbria for location shots and that care was taken to construct a convincing colliery at the Twickenham studios. The American influence could also be seen in the use of a narrator with a mid-Atlantic accent, the general absence of north-east accents, the ludicrous depiction of trade unionism and, once again, the emphasis on the hero's salvation. But what contemporary critics preferred to emphasise was the remarkable way in which British working-class life had been put on the screen. Graham Greene thought Carol Reed's film as good as *Kameradschaft*, while the *Daily Express* considered it a film about real people with the authenticity of grime and coal dust in every frame.[9]

It had been the documentary directors who first established coalfields as both photogenic and dramatic, and their influence on these two Cronin films is plain to see. The critics all praised the authenticity of the colliery scenes in these films, and yet with hindsight we can see that they were not perhaps the most important feature of what the British studios had achieved. Rather, what stands out about both films is that they were better written, they told a tougher story and they were better acted. In *The Citadel* Robert Donat had suggested that he was ready to become a star in the American style, while in *The Stars Look Down* it was the support playing of Margaret Lockwood and Emlyn Williams as two working-class characters who care little for the miners but who attempt to 'chisel' their own way out of the Depression that established the real whiff of social authenticity. It was an American-inspired professionalism that allowed critics to detect in the films 'the strengthening and the thickening' of the native product that they had long yearned for.[10]

The revolution which had taken place in the social content of British films between 1938 and 1940 was perhaps best summed up in Graham Greene's review of *The Proud Valley*, in which he complained that pit-head gear had become one 'of the great platitudes of the screen'. In fact Greene thought very little of this 1940 film: he felt that Pat Tennyson's direction was uneasy and he had taken a dislike to Paul Robeson's 'fat sentimental optimism' which was offered on this occasion in the form of 'a big black Pollyanna'.[11] More typical of the critical response was that of *The Picturegoer*, which concluded a review entitled 'Welsh Miners Come Into Their Own' with the observation that 'when British producers get down to the essentials of life they appear to be more successful than in any other medium'.[12] *The Proud Valley* certainly depicted the 'essentials' of coal-mining life, for we are shown the everyday dangers of the job as well as the fight to keep open a mine scheduled for closure. What is interesting about Tennyson's film is that he chose to examine a social problem in more of a British idiom. Compared to the Cronin films, the traditional weaknesses of the British cinema are far more apparent: the dialogue is weaker, the acting poorer and the pit village is essentially depicted in caricature. The debt to Gracie Fields is quite obvious, as is the English romanticism and sentimentality of the director. But the storyline is strong and, however sickly, the choral singing is used effectively to suggest and condone working-class solidarity.

In time it became known that the censors had insisted that the script of *The Proud Valley* be changed so that the continued survival of the mine was determined by wartime demand rather than by workers' occupation. Of course, by 1940 most critics must have been aware that the improvement in British cinema had largely been made possible by the censors' approval of stories with an industrial setting, which they had done only rarely pre-war, although it is still surprising how little critics spoke of the political constraints on film production.[13] The fact that a new era had well and truly dawned was only finally confirmed by the appearance in 1941 of *Love On The Dole*. Throughout the 1930s it had proved impossible to make a film of Walter Greenwood's novel, subsequently dramatised by Ronald Gow, but now there was to be unprecedented critical enthusiasm for John Baxter's film. Writers were all agreed that what they liked best was the film's unrelieved realism. Edgar Anstey found it so real that he had difficulty in believing that 'it came out of a film studio', while *Kine Weekly* described it as a 'documentary of compelling power' which told the truth 'honestly' and depicted authentically 'the working and living conditions of a typical drab pre-war English industrial town'.[14]

For years London critics had been unanimous in condemning British film acting, Ian Dalrymple once going so far as to suggest that 'we have not the acting personalities to persuade the mass audiences to support us'.[15] Now, quite unusually, there was widespread praise for the way in which *Love On The Dole*'s realism had been sustained by acting. It was William Whitebait in the *New Statesman* who drew attention to the vital point that a 'new set of actors' had made a 'striking' impact while 'never showing tuppence-coloured against the penny-plain background'.[16] Many critics reserved their highest praise for the twenty-year-old Scottish actress, Deborah Kerr, and in particular they stressed how effective she had been in that final scene in which she went off to be a bookie's tart so as to improve her family's fortunes. This was indeed a significant scene, for no other moment in film summed up so well wartime Britain's determination to move away decisively from the blandness of the

1930s. In 1938 Jane Morgan had written about the need 'for actors who have not had every spark of humanity ironed out of them by the strange conventions of the West End stage' and at that time disparaging remarks about the cut-glass accents of young actresses were almost *de rigueur*. Now Deborah Kerr was lavishly praised for the way in which she conveyed real intensity and anxiety.[17] It was appreciated that in some respects Miss Kerr was a typical British starlet but, as Ernest Betts suggested, other actresses could benefit from her stated advice that they should just be themselves.[18] Edgar Anstey saw *Love On The Dole* as proof that there was freedom of speech in Britain and that the country was fighting to defeat poverty as well as the Nazis.[19] For its part, *Kine Weekly* chose to stress that the film was not crude propaganda but rather a statement of artistic and social truth.[20]

Love On The Dole came as the culmination of a two-year period in which it had been felt that British films had been improving, and it is a marvellous experience to trace the growing pride as London writers compared the domestic product (and especially the four films discussed here) with what they now thought of as the less satisfactory Hollywood product. Ernest Betts saw Baxter's film at much the same time as he saw Bette Davis in *The Letter*; of course he enjoyed the American film – it was 'cracking' and 'first class entertainment' – but it was of 'no significance', whereas *Love On The Dole* 'blazes with it'. With Baxter depicting 'a nation showing fight', one could no longer be bothered with 'potty little murders'.[21] Such was the artistic distance travelled since the 1930s that Edgar Anstey felt able to put *Love On The Dole* alongside *Major Barbara* and *Kipps* while suggesting that 'a form of national expression was being evolved'.[22]

The trouble with critics, of course, is that every good film is heralded as making some kind of breakthrough and, once they have developed the notion of improvement or change in a particular direction, as films which fit into that notion appear they are used to sustain what appears to be a very natural linear development. For the film industry the reality is often more complex and haphazard – and indeed less prone to organisation in patterns. Such general remarks certainly apply to the first year or so of the war for, while critics waxed eloquent about landmark films, many people in the film industry itself experienced only confusion and uncertainty. For a brief moment it had looked as though there would be no film industry at all and then, when survival was assured, there was much dislocation and many cutbacks. What individual directors found confusing was that, while journalists were helping to sustain a general public expectation that there was about to be a golden age for the British cinema, there seemed to be no strong lead given by either the industry or the government.[23] Directors sensed that the new national mood had provided a fitting subject for an indigenous cinema and they also sensed that people were tiring of some of Hollywood's excesses. Uncertainty remained, however, because the industry had not yet fully interpreted either box-office trends or the wishes of the politicians. All the rhetoric invited great British films, but many of the early pressures of war seemed to sanction either mindless entertainment or government-inspired propaganda.

The director Michael Powell let it be known that he and his colleagues were not prepared to work on 'tuppeny-halfpenny subjects about blondes and jazz and what happened down Argentina way' and that they would all be off to war work if they were not given films that meant something, that were 'real'.[24] In conversation with Ernest Betts, the directors Anthony Asquith and Leslie Howard outlined the difficulties they had faced before moving on to talk about their own expectations. In general they were optimistic. Asquith was sure that the entertainment film would be able to take 'propaganda' and 'documentary' themes in its stride, while a very excited Howard talked of how, after years of filming other people's ideas, he was now making films according to his own. Howard's line was that 'there is a great conflict of ideas; why can't the cinema join in this?' The asking of that question indicated that the two were campaigning; they were hoping to use the new possibilities in their own way and were hoping to move British cinema in the direction demanded by the critics. Both men, said Betts, were demanding quality instead of trivia, both thought that 'the proper job of film was to tell the world what sort of people we are', both thought that it was 'time we had social significance on the screen'. In short, concluded Betts, 'they want the cinema to grow up'.[25]

In the general uncertainty that war had occasioned, it seemed to many that it was the documentary directors who were in the best position to make significant films. There was soon a steady stream of films depicting the involvement of the British people in the war. These varied from short films simply conveying information or explaining jobs that had to be done, to more ambitious productions which depicted military actions by concentrating on particular units or groups and which in some instances took the form of dramatised documentaries, with prepared scripts and with the characters played by actual serving men and women. There was much popular and critical acclaim for these more ambitious documentaries and especially for the new genre of dramatised documentary which it was appreciated had been brought into existence by government agencies. In May 1940 the *Documentary News Letter (DNL)* expressed pleasure at the government's initiative and commented on how the use of 'real people' had helped to overcome the traditional artificiality of the British cinema. It also expressed pleasure at the way in which the public itself was showing so much interest in what it revealingly called 'the war-time drama of the common people'.²⁶

Perhaps the contemporary impact of the new British documentary was best summed up in the recollections written just after the war by the critic Dilys Powell. She remembered her reaction to Harry Watt's *Target for Tonight* (1941):

> The actors were serving airmen, the dialogue was simple, realistic, ironic in the English manner – but somehow imagination had eradicated a plain story of the everyday experience. Here was a new genre in the cinema, a fact, a fragment of actual life, which still held the emotional tremor of fiction.

Miss Powell recalled how in 1943 and 1944 London audiences had been stunned by the brilliance of Soviet documentaries, but she did feel that the British *Desert Victory* and the Anglo-American *Burma Victory* and *The True Glory* had stood comparison. With the latter film, coming at the end of the war, she had no doubt that the Soviets had been well and truly superseded, since Carol Reed and Garson Kanin as directors had brilliantly depicted 'the common experience of an army of human beings': 'the fighting man had spoken for himself' and thereby 'a historical document had become more – a human document'.²⁷ By 1945, therefore, Dilys Powell had become one of the great advocates of this new genre and, like other enthusiasts, she delighted not only in the excellence of individual films but also in their popularity. At one point she recalled how she had gone to an isolated Welsh mining town and seen how 'at the end of the day's work, miners and their wives sat rapt and silent through a documentary record of the making of an airscrew'.²⁸

This somewhat patronising and overstated story possibly suggests that Miss Powell was a little carried away by her enthusiasm for this new realism in British films. It may well be that middle-class and intellectual critics tended to exaggerate the popularity of non-fiction films, and certainly close inspection suggests that through-out the war there was always a certain uneasiness about the cinema of actuality on the part of both the exhibitors and their regular customers. In 1941 Charles Kohn, the manager of the Granada Woolwich, told Ernest Betts that film taste was being made in air-raid shelters and that the mood was very much for escapism.[29] In 1943 Roger Manvell commented on how audiences were greatly embarrassed by documentaries and how they just 'laughed their heads off' if they saw themselves on the screen. He had noted in particular that when an actor had sworn in *In Which We Serve* the audience had been immediately disorientated and confused be-cause a taboo had been broken: the effect had been as if someone had taken their 'uglier underclothes off in front of a comparatively well-dressed assembly'.[30] In a 1948 account of London's cinemas during the war one observer recalled that war subjects had been unpopular until 1942 and that in general 'the British public as a whole has never been cajoled into loving the documentary'. He was quite prepared to admit that *Target for Tonight* and *Desert Victory* had been exceptions, but his argument was that all the Herculean efforts of the Ministry of Information had not been able to counter the public's intolerance of war films.[31]

What one senses with wartime documentary is that, while the genre gave immense pleasure to individual directors and critics, the response of exhibitors and audiences was rather different. There would certainly have been respect for the best British documen-taries, but there was no widespread enthusiasm for the genre as a whole. Audiences, above all, wanted to be entertained. They could take a certain amount of hard information, but there would have been much support for *DNL*'s view that far too many films had only 'a purely ephemeral how-the-wheels-go-round interest' and that, if only the uniforms had been changed, they could have served the Germans or Japanese just as well.[32] There was certainly a dislike of films which dealt with what was called 'social developments' and it is revealing that so few films of that sort were made. Even more, there was dislike of propaganda, although the strongest feelings in this respect came in the form of opposition to those feature films which had a very obvious propaganda point. Several accounts and surveys bear witness to the way in which crude propaganda had alienated British audiences from many Hollywood films at this time.[33]

Regardless of the popular response, the critics continued to be impressed by British documentaries and in 1943 they acclaimed two films by Humphrey Jennings which were considered to have achieved new levels of excellence. Of *Fires Were Started*, *DNL* stated that it offered 'the best handling of people on and off the job that we've seen in any British film' as well as 'maybe for the first time – proper working class dialogue'. It was felt that this was 'a fine and fruitful record of a way of living and doing a job that *did* work and of a discipline that came from the job itself'.[34] Jennings had indeed made a marvellous film, one of the best ever made about work and about London, but, as the *DNL* critic rightly spotted, there are moments in the film which remind us of how and why the film was made. It was an official film and so we have to be shown how well all the classes work together, and the story has to be given a rather crude upbeat ending as the munition boat sails out of the docks. The handling of the London firemen is assured, but the *DNL* noticed that there were moments when the director went 'all arty' and shots of firemen playing the piano, reading and reciting are there more as a projection of his own idealised view of the working man. It may well be that these 'arty' assertions, and the very freshness which critics liked in the handling of ordinary people, were indications of Jennings' own unfamiliarity with working-class people. Just as with Stephen Spender's book *Citizens in War*, *Fires Were Started* is a record of how an intellectual poet responded to a new familiarity with workers in conditions of domestic crisis.[35]

In *The Silent Village* Jennings used the story of a Nazi takeover of a Welsh mining village to pay tribute to those Czechs who had been slaughtered at Lidice. It is a beautiful and very moving film but, although it does feed off the reality of a semi-rural mining town, the community it depicts is far more an idealised and intellectualised version of the pastoral. Jennings was delighted that the local miners' leader (with whom he had been put in touch) was 'a Tolstoyan figure' and at a later seminar on documentary he reported that he had found people 'extra helpful and extra charming in wartime'. He suggested that this was because they were 'living in a more heightened existence' and were 'more prepared to open their arms and fall into somebody else's'. It seemed as if Jennings was directly taking up Priestley's pre-war point about the British working class being less interesting than the American. Yet during the war they became 'better film material and the emotion that they themselves are feeling is part of the emotion we indeed are always attempting to use and to propagate about life'.[36]

Ordinary people had thus made their début in British films. However, they had not done so on their own terms, but as part of controlled images of the war. It suited both officials and middle-class romantics to depict a happy people going about their often vital tasks with only an occasional grumble. Paul Rotha's *World of Plenty* was a comparatively rare example of a political film that refused to be celebratory. In 1947 Doreen Willis conceded that wartime documentary had 'helped to orientate people to the complex workings of industrial society whilst assisting them in the fight for a better deal', but she found it strange that the documentary concept of 'the creative interpretation of actuality' had produced so few shots of 'sweaty faces, slum housing, and the gyration of machines'. At the same time she found it 'almost breathtaking' that 'an organised audience of 8 million trade unionists and 9 million co-operative families had been ignored'.[37] To a good radical like Rotha it was clear that British documentary had lost its way in the war when sentimental patriotism had prevented the production of films of 'social good purpose'.[38]

While the critics argued, one suspects that the public at large always thought of documentary films as being worthy rather than striking or entertaining. For most, including the critics, it was simply the case that documentaries were less important than feature films. Dilys Powell nicely summed up the consensus view when she argued that 'ultimately it is on the quality of its entertainment films that the prestige of a national cinema must rest', for we judge a country's literature 'not by its text-books . . . but rather by its imaginative works'.[39] The release of *Love On The Dole* in 1941 had suggested that at last Britain was to break through to a socially significant cinema, but things were not quite to work out that way. Looking now at all those enthusiastic reviews of John Baxter's film, one can only conclude that there must have been considerable subsequent disappointment, for there was never to be any serious attempt to build on the foundations laid by it.

In 1941 *Kine Weekly* had suggested that it was John Baxter's childhood experience in the industrial north that had given him the insights and empathy that had shaped *Love On The Dole*, but sadly his subsequent work was never to be quite as satisfactory and it certainly received far less critical attention. His other 1941 film had been *The Common Touch*, which was made as a tribute to 'the humble people of our great cities whose courage and endurance has become the basis of national survival'. In fact the story is absurd and the middle-class characters are all hopeless caricatures. There is at least a wonderful range of working-class or rather lumpen Cockney characters led by Edward Rigby, who ends the film by declaring that the post-war world would be like "eavan on earf". The Cockney types give the film some real ballast, but we are back in the world of Dickens and of Victorian music hall rather than in the East End during the blitz. It could well be argued that the contemporary East End idiom was still essentially Dickensian, but surely a tribute to city dwellers in wartime needed to move away from such well-established theatrical and cinematic clichés?

In his 1944 film *The Shipbuilders* Baxter offered a fuller picture of working-class life, and Edgar Anstey for one praised its depiction of so many aspects of Glasgow life including unemployment, dereliction, football and the general meanness of the streets. For Anstey, though, these virtues had to be set alongside the film's untidy construction, sentimentality and political naïvety. There was no hint of Clydeside's militancy and, according to Anstey, 'the economic issues were simplified down to a point at which one is left feeling that every feat of economic and sociological organisation can be achieved by kindness'.[40] Baxter had been made and unmade by the war. That slight relaxation by the censor at the start of the war had allowed him to make a film that had caught the critical and popular mood. Thereafter he was indulged and permitted to make low-budget class dramas that allowed expression for his sentimentality.[41] Meanwhile both the studios and the authorities became interested in the production of more prestigious films.

The reputation of British cinema during the second world war was to rest on a small number of films which, without in any way endangering morale, nevertheless depicted the war and the involvement of ordinary citizens in it in what was taken to be an honest way. With hindsight we can see that many aspects of the war were neglected and there was never any real attempt to communicate the *whole* truth. But there was sufficient integrity and vitality in these films to convince contemporary audiences and critics that Britain now had a worthwhile feature film industry. Crucial in this respect was the avoidance of those crude and implanted propaganda messages which frequently spoiled American wartime films for British audiences. More positively, the studios managed to develop conventions and styles which never approached total realism but which nevertheless conformed very closely to the contemporary idioms of many British people. Fundamental to this achievement was the contribution of actors and writers.

Early in 1942 Edgar Anstey argued that 'screen-acting must be above all a pursuit of naturalism', adding that 'British acting like British production as a whole has gone on steadily overhauling Hollywood'. Thinking very much of George Carney's performances for John Baxter, he suggested that 'the most pronounced advance has been amongst the small-part players' – precisely the department 'where British production once was weakest'.[42] This view rapidly became an orthodoxy and both critics and trade papers began frequently to refer to 'brilliant characterisations' and 'fine portrayals'. With writers creating more sharply-defined and more varied bit parts, a veritable repertory company of British actors, many of them young and new, emerged to flesh out films and to give them a quite noticeable freshness. There was often praise for good performances by unknowns, but alongside them the old faithfuls had been given a new lease of life.

Much of this highly praised wartime acting was not to stand the test of time; where contemporaries had seen freshness, later audiences were to see stereotypes. The phrase 'repertory company' became more apt because that is very much how many British actors were to appear to later generations. They come down to us, in Charles Barr's phrase, as 'a working class stock company' because they turn up in film after film playing wisecracking Cockneys, dour Scots, garrulous Welshmen, down-to-earth northerners or plain old country bumpkins.[43] Affectionate memories of these wartime films became very much part and parcel of an entire generation's sense of national lore. Even at the end of the 1985 coal dispute the columnist Alan Watkins reported that the television interviews with miners he had seen reminded him of those old war movies with their 'dour and largely incomprehensible Tynesiders . . . their grim but great-hearted Scottish chief engineers and their comic and indomitable Welshmen', the latter in particular being remembered as usually dying of shrapnel wounds halfway through the films.[44] Certainly there was affection for such character portrayals, but there was also an awareness of their theatricality.

Later audiences found their chief source of pleasure in identifying the faces of the ubiquitous bit players. We always expected to see them, but not for one moment did we expect them to create a totally original character. The studios were simply not equipped for that kind of breakthrough for, as Sue Aspinall has recently suggested, it was 'the unfamiliarity of middle class writers, directors, producers and actors with working class life' that led to a dependence on 'familiar stereotypes from comedy or music hall'.[45] It was precisely this point which had been documented by Christopher Isherwood in his autobiographical novel *Prater Violet*, written during the war as a portrait of English film-making in the 1930s. Isherwood recalled the problems of writing dialogue for ordinary people. For example, of a man selling sausages, 'Shakespeare would have known how he spoke. Tolstoy would have known. I didn't know because, for all my parlour socialism, I was a snob. I didn't know how anybody spoke, except public schoolboys and neurotic bohemians.'[46] In his despair the fictional Isherwood fell back on copying other movies and emulating music-hall dialogue.

Possibly things never moved beyond this approach in British studios, but even so the quality of writing *did* improve in the war years and it was this, as much as anything, which explains why critics were suddenly noticing better acting performances. The debate over the quality of this acting can be resolved once we realise that there was a coming together of individual actors and better scripts. What the writers had done was to produce a conversational style which avoided anything that was overtly political but which nevertheless suggested that ordinary people had lives and values of their own, that they were not going to be cannon fodder, that they were not pushovers and that, if there was such a thing as Britishness, then it was to be found precisely in the spirit, humour, slight irreverence and sheer incorrigibility of ordinary people. Film-makers were aiming for a new naturalism but, given the conventions of British acting and the types that acting recruited, it was not so much naturalism that resulted but a filling-out of the stereotypes as actors more confidently delivered their better lines. The scripts now had more 'edge' and wit, and a thoroughly professional crew of actors responded to this encouragement. There was no great breakthrough in terms of naturalism or acting technique, but in the second world war British actors – and especially comedy actors – did make the most of the lines they were given.

Ealing specialised in this kind of thing and it was here where, in time, the depiction of ordinary folk became a major strand in a new kind of British film. In *The Foreman Went to France* (1942) the studio risked making an adventure story about ordinary workmen. In the film there is some mild criticism of official bureaucracy and red tape, but its impact rests on working-class dialogue – and especially on the role of Tommy Trinder as a wisecracking Cockney. A contemporary reviewer referred to the 'comedy flashes' of Trinder, and 'flashes' is indeed the right word, for here was a classic example of how such authenticity and vitality as there was in wartime films emerged more from witty asides and wisecracks than from the plot as such. The commitment to naturalness was there, but to go too far in that direction was to risk flatness in the film and to encounter the more fundamental problem of what workers said when they were not being witty or making ironic complaints. Ealing's *San Demetrio, London* (1943) was a worthy and honest tribute to merchant seamen that was somewhat spoiled by poor special effects and by a failure to breathe life into sustained bouts of working-class conversation. True, we are given merchant seamen who are the quintessence of ordinariness: they are droll, stocky, sexless and feisty, but they call each other 'chum' and are allowed such flashes of music-hall wit as:

'Have you seen him smile?'
'I did once; of course, it might have been a touch of wind.'
'I've left my teeth on board.'
'You can borrow mine when I've finished.'

This is a film in which it was the writing that failed. Far too often the phrase 'that's torn it' was the only response to a crisis, and we are given an ending of sheer corn when Mervyn John (a Welshman playing a Scot), who is dying, pretends to see a pair of stockings that can be given to his wife, whereupon the assembled crew give him a rendering of 'I belong to Glasgow'. This particular crew was certainly a collection of 'common old working chaps', but they needed better lines and to be more interesting and dramatic in themselves to be really convincing. In low-life films it was essential that dialogue and plot prevented the whole thing from becoming low-key.

If this was true of military and action films, it was even more so of social melodrama. In 1943 Sidney Launder and Frank Gilliat made *Millions Like Us* as a tribute to ordinary people on the home front, and in particular to the female employees in munitions factories. A contemporary reviewer of the film considered that it presented 'telling realisations of wartime conditions and that it pulsated with the very spirit of wartime Britain'. Perhaps that critic detected the spirit of the people in the posh voices of the starlets in their upper-working-class houses, or in the hopelessly exaggerated acting of a wealthy socialite and a poor Geordie waif, or even in the almost painful ordinaryness and baby talk of the young airman (played by the ubiquitous Gordon Jackson). But it was far more likely that he detected it in the accompanying humour and wit. Right at the start of the film audiences were asked to recall those pre-war days when eggs came out of shells and the government took 'only some of your money'. Later a member of the Home Guard fortifies himself with a drink: 'the only fortification we've got'. The father of the film's family comments on his meal: 'what's in this sausage is a mystery and I hope it's not solved in my time'. The best serious moment comes when the Welsh actress Megs Jenkins reflects on how the wartime hostel used by the factory girls was so much better than the conditions she had experienced in the mining districts just a few years previously. Much of the national mood is summed up in her comment that 'it took a war to do it, but if somebody is going to develop a social conscience I'm not going to sneeze at it'. Neverthe-less it is the wit that one remembers. The equally ubiquitous Basil Radford and Naunton Wayne, best known for investing test match scores with liturgical significance, are here found laying mines along a beach. Wayne dryly and casually suggests to Radford that 'we must remember not to bathe here after the war'. This was the kind of writing which the British did best. It was the very stuff of British realism.

Towards the end of the war Sidney Gilliat made *Waterloo Road*, a film very much about the people and in particular those described by Alistair Sim in the opening shots as 'the little people'. Sim plays a doctor who narrates the film and the main point he tries to get across is that in the war 'the little people had their battles too'. Here we are given a creditable tribute to ordinary people and the film effectively conveys the point that certain groups in society had been greatly inconvenienced and disorientated by the war. The working-man hero admits that he was 'doing nicely before the war' and prior to his call-up he had been working in a locomotive repair shop, when he had been looking forward to qualifying as an engineer and then to taking his wife to a new house in a suburb a long way from Waterloo Road. His wife also felt thwarted by the war and Sim warns that women become rebellious 'if their beaver instinct' is denied. Most spectacularly, the film admits that there was a group of 'spivs' in the country who had dodged the war and spent their time in bars, in pin-table saloons and at the pictures 'picking up a few hints from Victor Mature' and 'jitterbugging at the Alcazar' with the wives and girlfriends of serving men. According to the narrator, 'these people

would swear away their old grandmother for a packet of Wood-
bines'.

Waterloo Road was a strikingly frank film and it had a real sense of
place, for it was very much a London film. Its creditable authenticity, however, does not go unchallenged because of some traditional British film-making faults. John Mills created the role of the
ordinary soldier at the centre of the plot only by being totally lack-
lustre, and his attempt at realism rests upon a sustained and intense
earnestness. He is completely mismatched with a very sexy Joy
Shelton who, like so many other English actresses, is just far too
posh and harsh for the working-class family in which she is placed.
Stewart Granger was suitably oily in a lounge-lizard sort of way as
the spiv Ted Purvis. Here was one prize fighter whose nose had
obviously never been hit, and at the end of the film he collapses into
smiles and sentimentality, thereby surrendering any real edge that
he had earlier worked so hard to achieve. The 'stars' are not quite
right for the film but it remains authentic because the Cockney idiom
has been mastered by the supporting cast. As was so often the case
in British films, music-hall patter keeps us on firm ground. In a
marvellous pub scene (and how few of those there have been) the
song 'La Donna e Mobile' is instantly translated to 'Woman is
Mobile' and is therefore authoritatively attributed to Mr Bevin.
Ultimately the charm of the entire film rests on its humour as well,
perhaps, as on its pretty girls, since the beautiful Jean Kent really
does steal the whole show.

The approach to realism was a matter of convention and
technique. What critics liked best were films which showed
ordinary people becoming fighting men or putting up with the
ordeals of war. Both Noël Coward's *In Which We Serve* and Harry
Watt's *Nine Men* were highly praised, but it was Carol Reed's *The
Way Ahead* (1944) which was instantly acclaimed as the most
successful British war film. The film's press book had announced
that 'this would be a plain tale of typical Britons of this generation
who were called from the plough, the bench, the office: the man
with the white collar, the man without a collar' and so on. Every
possible angle was to be covered. 'Yesterday he was your husband,
my son, their brother, the man next door, the chap over the way,
that lad from the village.' Audiences would be shown how 'a travel
agent's clerk, a boilerman, a road-house playboy, a Welsh rent
collector, a Scottish labourer, a shop assistant, a man with nervous
indigestion, a man who wanted to go to the Navy and other relevant

characters were made into soldiers'. There was also an important clue to the production team's approach when the press book reminded its readers that 'when the British civilian goes to war he takes with him those qualities of rueful pessimism, of humour, and of broad humanity which make him in the end one of the most formidable fighting men of the world': 'There has been much talk of Tommy Atkins. Here is his film.'[47]

Although this hype was ambitious for a British film, the production team was able to deliver the goods. What was crucial with *The Way Ahead* was the quality of the writing. Eric Ambler and Peter Ustinov had provided director Carol Reed with material that had all the wit, pace and irony of Hollywood at its best. David Niven, Stanley Holloway and the stock company had been given something they could really work with, and there was a general feeling that the film's tantalising, ambiguous and controversial ending was both meaningful and successful because it rounded off such a well written story. To C. A. Lejeune this was a 'real script', the dialogue had a 'cutting edge' and 'few films had brought the audience so close to the people on the screen'. For her *The Way Ahead* had been a startling experience: it was a film which 'plays and talks like life'.[48]

The critical consensus was that Carol Reed had made a great film, but the responses to *The Way Ahead* raised several questions about the British film industry. In a sense this very effusion of praise was a reminder of how cool the response had been to so many British films. Certainly the praise for the script was meant as a condemnation of all those other films that had merely relied on wit and jokes to see them through. C. A. Lejeune perceptively argued that British actors needed a good script, as they could not rely on the exuberance and ingenious creativity of a Cagney who could always transcend his material. But the really big question was whether the skills that had gone into the making of this great war film could now be applied to a domestic subject and, in particular, to the process of demobilisation. Would there be a good film, Lejeune wondered, showing how a good soldier could be turned back into a good civilian? For her this next chapter threatened 'the gravest reorientation in history'.

Lejeune's speculations neatly convey the sense of social challenge that many were experiencing in 1945, but what is interesting in artistic terms is the clear implication that making war films was one matter but making films about everyday life was quite another. It had, after all, been relatively simple to show ordinary people at war.

Dilys Powell knew that to be true, and for her wartime films had been but a step towards maturity and realism. The films themselves had been uneven but at least they constituted 'a movement towards a national subject'. What the war had done, she suggested, was to set the English film on the path 'in which masterpieces may be created'.[49] The *DNL* agreed, adding that although the British film industry was not yet 'a medium of expression' for the British people and the British view, it was nearer to being so than at any other time before.[50]

In 1945, then, as in 1927, critics were waiting for British films to become 'a medium of expression for the British people'. In the years following *The Way Ahead* there was always to be a general feeling of disappointment that British cinema did not achieve the greatness that its wartime record had promised. Not that anyone doubted that British films were better than ever before, since this was after all the period when *Brief Encounter* and *Great Expectations* and many other excellent films appeared. Scripts, acting and production values were all of a new international standard, and yet critics still felt that something was missing. What was in fact missing was a social cinema, a cinema that went beneath melodramatic surfaces. The praise that had been hoarded in expectation of a cinematic break-through was transferred wholesale into the critical response to Italian Neo-Realism. Here was a naturalness and sense of place that the studio-bound British film could never hope to achieve. The disappointing truth was that British films were as bland and theatrical as ever, and only the occasional film like *It Always Rains on Sunday* hinted at other possibilities.

With hindsight we can see that the second world war had created a temporary and somewhat artificial situation in which better stories and elements of realism had been sanctioned. What it did not do was to change fundamentally the context in which British feature films were made. That melodrama should be the conventional mode of the national cinema was virtually prescribed by the American domination of the British market, by the Anglo-American financial control of studios which were pressurised into films that would do well in America, and by a system of censorship that precluded political or social awareness. The formidable array of constraints might have been circumvented had there been any genuine element of independence in Britain's indigenous film culture. There must have been some witty conversations in those pubs off Wardour Street, while beautiful young starlets and the first class technicians must have had their moments of fun in those studios that a cosmopolitan group of tycoons had constructed in leafy suburbs along the Thames. But was there ever any serious thinking about what British films should or could be? Rodney Acland, Christopher Isherwood and other observers of that sub-culture have left an impression that British movie-making lacked any real seriousness and was vehemently anti-intellectual.[51] In conversations dominated by financial considerations and witty banter there would only be the occasional recognition that poor scripts and repertory company acting were cutting films off from the most vital aspects of the national experience. Surely what was needed was a clearer sense of genre and a clearer understanding of how the motion picture camera demanded an acting style that relied on an inner tension and dynamism?

Perhaps in that very pleasant and very innocent film sub-culture there were those who had resigned themselves to the bland and melodramatic nature of British films because they had read J. B. Priestley. Perhaps indeed British life was less interesting than that in America. Perhaps British cinema dealt in caricatures, stereotypes and charades because so much of everyday life was like that. Perhaps actors failed to behave naturally in front of the camera not because they had been trained in a provincial rep, but rather because as real people they had been trained to disguise emotion and to address other people, and especially their betters, in a highly formal and well-rehearsed way. Perhaps British cinema had not found a satisfactory rhetoric or mode of discourse because so many British people still existed in sub-cultures that could not possibly form the basis of successful films. In time some of these issues at least would be resolved, but for the time being reasonably entertaining British comedies and melodramas continued to take their place alongside that massive and never-ending supply of Hollywood films. More often than not, Hollywood products appeared more stylish, more real and more meaningful than the domestic product.

Notes and References

1. G. A. Atkinson, *Sunday Express*, 20 March 1927 (Sydney Carroll collection, British Film Institute (BFI) Library, London).
2. 'English films and English people', in *World Film News*, I (November 1936) 8.

3.   Peter Stead, 'Hollywood's message for the world: the British response in the 1930s', in *Historical Journal of Film, Radio and Television*, I (1981) 1.

4.   Arthur Vesselo, *Sight and Sound*, 5 (1936) 18; J. B. Priestley, *Rain upon Godshill: A further chapter of autobiography* (London, 1939) p. 82.

5.   'The course of realism', in Charles Davy (ed.), *Footnotes to the film* (London, 1938) p. 158. Reprinted in F. Hardy (ed.), *Grierson on Documentary* (London, 1946) p. 143.

6.   J. B. Priestley, *Let the People Sing* (London, 1939) p. 83.

7.   'Americans share in British fame', in Terry Ramsaye (ed.), *Fame* (London, 1937). In this article Aubrey Flanagan analysed the popularity of Fields and Formby movies with British audiences.

8.   *Daily Herald*, 23 December 1938.

9.   Graham Greene in the *Spectator*, 26 January 1940, reprinted in *The Pleasure Dome* (London, 1972); *Daily Express*, 19 January 1940 (Carol Reed collection, BFI Library).

10.   The Americans were also impressed and, of *The Stars Look Down*, *Liberty Magazine* commented that it 'could never have happened in Hollywood' (16 August 1941). See the Carol Reed collection at the BFI for American reviews.

11.   *Spectator*, 15 March 1940, and *The Pleasure Dome* (op. cit.) p. 275.

12.   *Picturegoer and Film Weekly*, 23 March 1940 (Balcon collection scrapbooks, BFI Library).

13.   The changed ending was mentioned in a review by Dilys Powell in *The Sunday Times*, 10 March 1940 (Carol Reed collection, BFI Library).

14.   *Kine Weekly*, 10 April 1941 (BFI Library file).

15.   Ian Dalrymple in the *Spectator*, 28 January 1938 (Balcon collection scrapbooks, BFI Library).

16.   *New Statesman*, 7 June 1941.

17.   Jane Morgan in the *Daily Worker*, 14 February 1938.

18.   *Sunday Express*, 1 June 1941.

19.   *Spectator*, 6 June 1941.

20.   *Kine Weekly*, 10 April 1941.

21.   Ernest Betts, *Sunday Express*, 1 June 1941.

22.   *Spectator*, 6 June 1941.

23.   See N. Pronay and J. Croft, 'British film censorship and propaganda policy during the second world war', in J. Curran and V. Porter (eds), *British cinema history* (London, 1983) pp. 144ff.

24.   Powell was interviewed by Ernest Betts in an article 'The Shelterers Verdict' in the *Sunday Express*, 20 April 1941 (Betts collection, BFI Library).

25.   *Sunday Express*, 16 March 1941.

26.   'The man on the screen', in *Documentary News Letter (DNL)*, 1 (1940) 5, p. 3.

27.   Dilys Powell, *Films since 1939* (London, 1947) pp. 14ff.

28.   Ibid., p. 39.

29.   Betts, 'Shelterers Verdict', *Sunday Express*, 20 April 1941 (op. cit.).

30.   'They laugh at realism', in *DNL*, 4 (1943) 3, p. 188.

31.   'A filmgoer's war diary', in Guy Morgan (ed.), *Red Roses Every Night* (London, 1948) p. 70.

32. *DNL*, 4 (1943) 4, p. 200.
33. See 'feature film propaganda', in *DNL*, 3 (1942) 5 and *The Bernstein Questionnaire, 1946–57* (London, 1958).
34. *DNL*, 4 (1943) 4.
35. Stephen Spender, *Citizens in war – and after* (London, 1945). Note in particular John Hindo's 48 colour photographs.
36. Humphrey Jennings collection, BFI Library, files 8 and 16.
37. 'Why no labour films?' in *DNL*, 6 (1947) 55.
38. Paul Rotha, *Documentary Diary* (London, 1973) p. 286.
39. Dilys Powell, *Films since 1939* (op. cit.) p. 19.
40. *Spectator*, 17 March 1944.
41. For Baxter see Jeffrey Richards, *The age of the dream palace: cinema and society in Britian, 1930–39* (London, 1984) p. 299.
42. *Spectator*, 2 January 1942.
43. Charles Barr, *Ealing Studios* (London, 1977) p. 37.
44. 'All of a sudden it's peace around the world', *Observer*, 10 March 1985.
45. Sue Aspinall, 'Women, realisms and reality in British films, 1943–53', in Curran and Porter, *British cinema history* (op. cit.) p. 279.
46. C. Isherwood, *Prater Violet* (London, 1946) p. 37 of Penguin edition.
47. *The Way Ahead*, United Kingdom press book (BFI Library). In the American press book for the film exhibitors were reminded that it 'is the story of our G. I. Joes too'.
48. C. A. Lejeune, *Chestnuts in her lap* (London, 1947) p. 136.
49. Dilys Powell, *Films since 1939* (op. cit.) p. 20.
50. *DNL*, 5 (1944) 1.
51. Rodney Ackland and Elspeth Grant, *The Celluloid Mistress* (London, 1954); Isherwood, *Prater Violet* (op. cit.).

5

British Cinema and the Reality of War

Clive Coultass

In notes written for a student screening of the feature film *The Next of Kin*, which he had directed in 1941 for Ealing Studios and the War Office, Thorold Dickinson had this to say about its preview at the Curzon cinema in London:

> The first version of *The Next of Kin* was so explicit that it sobered the troops who saw it and sickened many of the civilians, some of whom were carried out in a dead faint. The military cinema manager had to indent for a case of brandy and often called me from his office across the road to come and help him talk people back to calmness. The worst case we had to deal with was a most intelligent woman civil servant who had two sons serving overseas. She said that until her sons came back to Britain she would never sleep again. She insisted that all the scenes of fighting in the film were taken in genuine battles, that all the Germans were real Germans in actual military operations. I tried to explain that I alone had placed the cameras and instructed the performers, but she said I was lying and that the work was inexcusable. In the end we had to summon a military psychiatrist.[1]

The Next of Kin had started as a military training film on the subject of careless talk and, with encouragement from Michael Balcon, had grown into a full-length feature designed for general distribution.[2] The main story was about the leakage to the enemy of information concerning a raid by British troops on German installations in north-west France and, coincidentally, its completion early in 1942 just preceded a naval and commando assault on the dry dock at St Nazaire. The genuine operation achieved its objectives, with an acceptable level of casualties, at a time in the war when reverse and humiliation had become the common pattern of Britain's military effort. The fictional raid also had a limited success, but the forewarned Germans had inflicted heavy losses on the British, just as they were to do in the major attack on Dieppe in the following summer. Churchill had not wanted the film to be issued and, according to Dickinson's account, his aides insisted on the removal of some twenty seconds of film at the end. The military authorities, for their part, anxious that the message should be brought home to their soldiers and to the public, were more content to see the film screened.

The reactions described by Dickinson seem now to be extraordinary and can perhaps be partly explained by the relative 'illiteracy' of the public in visual terms when presented with images which the present-day observer would see as being realistic but hardly unusual or offensive. The sequences in question which caused so much shock had shown the corpses of British troops as whole units were massacred by an enemy that had been waiting in concealment for their landing. To depict death on the screen to that degree was unprecedented for a British wartime film, whether feature, documentary or newsreel, and official policy throughout had been to avoid the filming of casualties, a situation which had above all affected those cameramen of the Service Units and commercial newsreel companies whose job was to shoot the actuality sequences of the war which would most instantly be seen by the public. Individual death did occur in many British films from the second world war, and the loss of numbers of men was also acknowledged in features like *In Which We Serve* and *San Demetrio, London*, but only at a distance as ships are sunk at sea and not in the kind of bold close-up which Dickinson had employed to such obvious effect. The making of *The Next of Kin* can only be explained in the context of the army's anxiety about betrayal and the need to create more understanding about the activities of its security police. It was a fine line that had to be drawn, as Churchill realised. The Prime Minister's capacity to interfere with film projects has become legendary through the case of *The Life and Death of Colonel Blimp*.[3] With *The Next of Kin* there was possibly even greater justification for his fears. The man who had initiated the Gallipoli campaign in 1915 was able to appreciate the enormous hazards of the proposed 'second front' which the Russians and Americans were impatient to have him support, while he was unhappy about a film which might adversely influence the morale of the troops. Most of the script of *The Next of Kin* had not been far removed from the plots of other wartime spy thrillers, but its ending was a curiosity, an experiment not to be repeated.

Early British wartime films had shown little sense of reality at all – from the comical expectations of *The Lion Has Wings* (1939) that barrage balloons alone would frighten off German bombers to the fantasy heroics of *Ships With Wings* (1941) with its caricature characters and shoddy sets. It is clear that any movie which told the truth about war would be nine-tenths of the way towards being an anti-war film. It is equally obvious that the authorities, intent on maintaining support for a conflict which most people believed anyway to be a struggle to preserve their democratic way of life, had no intention of allowing any such productions to pass their censorship – even if there had been those in the film industry with sufficient independence of mind to promote projects of that nature. Moreover, the memory of the previous war still weighed heavily on all but the very young. Early features like *Pastor Hall* (1940), *Freedom Radio* (1941) and *Pimpernel Smith* (1941) put forward the mirage of Nazi society collapsing from within, an event which would spare the Allies the need to go through bloodbaths of the kind which had been commonplace in the first world war. Dunkirk and the blitz blew away the cobwebs of complacency and inertia, and the documentaries of 1940–1 at least were able to come to terms with the new spirit of endurance and resolution, even if in so doing they carefully papered over the cracks in British society. The commercial industry duly followed suit with home-front movies like *Salute John Citizen* (1942) and *The Bells Go Down* (1943), which showed the people as a united band of citizens at war. An appeal to the only possible saviour in the long term, the United States of America, was made with *The 49th Parallel* (1941), officially subsidised in order to demonstrate to Americans the ideological gap between Nazism and western democracy.

The public had never taken wholeheartedly to war films (though a select few of them were a success at the box office) and their principal mood had remained one of simple escapism. In any case, American productions dominated the distribution circuits. The last phase of the war saw the British industry turning away from war themes; the future became a major preoccupation of the documentaries and even of features such as *They Came to a City* (1944) and *Waterloo Road* (1945). Suburban family life came to be looked at nostalgically in *This Happy Breed* (1944), personal relationships were affected by the upheaval of war in *Perfect Strangers* (1945) and *Brief Encounter* (1945), and there were examples too of costume dramas, comedies and straightforward thrillers, all of which grew out of the assessment by the film producers of a new mood amongst their audiences that the tribulations of five years of war were behind them and that a war-weary people was searching for laughter and relaxation as it made its weekly visits to the cinema.

For some measure of reality in the films which were actually made during the course of the second world war, one must therefore look to the middle period of 1942–3. Early illusions about the ease with which Nazi Germany might soon fold up had long since gone and Britain had been forced to face up to a succession of military defeats in the Mediterranean, North Africa and the Far East. This change in the war situation by itself determined a freshness of outlook which the cinema could not ignore, and official encouragement provided a further impetus towards a morale-boosting view of the British as a people united in a common sense of determination, no longer content to sit back and just survive, but now to move forward to victory as part of their Grand Alliance with the Americans and Russians. However, the example of *The Next of Kin* should not mislead one about the general outlook of the military establishment – not normally enlightened when it came to offering support for film projects, a fact which was acknowledged by Ronald Tritton, the civilian publicity officer at the War Office. A proposed production with the title *The People's Army* ground to a halt when the colonel of the regiment with whom the film-makers were supposed to be working took the view that the title sounded like some kind of communist propaganda and, at a meeting to discuss future progress, another senior officer expressed the view that films on the army ought to show soldiers in the course of their ordinary day-to-day activities, for example showing them 'watering their horses'.[4] Only the unexpected popular success of the Army Film Unit's *Desert Victory* early in 1943 caused a change in appreciation of the value of film in some such circles.

As a military-type instructional film, *Kill or Be Killed*, made in 1942–3 by the independent company Realist, was intended on one level to demonstrate techniques for dealing with individual enemy snipers. As it was directed by Len Lye, a New Zealander who had worked with the GPO Film Unit before the war and who had made his principal reputation as a maker of animated films, the film gained a further quality as a stark document about the real essence of war: the bleak process of man-to-man combat with death at the end of the road for one or more of the participants. It has some elements which are less than satisfactory in the realist context: for example, the German sniper and his colleagues look as though they have been kitted out by a theatrical costumier (as no doubt they were). Also, the sniper's thoughts, as spoken by Marius Goring mixing English and German with a fake accent, would have been best left out. 'It's that damned Tommy', he says, while the British sergeant pronounces as his intention for the game they are playing, 'Hell, I'm going to get that Jerry, blast him, before he gets me.' According to Roger Manvell the British cinema audience was surprised by words like these, to which they were unaccustomed in their cosy cinema surroundings.[5] (They reacted with similar embarrassment to swear words in *In Which We Serve*.) Finally, the English countryside used as the location of *Kill or Be Killed* reminds one of no actual war front on which British forces were engaged, although this possibly adds to the faintly surreal feeling of the film as a whole.

In fact the spoken words are all thoughts in the minds of the two principal characters. Although Marius Goring speaks for the German, he is played by Alistair MacIntyre, who had been an actor in civil life and was now an army captain. Oddly, MacIntyre speaks the words for the British sergeant, performed in the flesh by Duncan Chisholm, formerly head gillie for a large game park in Inverness-shire. Chisholm was an expert marksman and deer stalker, and at the time of appearing in the film was recovering from temporary deafness caused in an exercise while training. The German sniper fires at a British mine-laying party, narrowly missing the sergeant. Thereafter the British soldier sets out on a hunt to trap him and he employs a number of devices which are lessons in ways of camouflage and deception. As he crawls forward through the foliage, the camera cleverly follows his movements. Lye and the cameraman (Adrian Jeakins) had thought that an orthodox rigid runway would provide lifeless tracking shots and so they supported the camera by fixing its leather handle to a rifle and carried it forward in this fashion. The sergeant succeeds in shooting the German and props up his body, head tilted against his weapon, to use as a decoy for his comrades. Blood oozing from the man's mouth was simulated using blackcurrant purée and apparently MacIntyre found it hard to pretend he was dead because of the number of wasps he attracted to the scene. When the other Germans (five of them) arrive the British sergeant coolly disposes of them one by one. In order to make the action convincing, Lye and Jeakins fitted a mask with the appearance of a rifle sight to the front of the camera. When Jeakins got one of the 'Germans' in his viewfinder, he would call out the man's prearranged number, and Lye would repeat it as a cue for the actor to fall down while he simultaneously jerked the mask sights to simulate a rifle kick as the German dropped dead. At the end of the film aircraft pass overhead and the camera cuts repeatedly between the bodies of the dead Germans and cartridge cases on the ground, a technical trick reminiscent of some of Lye's more complex films and one which reinforces the impression of surrealism. It is a factor which helps to lift *Kill or Be Killed* from the level of a simple training film to a more abstract plane, as a statement about the violent nature of war.[6]

Military training was also the starting point for two longer films about the army. One of them, *The Way Ahead*, released in 1944, became one of the most successful British features at the box office and it had been created (with encouragement from the MoI) as a propagandist production about the concept of the ordinary citizen turning himself into a soldier, a prop for the official view of the nation's unanimity in wartime. Ealing's shorter *Nine Men*, issued at the beginning of 1943, began from a different base more directly derived from the traditions of the British documentary movement, one of whose aims throughout the 1930s had been the depiction on screen of a form of realism which was generally absent from the commercial industry. Cavalcanti left the GPO Film Unit in 1940 for Ealing, where his influence helped that studio's attempt to provide a genuine kind of representation in cinema of British people free of the class stereotypes of the past. *Nine Men* was directed by Harry Watt, who had followed Cavalcanti in 1942. Its basic story, that of an isolated stand by a small group of British soldiers in the desert against a larger Italian force, was written for the screen by Watt himself and was filmed by him in the same type of careful, conscientious style which he employed in his GPO and Crown Film Unit documentaries. Location shooting took place in an area in Wales which convincingly reproduced the sand dunes of the North African desert.

For the first time in his film career Watt was making use of some professional actors, but he deliberately avoided star names and looked for those who would be able to play what were in fact the people who made up the members of a real British infantry unit, men from mostly working-class backgrounds, both regulars and conscripts. As in his Crown documentary *Target for Tonight* (1941), he paid attention to diversity of accents (though in fact army regiments were more highly regionalised, made up as they were from a preponderance of men from a single county or adjacent group of counties). In fact most of the recruits characterised in *The Way Ahead* were actually middle-class in origin and David Niven's upper-middle-class demeanour was not strictly right for the role he played as garage owner and territorial officer. Watt's approach for *Nine Men*, however, was quite different. He selected the stage actor Jack Lambert for the part of the Scottish sergeant, and two other Scots, Grant Sutherland as Private Jack Scott, a Glasgow policeman who had been dismissed from the force, and Gordon Jackson as the 'young 'un' who is believed to be younger than his stated age of nineteen. A Geordie, Jack Horsman, was chosen to play former Durham miner Joe Harvey. Bill Blewett, the Cornish postmaster who had been featured first by Watt in his GPO documentary *The Saving of Bill Blewett* (1936), became Bill Parker, a regular soldier. For the Cockney Banger Hill, Watt tested an amateur actor, an NFS fireman called Fred Griffiths, but in the end he came down on the side of experience, giving the part to Frederick Piper (who was to be the bo'sun in *San Demetrio, London*). Watt found himself so prejudiced in favour of working-class reality that he had to be persuaded by Cavalcanti that he should have at least one middle-class recruit for the plot to be truly representative, and Eric Micklewood was picked to play Private Gordon Lee, the 'booky', a Cambridge man.[7]

Dialogue in *Nine Men* was cut to a minimum, registering mainly commands and reactions. The survivors of the group hide in a stone hut which is besieged by the Italians. There are no reposeful moments, although in the hands of a more traditional (and arguably more imaginative) writer the plot might have been expanded from its 65-minute compass to the length of a full feature if it had attempted to say more about the individual soldiers and their lives during those periods when they were simply watching and waiting. Watt's puritanical dedication to the most literal form of realism allows for none of this. Apart from a brief exchange between Parker and Scott about life on the streets of Glasgow, there is no room for expansion in the script, and this tautness secures conviction on one level as a documentary account of action but also denies it the opportunity of making a more searching and symbolic statement about the nature of war from a further plane of artistic fulfilment.

Perhaps this is why some of its critics at the time considered it 'naïve'. Audiences were not accustomed to this cerebral style in a fiction film and they responded with more enthusiasm to the panache and humour of a production like *The Way Ahead*, in which the main parts were taken by familiar screen actors who conformed more to the requirements of a public taste which fell short of a need for outright realism.

In the final sequence of *The Way Ahead* the British soldiers move forward, bayonets fixed, through smoke and dust to engage the enemy, while the end-title announces that it is in fact 'the beginning'. In *Nine Men* actual close combat is directly witnessed. The first Italian attack on the hut has medium camera shots of the men firing through the apertures, seen from both front and rear, and close-ups of the rifles themselves, the triggers being pulled, fresh magazines being pressed in after each of the Lee Enfield's six rounds has been spent. When the enemy has retreated, the film's images show relaxation and relief on the faces of the soldiers; they wipe the sweat away; one spits onto the ground. There is a moment's silence and then a release of tension as they chat excitedly about what had just happened:

'Young 'un': Here, you should have seen the bloke I got with my pursuer. He jumped about seven feet in the air and stuck his head in the sand like a bleedin' ostrich.
Hill: Did you see the bloke who dropped his tin hat and tried to pick it up? Blimey, did I catch him bending.
Harvey: When I got the big fellow with the skinny legs I saw the look of surprise from here.
Scott: Now wait a minute. You should have seen the one I got in the shoulder . . . he stopped dead. Absolutely beautiful it was.

The sergeant interrupts: 'All right, we haven't won the war yet.' The only line which strikes a false note occurs earlier when Harvey receives a glancing blow from a bullet on his helmet and, as he falls back, the sun casts a glow round its rim. The wounded and delirious Dusty Johnstone cries out: 'Since when did they have saints in Hell?'

In the final action of *Nine Men*, just before the beleaguered group is rescued, the British soldiers go out to engage the Italians in a dire bayonet-to-bayonet struggle and again the camera pinpoints the clash of weapons and the faces of the men as they come together in this primitive form of 'kill or be killed' game. The soldiers call the enemy 'macaroni munchers', but the film does not parody the Italians, seeing them instead as worthy combatants – a departure from the practice of so many other British films. It was a form of treatment in line with Harry Watt's intentions: to make a straight-forward 'record' of a credible incident in the North African campaign. To have put into the plot a character like the Peter Ustinov café owner in *The Way Ahead*, who pours wine on to a soldier's machine gun when it overheats, would have disturbed that sense of simple naturalism. At the same time, by having the story narrated by the sergeant to a group of new recruits, persuading them of the necessity for adding a bit of 'oompetypoo' to their battle eagerness, Watt linked the affair to the experiences and expectations of citizens in training for war.

The British have never been an army-minded people: their front line had always been the sea. Thus the Battle of the Atlantic turned out to be the nation's most sustained and successful – if unspectacu-lar – campaign of the second world war. The extent to which Cavalcanti and the documentary movement had influenced Ealing was demonstrated by *San Demetrio, London*, a very faithful adap-tation from an official publication which had narrated the true story of a damaged tanker being saved by a part of its crew. It was, however, entirely shot in the studio, and so the basis from which it started was different again from that which inspired the making of the Crown Film Unit's feature documentary *Western Approaches*, a film which although not finished until late 1944 had belonged both in its conception and in the main process of production to the middle part of the war. Following the GPO/Crown traditions, its director Pat Jackson made the film entirely with amateur actors, playing themselves, but it was unusual for the time in that it was filmed in Technicolor. It had one other innovative feature for a British wartime film: Germans in a U-boat (actually Dutch naval men) speak in German and their words are translated with subtitles.

Some of the work was done at Pinewood, including the interior sequences for the U-boat, which involved the scene of its sinking at the end of the film when the trapped men struggle against the rising tide of water as their vessel slides below the surface. At the time this was most unusual: there is no parallel, for instance, in the post-war Ealing production *The Cruel Sea* (1953). Yet this enemy angle was an essential ingredient in a plot which has the U-boat shadowing a lifeboat with survivors from the torpedoed *Jason* in the hope that its wireless signals would attract another target. This tactic works, but the British freighter *Leander* is able to turn the tables on the submarine by sinking her with gunfire.

Most of *Western Approaches*, however, was filmed actually at sea. The project had begun as a story on the transatlantic convoys, and the film unit travelled to New York to accompany a convoy back to Britain. In addition to the required shots on the docks, of the merchant ships and their escorts, Pat Jackson (who himself played one of the *Leander*'s junior officers) was able to have the freighter stopped for a time while the crew simulated abandoning ship. In the plot the *Leander* has been hit by a torpedo and, once it appears that the crew has left the ship, the U-boat moves in for the kill. In fact the captain and two others are still aboard and they man the ship's defensive armament. The navy co-operated by providing a real submarine for the surface shots and by effectively faking explosions as the shells from the *Leander*'s four inch gun hit its target. Whereas realistic feature-type films such as *Nine Men* and *Fires Were Started* had relatively simple stories, as soon as the extra dimension of the U-boat was added in *Western Approaches* it gained in complexity, acquiring a certain suspense quality, and in this respect it was something of a departure from what had been accepted practice in the documentary movement.

In terms of the shooting schedule, the most painstaking sequences of all were those filmed inside the *Jason*'s lifeboat. Jackson had recruited a score of real seamen and took them with his film unit to Holyhead. From there they set out to shoot, over a period of several months, the lifeboat scenes, some from within the boat itself and others from an accompanying launch and drifter. The decision to make the film in Technicolor required the use of a heavy triple-negative camera, operated by Jack Cardiff who had been recruited by Crown from the industry, and at times this, together with the sound equipment, had to be crammed into the boat along with the amateur actors and film crew. The plot made it necessary to shoot in the Irish Sea during some periods of rough weather, and the whole experience of filming while putting the seamen-actors through the routines of rehearsing their dialogue was a demanding undertaking for the director and his assistants, clearly more arduous than the making of a similar sequence in *San Demetrio, London* in the studio at Ealing.[8]

The *San Demetrio*'s lifeboat contained survivors who were played by professional actors, some less well known to the public, others more so (among them Ralph Michael, Walter Fitzgerald, Robert

Beatty, Mervyn Johns, Gordon Jackson and Frederick Piper). It is difficult to argue that the use of genuine seamen in *Western Approaches* increased the sense of 'realism' as such, but it can justifiably be said to be more 'authentic'. And Pat Jackson succeeded in bringing out the real personalities of a few of them. There is, for example, the obstinate and stubborn Bob Banner from Merseyside who describes how the vessel sank and how the U-boat machine-gunned some of the men as they were abandoning ship. He himself had gone under the water with the *Jason*:

> I was going down and down and down and I could feel pressure on me here, you know, and in my ears, and I thought to myself 'this is it' and I think the boilers must have went and I shot up to the top and I had my eyes open and I was looking up and I could see the sky getting brighter and brighter, you know, at the top of the water and I come up to the top and by God I thought I was an aeroplane. I ruddy near came right out of the water and I looked around me, all that was left was a few spots of oil, not a damn soul anywhere and I started to holler and you know the rest.

As the men tire, Banner sings to try and lift their spirits. Several days later, when the *Leander* approaches them, the sick Rawson spots the U-boat's periscope but most of the sailors think he has imagined it. Captain Pycraft, however, is not prepared to take any chances and turns the lifeboat away from the rescue vessel. Banner threatens to lead a mutiny against him: 'It's our lives you're taking chances with and we're not going to stand for it, do you hear? There you are, risking all our blooming lives just because a man off his head thought he saw a U-boat. There's twenty-four men in here, mister!' The captain does, however, win the others round and the argument is resolved when Banner himself sees the submarine. Another personality in the lifeboat is a journalist, Tosti Russell, the son of an operatic impresario who had become an American citizen and had gone to sea to gather material on the Battle of the Atlantic. He asks: 'But what is it that makes you all go back to the sea? What's your reason Fred?' Fred Armistead, a steward, replies:

> I don't know really. Maybe it's because you always want something you haven't got. You see, it's like this with me – when I'm at home I miss the sea and when I'm at sea I miss the missus. In fact, between you and I, I don't know which I miss most. Now

when I do come home from a trip, me and my old dutch hit it off a treat but she just can't see me about the house too long. And that goes for me in a way.

Compared, then, with *Nine Men*, the script of *Western Approaches* moves a small way towards exploring the lives of some of its characters, banal though they might appear to be, but it does not go as far as one would have expected in a mainstream feature film. The documentary method was more concerned with immediate, workaday conversation, not with the embellishments which added more depth and fantasy to people's lives. (The contrast in style can be studied in more detail with the two Fire Service films, Ealing's *The Bells Go Down* (1943) and Crown's *Fires Were Started* (1943).) In terms of portraying the reality of the war at sea it took a small step, one which was perhaps as far as audiences between 1942 and 1944 were prepared to accept. The men in the lifeboat were seen in a situation which called for grit and perseverance, qualities greatly admired in the tight-lipped British context. Death of their shipmates was referred to in retrospect rather than being represented on screen. A naval gunner does die on the *Leander* (just as the greaser Boyle dies on the *San Demetrio* after carrying on for as long as his injuries allow) but it is a moment which is passed over cursorily. Not the least of the virtues of *Western Approaches* is the way in which it brought to the attention of the public the sacrifices being made for them by a group of civilians at sea, distinguished only by their very ordinariness, different again from the glamorised naval characters of films like *Convoy* (1940) and *In Which We Serve* (1941).

The theme of battle against the U-boats was tackled again in the Ealing production of *The Cruel Sea*, directed by Charles Frend (who had also directed *San Demetrio, London*) and released in 1953. Based on the popular novel by Nicholas Montserrat published a few years earlier, the film was scripted by Eric Ambler, who had contributed to the writing of *The Way Ahead*. It was thus made as a retrospect within the first decade after the war. For its time the novel was more candid about one aspect of war than any other book to originate in Britain in the 1950s (though it had nothing like the sophistication of Norman Mailer's *The Naked and the Dead* about Americans at war). It is not surprising that it should have been about the sea, so close to the sentiments of a maritime people, and its account of the horrors of the Battle of the Atlantic left a powerful impression on its reading public. Even so, Montserrat introduced a layer of artifice by personifying the sea in his title and by referring in his introduction to 'its moods, its violence, its gentle balm, its treachery, what men can do with it, and what it can do with men'. And later: 'the men are the stars of this story. The only heroines are the ships and the only villain the cruel sea itself.' Poor sea! The caption for the film wisely added 'which man has made crueller' to the last sentence.

The film did not reproduce the most gruesome moments in the book, the episodes of 'the dead helmsman' (adrift in a lifeboat), 'the burnt man' (a death agony), 'the skeletons' (corpses floating in their lifejackets) or 'the burning tanker' (the crew gradually trapped by the flaming oil). It was not prepared to offend public taste with that degree of naturalism. The most harrowing part of the film version is the sequence where the corvette *Compass Rose* follows an ASDIC contact and discovers that men from a torpedoed ship are swimming above what seems to be a submerged U-boat. The convoy has been almost wiped out by submarine attacks against which its few escorts appear to be helpless, a truthful reflection of a period known to U-boat crews as the 'happy time'. The captain of the *Compass Rose* Lieutenant-Commander Ericson, makes the decision to drop depth charges in the knowledge that he will kill the men in the water. Immediately afterwards the ASDIC contact is lost. There are some subtle differences in the way the incident was treated in the novel and the film. 'Bloody murderer!' a sailor calls out to the bridge in the Ealing version, a touch which increases the emotional impact. But the book makes it clear that Ericson believes in the end that there had been no submarine after all, and that the sonar contact might have been with the torpedoed ship as it sank to the bottom. This was a conclusion which the film script could not face. On screen Ericson, played by Jack Hawkins, insists that there must have been a U-boat. In harbour at Gibraltar, after a heavy drinking session, he tearfully tells his first lieutenant, who has himself been trying to shoulder the blame for the incident: 'No one killed them. It's the war, the whole bloody war. We've just got to do these things and say our prayers at the end.'

Whereas *Western Approaches* had been set entirely at sea (apart from the convoy briefing scenes), *The Cruel Sea* followed the lines of Montserrat's novel by sketching some details of the sailors' lives at home. In the book Ericson's first lieutenant, Lockhart, starts an affair with a Wren, second officer Hallam. They talk about marriage after the war, they make love and she becomes pregnant, but it all ends tragically with her death in an accident. The coy British cinema convention of the early 1950s did not permit them to go to bed. Lockhart and Hallam, played respectively by Donald Sinden and Virginia McKenna, have a traditional screen romance with a happy ending. In the book Hallam's death had been the turn of the screw which completed the framework of the agony and bleakness of war, but the film script had backed away from it.

Compass Rose is torpedoed with few survivors. Ericson goes on to command the frigate *Saltash Castle*, Lockhart joining him again as first lieutenant. While the captain is obsessionally pursuing a U-boat which no one else believes to exist, he talks to Lockhart about his feelings on the war at that stage, dialogue which is lifted from the novel (although from another part of it):

> It's getting to be a different kind of war, Number One. The people in it have got different too. At the beginning there was time for all sorts of things – understanding people, making allowances for them, wondering whether they were happy, even whether they like you or not. Now the war doesn't seem to be a matter of feelings any more. All that finished with *Compass Rose*. Now it's just a matter of killing the enemy. I suppose you think that's all wrong and a man should never allow himself to be dehumanised by war? . . . After the war, I'll be as sweet as you like to everybody, including you . . .

Ericson's sentiments express the basic view of both the novel and the film about the war which the British have been fighting.

It has been noticed that the film in some respects failed to carry forward the degree of realism which the book had conveyed – not a very surprising development, since cinema in Britain has always lagged behind literature. The convoy scenes and sequences of ships sinking had been shot in the studio tank at Ealing (there were also a few newsreel shots) and in terms of style the film related closely to Frend's earlier *San Demetrio, London*. Its black and white cinematography was adequate for its needs and, on balance, it gave a faithful account of the privations which had been suffered by men involved in the struggle to keep the sea lanes open. It did not advance from the realism of *Western Approaches*. It was too restrained to become a complete anti-war movie. The kind of war which book and film represented was a necessary war, a fight for survival with the sea itself providing a metaphor for Britain's epic endurance through the years 1939–45.

The Cruel Sea was perhaps the last British film to be sufficiently close to the events of the second world war to retain a high measure of authenticity. There have been dutiful reconstructions like the blockbusters *The Battle of Britain* (1969) and *A Bridge Too Far* (1977), but their style is remote from the period which they have tried to recreate. British cinema's attempt to capture the reality of the war almost began and ended with the period of hostilities itself, and flourished particularly between 1942 and 1943. The attempt was circumscribed both by the attitude of the authorities and by the conventions which were familiar to audiences of the time. Most of the notable directors of features during the war had had no experience of the documentary movement, although some, like Roy Boulting and Carol Reed, were to make outstanding non-fiction films. Almost all of them, however, were influenced by its methods. Gilliat and Launder's *Millions Like Us* (1943) derives directly from the Rotha production of *Night Shift* (1942). Leslie Howard went through a remarkable transformation of style from *Pimpernel Smith* (1941) through *The First of the Few* (1942) to his near-documentary film about army servicewomen, *The Gentle Sex* (1943). It is more surprising that Harry Watt virtually abandoned the whole area after *Nine Men*, though he was to bring some of his experience in handling realism to his film set in Australia, *The Overlanders* (1946).

Cavalcanti himself directed for Ealing only one very singular feature with a war theme, *Went the Day Well?* (1942). The story by Graham Greene on which it was supposed to be based was in fact totally different both in content and spirit, and Greene himself never saw the film.[9] Written as it had been before the summer of 1940, the story depicted a group of Nazi invaders as amateur bunglers, an attitude which probably arose out of the phoney war period. By the time of the film, in 1942, they had turned into ruthless paratroopers disguised in British uniforms, while the community in the village which they try to hold reacts with its own form of counter-violence. *Kill or Be Killed* had started as a project which would teach not only soldiers but also the irregular Home Guard force how to cope with individual enemy snipers in the event of invasion. *Went the Day Well?* was an extension of this uncompromising message and, in spite of much that has been written about it in retrospect as an anti-war film, it did not say anything radically different from the determined postures which had been adopted by a number of the documentaries. (It even had a striking antecedent in *Miss Grant Goes to the Door*, made in 1940.) Both it and Powell and Pressburger's

Colonel Blimp had the same purpose, namely to persuade the public that the Nazis have to be defeated by their own methods. It is this mood which is the crucial factor in understanding the few British films of the central part of the war which tried to readjust realistically to the state of the nation at that time.

Beating the enemy on his own terms did not include frankness about the most controversial area of the British war effort, the strategic bombing offensive against Germany. The subject of indiscriminate bombing had been discussed in a scene showing a press conference in Ealing's *The Big Blockade* (1942), a film which still promoted a number of illusions about how Germany might be defeated. The representative of the Ministry of Economic Warfare who fields the questions in this scene is heard arguing against such a policy. A bombing sequence in the same film gives the impression, as *Target for Tonight* (1941) had done, that the RAF could strike specific objectives in the dark with ease. In fact, at the time of the release of *The Big Blockade* early in 1942, Bomber Command had despaired of being able to hit anything except a whole city. The newsreels kept up a barrage of revengeful comment about the bombing, but only one small film, *The Biter Bit* (1943) directed by Alexander Korda, gave a hint of its more drastic effects on civilians while also providing a justification for such action. Military historians have indicated that the death of around 55 000 aircrew, the élite of the British fighting services, was as severe a loss as the decimation of the officer class in the first world war.[10] It is interesting to note that the feature films did begin to have airmen killed on duty, though always off screen (*The Way to the Stars* (1945) is the best known example) and the theme was taken no further, not even in any post-war production.

If British cinema had any collective purpose during the second world war, it was that of putting forward – in features and documentaries alike – the image of a people working together with the kind of unity which Winston Churchill had asked from them. A few film-makers, mostly from the documentary movement, also saw social improvement as being one of the nation's goals. The virtues which were lauded on film were those of bombed-out citizens in the blitz, merchant seamen cast adrift in the Atlantic or recruits of the people's army with their backs to the wall. What mattered was stoicism, resolution, togetherness. It had become possible, though not very common, to put working-class characters on the screen without seeing them as comic caricatures. But the

quality welcomed most of all in the British war film was understatement. Although the high street public seems to have liked *The Next
of Kin* (judging from a Mass Observation report), the reactions to it
of its establishment preview audience showed how much it was the
exception to the rule. When inertia and conformity set in again as
soon as the war was over, the industry's brief flirtation with the
reality of the war came to an end.

Notes and References

1.   Notes written for the University of East Anglia. One might allow for a
      possible degree of exaggeration in Thorold Dickinson's recollection
      of the event.
2.   The script for *The Next of Kin* was written by Dickinson in co-
      operation with the Ealing staff writers Angus Macphail and John
      Dighton, along with the military supervisor, Captain Sir Basil
      Bartlett.
3.   This celebrated case is discussed in I. Christie (ed.), *Powell, Press-
      burger and Others* (London, 1978) and by J. Richards and A. Aldgate
      in *Best of British* (Oxford, 1983).
4.   From the unpublished diaries of Ronald Tritton, extracts from which
      have been made available to the Imperial War Museum, London.
5.   Roger Manvell, 'They laugh at realism', in *Documentary News Letter
      (DNL)*, 4 (1943) 3, p. 188.
6.   Production details for *Kill or Be Killed* can be found in PRO INF 6/479.
7.   Harry Watt, 'Casting *Nine Men*', in *DNL* 4 (1943) 2, pp. 179–80. Fred
      Griffiths was retained for a few lines at the beginning of the film, as
      one of a number of grousing recruits, but he was to win more fame as
      the former taxi driver who sings 'One man went to mow a meadow'
      in Humphrey Jennings' *Fires Were Started*.
8.   Production details for *Western Approaches* can be found in PRO INF 6/
      370.
9.   Graham Greene's 'The Lieutenant Died Last' was originally pub-
      lished in 1940 and reprinted in Hugh Greene, *The Pirate of the Round
      Pond* (London, 1977).
10.   The argument has been made most strongly by John Terraine in *The
      Right of the Line* (London, 1985).

6

British Historical Epics in the Second World War

Nigel Mace

The scene is the sunny terracing of an English country house where, among the spectators, its owner Mr Ranalow (played by Felix Aylmer) is in conversation with Ivan Kouznetsoff (Laurence Olivier) from Nijni-Petrovsk. A historical pageant is about to be performed:

> *Ivan*: But vhy do you hev it if you do not like it?
>
> *Ranalow*: We English, my dear fellow, have a regrettable tendency to indulge in matters historical and so, this afternoon, you will see the Roman occupation of Britain, the Black Death, an Old English Fair, Welcome to Queen Elizabeth and the stagecoach bringing the news of Waterloo . . .

Although the territory covered by British historical epics during the second world war was less extensive than that promised to the puzzled Russian engineer by the paternalistic shipbuilding magnate in Anthony Asquith's *The Demi-Paradise* in 1943, it may well yield conclusions no less definite than those which close the first Barchester pageant in that film. As the promised coach draws to a halt, a gentleman passenger leaps to his feet, hat raised to cheer, and cries 'The Battle of Waterloo!':

> *People*: Yes, yes. Who won it?
>
> *Gentleman*: *(after a hushed pause)* WE did!

Mr Ranalow, turning to his neighbour with an amused sigh, says 'For one awful moment, I thought we'd lost!' To discover whether wartime British historical films offer even so clear a view of British history as this, and to explore why it may be of historical significance whether they do or not, we should begin with the implications of Ivan's question.

101

Despite their obvious failings, the case for studying historical films, that is feature films dealing with relatively remote, even pre-cinematic, periods of the past, has been well made by Pierre Sorlin. It is a case which exists at two levels. First there is the way in which such films may be seen as selecting and recasting past events to reflect the circumstances of the time of the film's production. As Sorlin maintains, 'an historical film is a reconstruction of the social relationship which, using the pretext of the past, reorganises the present'.[1] Nor is this merely one historian's construction. *The Times*, in its review of Carol Reed's *The Young Mr Pitt* (1942), used the following headline and opening paragraph:

PARALLELS IN HISTORY

The parallel between the wars against Napoleon and against Hitler are close enough to tempt any director in these days when films are all too prone to find in the past dubious and unexpected texts for lessons on present events. William Pitt, representing England in her earlier days of trial, suggests obvious comparisons with our present leader and the opportunities for a film of false history and easy glorification are all too plain.[2]

The second sense in which Sorlin has seen such studies as important relates to what he has called 'the cinematographic conception of historiography'[3] (here shortened to 'cinematic historiography'). By this he means us to understand that the cinema's versions of the past are themselves a part of the total body of material out of which historical traditions (that is, successive interpretations of the past) are made and which, for their own time, express such traditions. It is in these two senses that Sorlin can legitimately claim that 'it would repay our interest to analyse historical films in which we have a chance of finding a *view* of the present embedded within a *picture* of the past' (my emphasis).[4] Sorlin's own method was to concentrate on films 'produced during periods of tension rather than those that were released in a period of relative calm'.[5] This not only fits the war as a whole but also the specific period in which the major British historical films were released, namely 1941 and 1942.

The cinematic mobilisation of history in the second world war was much less all-embracing and much more selective than that suggested by the *Times* review. In Germany historical films were one of the main production categories throughout the war, with some sixteen titles, many of which were directly harnessed to the needs of the psychological war effort, such as Wolfgang Lieben-einer's *Bismarck* (1940) on the *Führerprinzip*, Veit Harlan's *Jud Süss* (1940) on the Final Solution, Harlan's *Der Grosse König* (1942) on manifest German destiny against Russia, or Harlan's *Kolberg* (1945) on final civilian resistance. Less specific than these were those films which, in the guise of artistic 'biopics', gave meaning to Nazi ideas on the *volkisch* nature of genius by annexing to Nazi history suitable 'stars' of high German culture, such as Hans Steinhoff's *Rembrandt* (1942) or Herbert Maisch's *Andreas Schluter* (1942). Among the western allies, however, history was less obviously, or at any rate less frequently, recruited. The now well-documented case of Henry King's *Wilson* (1944)[6] was a clear enough example in the United States, yet with the constant recreation and re-examination of American myths through the 'historical' vehicle of the Western, it becomes difficult to assign many other American films of the period to a sensibly discrete historical category. How, for example, is the historian to approach Raoul Walsh's film of Custer's last stand, *They Died With Their Boots On* (1941)? As Western, as biopic, or as historical film?

The British case is less complex. During the entire period of the war, there were only four films produced in Britain which were historical in the sense discussed here. We must discount both Olivier's *Henry V* (1944) and Korda's *Lady Hamilton* (1941): the former, for all its obvious jingoism, still had Shakespeare's play as its basic text, however much it was altered for the cinema; the latter was produced in Hollywood, and even Churchill's meddlesome enthusiasm[7] and Korda's supposed links with British intelligence[8] cannot be said to have made it a British production. Of the four films which remain, one does not merit consideration (Lance Comfort's 1941 film for British National, *Penn of Pennsylvania*) because it is not mainly concerned with the British past. This leaves Thorold Dickinson's *The Prime Minister* (1941), Carol Reed's *The Young Mr Pitt* (1942) and Norman Walker's *The Great Mr Handel* (1942). How did these films relate to people's contemporary sense of the crisis through which they were passing and to the existing view of the world which the cinema in Britain had been fostering for the previous decade?

The 1930s had seen the cinematic construction of a consensus view of Britain and of Britain's past.[9] This consensus was composed of celebration of the empire abroad, the resolution of conflict at home by consent and the consolidation of a class society in which progress was assured while its members kept happily in their respective places. These points can be illustrated throughout the decade, for example, by *Sanders of the River* (1935), *Say It With Flowers* (1936), *Sixty Glorious Years* (1938), *South Riding* (1938) and *Shipyard Sally* (1939). In most respects it can be argued that the experience of the second world war did little to erode this manufactured image of apparent consensus, and this seems especially true of historical films. Thus, while a small relaxation of censorship at last allowed John Baxter's *Love On The Dole* (1941) to be made, the Ministry of Information's desire to foster the notion of the 'people's war' resulted in not one historical film which dealt with a genuine people's hero or champion. There was no wartime Robin Hood, no Cromwell, nor even any hero of labour to proclaim the depth of the 'people's traditions' in the face of oppression. During the 1930s the overwhelming image conveyed by historical films had been that of the royal family and of Queen Victoria especially. Around these pivotal figures the lesser lights of mere prime ministers, inventors and adventurers had been allowed to appear, but as largely conventional props to the central tale. Now, with films which focused on politicians and on what the Bishop of London called in *The Great Mr Handel* 'a person of the theatre . . . who, as a Playhouse Person, is still described in law as a rogue and a vagabond', British cinema might be breaking fresh ground.

The chief restraint on doing so remained the very efficient system of political censorship established by successive home secretaries through the co-operative medium of the British Board of Film Censors.[10] Indeed, given the fact that *Sixty Glorious Years* had been partly scripted by both Robert Vansittart, Permanent Undersecretary at the Foreign Office, and by Lord Tyrrell, President of the BBFC,[11] we should expect to find every sign of official intervention in the production of films venturing into such subjects. Yet there is no trace of any of these films in the surviving files of the MoI or in the BBFC pre-production scenario reports. MoI files do, however, provide evidence that the companies responsible for these productions were co-operating fully with the ministry and with the censorship authorities in advance of films being shot.

An internal memorandum of November 1941, in the discussion between the MoI and the Censorship about the volume and practicability of censorship tasks, stated that there were currently 41 'public and private bodies consulting the film censorship' and among the complete list, which was appended, were Warner

Brothers, Twentieth Century Fox and Associated Pictures – the three parent companies of the productions in question.[12] Not all companies were seen as being equally co-operative, but those which were only seemed to the official mind to furnish grounds for treating the cinema with particular rigour. As an official at the Dominions Office put it in April 1942:

Indeed there would seem much to be said for insisting that all films . . . should be compulsorily submitted to Censorship . . . We know that it might not be easy to give effect to such proposals which amount to discrimination against film companies in favour of other producers of publicity material . . . There is a distinction to be drawn between the publication of opinions in print and an attempt to represent them in the cinema or the theatre. The stage and screen can present a case with much greater vividness and criticism so conveyed is therefore more likely to wound the sensitive. This is commonly recognised by the public and indeed by the film companies themselves who have voluntarily agreed to a domestic censorship of their own of a kind which newspapers presumably would not tolerate.[13]

Certainly the volume of film being viewed for censorship as early as October 1941 would indicate that virtually all films were being viewed on a post-production basis[14] in addition to such advice and guidance as might be sought or given beforehand.

In the case of *The Young Mr Pitt* Geoff Brown has recorded some of Launder and Gilliat's memories of script disagreements with Ted Black and with Lord Castlerosse, who was assigned the role of 'historical adviser' and provider of additional dialogue, in the course of which he gossiped about the War Cabinet.[15] This may indicate official interest, as may the fact that Maurice Ostrer, very much a Conservative partisan, was in personal charge of the production at the Gaumont-British studios in Shepherds Bush. However, it is not upon the discovery of some fresh evidence of official manipulation that the importance of these films rests, but upon their contribution to the cinematic historiography of the war years. The historical viewpoints developed in British feature films during the war were remarkable for the consistency with which they re-presented the past, whether it was the very recent past of the twentieth century or the remoter past of eighteenth- and nineteenth-century Britain. Indeed it can be shown that the cinema built up not several but rather one overwhelming historiography, a historiography which found its fullest expression in *The Prime Minister* and *The Young Mr Pitt*, but which found a passing outlet in other films also. These more contemporary references, though brief, gained significance from repetition and served to establish the view of the 'recently-lived' past with which historical films could interact throughout the war years.

The most recent of these references can be summarised and categorised under the following headings and are exemplified in many more films than can be noted here.

(1) Appeasement: This policy was uniformly criticised as shameful (as in *This Happy Breed*), as itself productive of war (as in *The Demi-Paradise*), as a betrayal of traditional English values (as in *The Life and Death of Colonel Blimp*) and as an abandonment of the British role as guardian of small nations (as in *One of Our Aircraft is Missing*).

(2) Rearmament: Here the line was that it was too little and came nearly too late (as in *The Way Ahead*) and that this was the fault either of a pacifist-minded public (as in *The Demi-Paradise*) or of the pre-war National Government (as in *This Happy Breed*, where Baldwin's newsreel image from the 1935 general election was evoked as a poster on a film van with the slogan 'I shall never stand for a policy of great armaments').

(3) The 'Prophet without Honour': Opportunities were rarely lost to reflect contrastingly and favourably on the role of Churchill before the war, and examples of this accompany the anti-appeasement and the pro-rearmament passages in both *The Way Ahead* and *This Happy Breed*.

Similarly, the domestic perspective of the inter-war years was from a proto-Churchillian Conservative standpoint. In *This Happy Breed*, for example, not only was the empire in India celebrated but, at home, the general strike was revealed to all – with loud-mouthed socialist youths and mentally unstable spinsters posing a threat of 'bloody revolution', defeated by a patriotic alliance of upper and middle classes. And in the years which followed, in the film, there appeared to be no Depression but only a steadily improving prosperity which socialised the intemperate socialist youth into bowler-hatted respectability.

Much harder to pin down clearly, but cumulatively and demonstrably present, was the assumption – common to pre-war films with social themes – that there was a natural understanding and sympathy to be discovered between a caring, traditionalist upper ruling class and the workers. This had shown through even in such 'newly liberal' films made on the eve of hostilities as *The Stars Look Down* (1939), where the 'old money' mine owner guides the rescue parties, suffers a heart attack while leading the rescuers and finally dies while trying to take the plans of the old workings, which greed had earlier led him to suppress, to the pit head. Nowhere was this assumption more clearly stated with reference to the wartime experience of the cinema audience than when, during the devastation of the London blitz, the city's screens showed *The Common Touch* (1941) with its evocative final speeches. The film closes with its upper-class, cricket-playing hero reading his property company's board of directors a lecture on the behaviour of their recent and usurping, *nouveau-riche* chief executive, the sinister Mr Cartwright. The hero, Peter Henderson, ends with a letter to the inmates of 'Charlies', a dosshouse which he had saved from Cartwright's grasp, and this is read out to them by Lincolns Inn, a former lawyer, fallen from grace but avuncularly bent on making amends. The down-and-outs whose responses we hear are Tich, Charlie's right-hand man, and Bill, the oldest inhabitant.

> *Henderson*: I'm sure we're all very sorry that Mr Cartwright and his friends have abused my father's trust – but they've been like many others who, given power, have only striven for more and, in so doing, have missed a golden opportunity of using it to benefit the whole community. Mr Cartwright and his friends should have known better.
>
> I have recently had an opportunity of witnessing how certain of our people acquit themselves when they are really up against it and I deem it a great privilege that we, with the property under our control, may pay them a small tribute by becoming the advance guard for the true development of our city, a development which considers first and foremost the requirements of the people who have to live in it.
>
> *[Cut to the cellar of 'Charlies']*
>
> *Lincolns Inn*: Dear Lincolns Inn, Please tell everyone that 'Charlies' will not be touched until we have found accommodation for the period of the rebuilding. On the same site we hope to see a fine new building with all the things you now miss – but

with the same spirit of 'Charlies' going on unchanged. I once heard it said, 'Any fool can smash things down but you've got to be clever when it comes to building them up again.' You are the fellows who have made me realise how true that is. So now, perhaps, I am better fitted to start on the work of rebuilding. I shall never forget what I owe you all. God bless you all. Peter Henderson.

Tich: That's the lad wot plaid the pianner. Remember, Bill?

Bill: Yaish. Oi remember.

Tich: All this talk abaht better fings. 'Omes and all that. D'yu suppose they really mean it? Or will they ferget?

Bill: No. *(pause)* I think they really mean it this time, Tich.

Tich: Blimey! It'll be like 'eaven on earf!

Bill: *(in close-up directly into camera)* An' whoi not?

[Music up. End]

Thus, while sponsoring occasional vague notions of paternalist improvement at home, the wartime cinema constructed a historical perspective on the inter-war years which, while favouring the values of the traditional ruling class, criticised those who had been (or who had usurped) their custodians and contrasted them with the percipience and abilities of 'old money' in general, and of Churchill in particular. This was the context for the historical films, in cinematic terms.

To consider the possibility of this partisanship in an intellectual sense, it may prove useful to reflect at this point on some of Sir Herbert Butterfield's words, published at the start of the sound era in cinema barely a decade before the war. He condemned 'the tendency in many historians to write on the side of Protestants and Whigs, to praise revolutions provided they have been successful, to emphasise certain principles of progress in the past and to produce a story which is the ratification if not the glorification of the present.'[16] He further maintained that 'it cannot be said that all the faults of bias (Whig) may be balanced by work that is deliberately written with the opposite bias . . . and though there have been Tory . . . partisan histories, it is still true that there is no corresponding tendency for the subject itself to lean in this direction'.[17] Clearly Whig history, in the partisan sense, could hardly have found expression in the tightly-controlled cinema of the 1930s although, in the more general sense of faith in progress, it might. The two main historical feature films of the war, however, did have an opportunity to grapple with the 'partisan' question directly.

Both *The Prime Minister* and *The Young Mr Pitt* dealt with the life and times of a Conservative or Tory Prime Minister and both did so in a way which, while challenging the then popularly accepted polarities of Whig, partisan history, did so by the very methods which Butterfield had seen as inherently Whig in the broader sense: that is, they harnessed social and political progress to their heroes and reinterpreted the past in order to fit with presently perceived truths. Both films, therefore, shared a number of themes in their structure which may be identified as follows:

(1) Concern for the interests of ordinary working people is at the heart of the Tory tradition.
(2) Party interest has never been uppermost among Tories, but rather a willingness to put country, talent and faithfulness to true Conservatism above the party.
(3) Dictatorships which arise from revolutions, be they national or populist, are Britain's natural enemies and Britain is Europe's guarantor against them.
(4) Appeasement and lack of military preparedness are grave errors to which the Tory Party has, historically, found rejoinders from within its own ranks.
(5) Both films make use of references to recent Conservative triumphs, but in a new sense, so that they are now recast to form part of acceptable Tory history.

Each of these themes merits more detailed examination.

1 TORY CONCERN FOR ORDINARY WORKING PEOPLE

In *The Young Mr Pitt* the entire film is set in a context of the depravity of a corrupt society, neglectful of its defences and of its humbler citizens' wellbeing. An early sequence shows a montage of shots of sensual, society pleasures and of the destitute, sprawled in the street or dangling from a gibbet, while the voice-over intones:

An age of highly-polished manners and rather low behaviour, of gay satins and miserable rags. The aristocracy get mellow on delicate wines, the poor dead drunk on gin at a penny a pint. Men are hanged for stealing a sheep while others grow fat on the proceeds of corruption.

A cut to the House of Commons is accompanied by:

> Wormwood eats into the army, navy and into Parliament where the unpopular coalition government of Lord North and Charles Fox sticks its head ostrich-like in the sands of time whilst the country sprawls aimlessly on a multi-coloured quilt of feckless folly.

With such a context set at the start of the film, Pitt's later defence of Fox (played by Robert Morley) and his own unspecified 'reforms' have immediate meaning invested in them, both in terms of social justice and as means of reviving the nation's defences.

Similarly, in early sequences of *The Prime Minister*, Disraeli (John Gielgud) is identified by Mary Anne Wyndham Lewis (Diana Wynyard) as a reformer, and he speaks of himself as such in his first conversation with Lord Melbourne (Frederick Leister). Immediately following this scene Disraeli observes to the young Victoria that she is queen, and as she says that 'these are dangerous times and so much wealth and so much suffering'. Disraeli, who has been communing with an elderly footman, is visibly moved.

Throughout both films it is made clear that it is the heroes' contemporaries who see them as the friends of the working class. In Pitt's case, he (Robert Donat) and Wilberforce (John Mills) are set upon in their coach by hired ruffians and are rescued by Dan Mendoza (Ray Emerton) and Gentleman Jackson (Leslie Bradley). Later, when being treated in their Pugilists' Academy, Pitt is reassured by Jackson that he is the people's man:

> Pitt: I'm used to defending myself against the representatives of the people but now it seems I must defend myself against the people themselves.
> Jackson: Surely you don't think what happened out there had anything to do with the people?
> Pitt: Well, there seemed to be plenty of people about!

Disraeli has frequent moments of benign contact with the workers, who respond in kind. Thus when a dangerous Chartist mob, whose members have been seen as arsonists in a previous scene, is listening to denunciations of Peel and of child labour and is being egged on by a humorously vulgar agitator (Will Fyffe) to 'tear down the whole rotten system', it is to Disraeli's carriage that the more moderate among them turn with friendly waves. Servants find it easy to talk to Disraeli, who answers the 'Lor', bless yer' type of remarks made by the watching coachmen on the occasion of his engagement to Mary Anne by throwing his own driver a sovereign. He also appears to pay his man so well that he is able to retain it as an unspent souvenir, which Disraeli asks leave to touch for luck decades later when he is about to bring down Gladstone (Stephen Murray) in 1874!

This notion of identification with the interests of ordinary people is carried further by showing the heroes' successes in general elections as though they were genuine exercises in popular democracy, the trimmings of largely picturesque and comical eighteenth-century corruption in *Pitt* still leaving quite untouched the impression that it is the whole people that is appealed to. These events also provide the necessary setting for establishing the former Whig heroes, Fox and Gladstone, as the villains of the piece.[18] On his first appearance Gladstone is dressed like the English eighteenth-century version of the gunfighter in *Shane*, the only man to appear at the garden party in a complete and forbidding set of black clothes – topped by a large black hat. Later he is vilified by working-class crowds who boo him during election sequences and chant the slogan: 'Gladstone protects the rich and taxes the poor.'

Disraeli's reforming acts are shown in a series of rising lap dissolves, a technique later used in the MoI propaganda film *Words and Actions* (1944) on the only occasion that the Beveridge Report appeared officially on the screen. Pitt's reforms are limited, he promises the king (Raymond Lovell), who says: 'You're a reformer. You like to change things. I hope we shall see no innovations in my time'; Pitt replies: 'We shall restrict them to those that are necessary.' The reforms, not surprisingly, remain unspecified, but an interesting parallel emerges with the way in which later policy developed on the question of the implementation of Beveridge. Churchill insisted on the line that the first commitment must be to victory and there was great delight shown within the MoI when Beveridge himself went on record as saying the same thing in a speech to Oxford Fabians in December 1942.[19]

This theme is already present in *Pitt* in a number of key scenes with Wilberforce and with Eleanor Eden (Phyllis Calvert). Thus, towards the end of Pitt's first burst of reform, he and Wilberforce lean on a country gate and survey the waving cornfields of the English rural idyll, a scene whose conservative message was familiar to 1930s newsreel audiences.[20] Pitt says: 'Quite soon, perhaps sooner than we think, all our dreams may come true. The first essential is peace and that we have. Peace – and then as surely as they're taking in their harvest over there the rest will come.' Even in such responsible hands, however, such scenes were shown to be inconstant, and the scene is followed by the demented *sans-culottes* and the outbreak of war. Later a wiser Pitt tells Eleanor in a conversation about peace talks, 'If you tell your dreams they never come true', to which Eleanor replies, 'In peacetime, all dreams come true.'

2 COUNTRY, TALENT AND TRUE CONSERVATISM ABOVE PARTY

In *The Prime Minister* this theme is developed strongly from the start of the film. As Melbourne says in his first meeting with Disraeli, 'there's more in politics than party. What matters in the end is to be working for England.' Similarly, Pitt's first action on his appointment as prime minister is to visit Brooks' Club and ask Fox to join his ministry, and the pinnacle of his domestic political success is seen to be when Fox is moved to offer to serve in his third administration.

Both films go out of their way to deny personal ambition as the motive for their hero's rejection of party orthodoxy and, instead, stress not only selflessness but also ability. Disraeli, for example, will not serve as premier until Derby goes to the Foreign Office, although he knows that they disagree on foreign policy. Pitt, surveying the abilities of his predecessors, observes as he discusses the problems of a hostile House with Wilberforce and Dundas, 'it's so long since a Prime Minister had a policy, they might find the novelty attractive'. This high-minded attitude to party partisanship does not, however, extend to their opponents, except at the very end when the superior lessons of true Conservatism have been taught. In *The Prime Minister* Disraeli, discussing Peel and Gladstone, not only says 'they'll change the party; their hearts are with the industrialists', but this is also followed by a rolling caption which includes: 'Later, Gladstone *openly* joined the Liberals, the great industrial party of England' (my emphasis). Clearly, then, coalitions of talent were only to be regarded favourably when they were led by the right people and who were faithful to the right values.

The attitude of both films to the equation that industrial development equals progress is consistent with their support for their heroes. Pitt appears almost to cause the industrial revolution by his mere existence, while Disraeli is cast as its humaniser. The imagery employed in the former case closely recalls at least one version of Tory history as well as forming a counterpoint to the opening montage of decadence already mentioned. Pitt, elected for the first time as Prime Minister, commences to reform and rearm:

> In Portsmouth, Plymouth, Rotherhithe and Chatham the sounds of shipwrights' hammers mingle with the sounds of chains hauling timber and in the rising cities of the north burn the first lights of the industrial revolution. The pace of Britain changes. Watt invents the steam engine, Cartwright the power loom, Trebethick the locomotive. . .

Writing in 1914 in *The Tory Tradition* in a chapter on Disraeli, Sir Geoffrey Butler, later director of the British Information Service in New York during the Great War, said of Britain in the early nineteenth century: 'it was not the England that men had known before the war. It was already in the grip of an Industrial Revolution. It had been a land of agriculture; it was now a land of industry; and in the north the sky already glowed with lighted furnaces.'[21]

3 BRITAIN, ENEMY OF DICTATORSHIPS AND FRIEND TO THE WEAK

This theme is almost inseparable from the anti-appeasement theme in *The Prime Minister*, being most strongly evident when Disraeli insists on bluntly telling the Turkish ambassador that 'Yes, we are breaking our word.' In *Pitt* natural enmity to dictators is made clear in the early scenes when the film cuts from Chatham's deathbed to the christening of Napoleon, and this intercutting continues at other appropriate points until, as a fully grown and menacing character played by Herbert Lom, Napoleon takes his inevitable place in the story. The obvious relevance was widely noted in reviews and its sense was reflected in other workings of history available to the public at the same time. Arthur Bryant's first volume of his

Napoleonic wars trilogy, *The Years of Endurance*, was published in the same year that saw the release of *The Young Mr Pitt*. In his preface Bryant wrote of British survival in the first phase of the wars and quoted the same speech of Pitt's which, in the film, is used as the occasion for Fox's belated offer of support. The passage ends: 'our still higher exaltation ought to be that we . . . hold out a prospect to nations now bending under the iron yoke of tyranny what the exertions of a free people can effect.'[22] The voice, remember, is not Churchill's but Pitt's; the year 1804 not 1940.

4 APPEASEMENT AS AN ERROR AND TORY REJOINDERS

It is on this theme that the sophistication of the films' messages is most apparent, for in both cases the folly of appeasement, though it is supported by the villains, is also crucially evident in Tory ranks. In *Pitt* the querulous Addington (Henry Hewill) fulfils the role from within Pitt's own cabinet, as do others in *The Prime Minister*. Here the leading spokesman for such ideas is a Lord Derby whose close physical resemblance to Lord Halifax, Chamberlain's foreign secretary, is unmistakable. Just as Pitt deals with his doubting colleagues with a speech in which he warns 'it's fight or surrender now. And we shall fight . . .', so Disraeli, in an early warning of the dangers to which Derby's line will lead, says: 'I tell you. Peace can be purchased at too great a price.'

It is in *The Prime Minister* that the most substantial anti-appeasement speech is made in a splendid set-piece confrontation in the cabinet:

Disraeli: Do I need to remind you gentlemen that we have a mutual aid treaty with Turkey guaranteeing her military assistance?

Cabinet Member: But surely, sir, before we resort to anything as desperate as mobilisation against a great power like Russia, we should try to make some attempt at appeasement?

Disraeli: Appeasement? Of an autocracy?

Cabinet Member: After all, sir, Germany is a civilised state; so is Russia; so is Austria – although some of the ideas of their rulers may be a little alien to us. But you can't condemn a whole people because of the opinions of its rulers!

Disraeli: In an autocracy, the leader *is* the people, and Europe at the moment is at the mercy of the most ruthless band of autocrats the world has yet seen. I know these dictators, these men of blood and iron. They are always in a hurry. Their God is power and its kingdom is on this earth. They are men without humility and without hearts. The virtues which we hold dear they call weaknesses, and what we love they despise. They hold themselves a race apart, finally ordained to rule the world to the exclusion of all others. That is a form of madness that must eventually destroy the world or be destroyed. It cannot be appeased by soft words or good neighbourliness. All civilised methods of approach to international agreements are signs of weakness to these men. They recognise one argument and one argument alone – *force* [here Disraeli slams his hands on the cabinet table] and that is the argument I beg you to use now with all my heart and all my soul, for the sake of peace and for the sake of England.

The cabinet does not take the advice, but Disraeli later shows the wisdom of the policy when he outfaces Bismarck. Similarly Pitt is seen to take on and defeat Talleyrand (Albert Lieven) in a series of exchanges in which the practical efficacy of anti-appeasement policies is shown, while the language is evocative of 1930s diplomacy. Talleyrand, for example, says: 'As to Savoy, it is scarcely a serious state', as well as: 'Mr Pitt, if Britain and France became military allies we could dominate the world.' When Pitt rejects this as a mere ploy to test his reactions, Talleyrand explains it was made 'in the language of your older diplomats, to find out how much intervention there was going to be in your non-intervention'. Pitt finally demonstrates the soundness of his anti-appeasement position when, by announcing the certainty of British intervention if Holland is attacked, he receives a reply from Talleyrand (whose face and gestures recall Ribbentrop) and says 'I feel sure that the neutrality of Holland will be respected.' The personal identifications within *The Young Mr Pitt* also include that of Addington with Chamberlain, a view which is supported in contemporary material. Bryant, who had been the editor of Chamberlain's speeches,[23] saw parallels in his preface to *Years of Endurance*. Surveying the period from the Peace of Amiens to the outbreak of renewed hostilities, he wrote: 'Like ourselves after Munich, our ancestors tried the experiment of living with and letting live a Europe in which there was no balance of power but only unilateral force. Within a year the experiment had failed.'[24]

More remarkable still is the fact that both films answer the unspoken question posed by the simple verities of the anti-appeasement position, namely 'why appeasement?', and in both cases it is shown to have been foolish but honourable. Addington's attempt to lead the world in beating swords into ploughshares, cruelly visually inverted in the film, is nonetheless seen as high-minded. Similarly, Derby's anxiety is shown to be the prevention of war which might arise from some crude and untrusting provocation. As one of his colleagues blurts out, 'say what you like. Bismarck is a gentleman!' Yet this high-mindedness, both films argue, is the unrealistic attitude of men grown soft; indeed, Kipling's poem 'The King's Task' can never be far from our minds when viewing these films. Addington has so lost touch with England's strengths that he cannot imagine where a great military leader can come from, while Disraeli, excusing the weakness of his pusillanimous ministers to Victoria (Fay Compton), says 'they have lived too long in the comfort of democracy' and suggests that they cannot therefore bring themselves to believe that they are being lied to.

5 RECENT TORY TRIUMPHS RECAST

If these films do represent a partisan Tory historiography in the making, then, given their strong emphasis on appeasement, both would have come to some sort of cinematic revision of the Munich episode. Both do this, and in strikingly similar ways, although *The Prime Minister*, dealing with problems of greater propinquity to that embarrassing event, carries the process further than *Mr Pitt*. In both films the hero's greatest parliamentary triumph, the domestic political climax of the story, is snatched from the jaws of defeat by the same device as in the real pre-Munich debate. Thus a piece of paper is passed along the front bench from behind the Speaker's chair to announce, in *The Young Mr Pitt*, the defeat of Napoleon at Aboukir Bay and, in *The Prime Minister*, the arrival of Disraeli's secretly mobilised Indian army troops in Suez ready to sail to Constantinople. As in 1938, both moments unite the House in cheering the Prime Minister. The famous or, as in the context of 1941–2, infamous circumstances of the Munich triumph are transposed to fit the climax of the boldness and the anti-appeasing preparedness of the films' Tory heroes.

The bold reversal of parallels is completed in *The Prime Minister* by the treatment of the Congress of Berlin, to which the script pointedly refers as a 'conference'. Bismarck's claims to disinterest are comically subverted by two shots of the shadow of his head, torso and menacingly enlarged outspread hands, raised in a gesture of apparent mediation, spread across a sand-table map of Europe. Disraeli's return in triumph makes the matter explicit. He is received by Victoria at Buckingham Palace, the only time in the film when she is not seen at Windsor, and after an exchange in which he makes his 'Peace with Honour' remark to which the queen replies: 'No, Peace *through* honour, I believe', he and Victoria emerge to accept the cheers of the crowd from the balcony. The entire sequence recalls the famous Munich newsreel special issued by Gaumont-British on 3 October 1938, which had ended to the strains of 'Land of Hope and Glory'. The feature film was bolder still and closed with the National Anthem, for which the cinema audience would have been accustomed to standing. The almost intangible exorcism of Munich makes it clear that, while new spirits were being conjured, the old devil of Chamberlain was also being cast out.

The new cinematic historiography which was emerging in these films was not necessarily recognised as such at the time. The potential for historical parallels was as much as most critics appear to have identified. Some, less elegant than *The Times*, merely referred to topicality. The *News Chronicle*, for example, commented on *The Prime Minister*: 'It is an absorbing narrative with Chartist riots and a glimpse of Will Fyffe as an agitator thrown in. There are too the inevitable topical allusions to dictators.'[25] Criticism on the grounds of historical 'inaccuracies' was remarkably rare and it was left to the *Picturegoer and Film Weekly* to mount the strongest attack on *The Prime Minister*: 'We frequently accuse American producers of distorting facts in pictures dealing with English history, but apparently our own movie moguls can be equally misleading judging by this biographical film of Disraeli's life.'[26] Despite this, the magazine gave the film a two-star rating (out of a possible four) and concluded: 'a strongly patriotic note is struck and a parallel is drawn between events then and those that are occurring today'.

Inevitably the big stars involved in both productions meant that many reviewers saw their main task as passing judgement on Gielgud's challenge to the twelve-year-old memories of George Arliss in the title role of Alfred E. Green's *Disraeli* (1930) or as assessing the attainments of Robert Donat in his first big role since

Sam Wood's *Goodbye, Mr Chips* (1939). Indeed *Pitt* was promoted to the trade in America as 'Mr Chips with a gun in his hand'. Few took up the most troubling question for the future of any historical film, namely: would the public go and see it? Given the casts, the prospects were good, and *Picturegoer* gave *Pitt* the treble honour of a front cover, a single page condensation 'freely adapted from the motion picture' and a special three-star rating. Gaumont-British, however, took no chances and the *Daily Mail* ran a review which, in addition to praising the film without reservation, quoted Commander Arthur Jarratt, the chief film-buyer for the Gaumont cinema chain, in its support. Under the headline '£250,000 Was Well Spent on This Picture' Jarratt confidently predicted that 'the picture to beat *How Green Was My Valley* [directed by John Ford, 1940] is *The Young Mr Pitt*':

> Some say that popularity is not a virtue. It is as vital to a picture as to a Prime Minister. A Prime Minister lives by popular confidence. A picture does not live at all until the public sees and likes it. The public will see and like *The Young Mr Pitt*.[27]

But perhaps the most interesting feature of the reviews is their frequent tone of intoxicated and naïve enthusiasm. As Goebbels said of propaganda, the most effective forms were those which were not even detected as such. Thus the *Daily Mail* called *The Prime Minister*:

> . . . a picture of high courage and good heart. It sets out to show the world something of the selfless devotion to duty which is asked of those who would serve Britain and which has been freely and gladly given.
>
> The implication of the picture is that high ideal has never been so exalted as it is today. That is a good thing to put into British films in these times. It is heartening. It is true.[28]

The Times, in a particularly pompous review, stated that

> *The Prime Minister*, though it takes one or two liberties with accuracy, over-simplifies complex issues and writes nineteenth century history with an eye on the present year 1941, does not take the advantage of the Disraeli legend as it might legitimately have done.[29]

This notion of restraint and of honesty or truth found repetition in reviews of *The Young Mr Pitt*: *The Times* suggested that 'Mr Carol Reed . . . may well stand amazed at his own moderation' which it believed had resulted in a film in which the main characters and drama were 'at least . . . thrown on to an honestly contrived screen'.[30] *Picturegoer*, which featured the film so prominently, echoed this, calling it 'a sincere historical picture . . . [which] has an honest motive in paralleling the dangers of those days with those of today'.[31]

Patriotically making allowances, therefore, star-struck and impressed by honestly-meant – if somewhat dubious – historical parallels, the reviewers and perhaps the public were induced to accept as entertainment a new cinematic historiography compounded not only of historical subjects but also of the stuff of current history. The war, its principal events, features and the years which led up to it, were the most immediate material for historical reflection. What is remarkable is that both subjects produced not many but only one tradition of British political and social history in the wartime cinema, which harnessed the dynamic of Whig history to the Tory cause and enshrined true Conservatism in the unrepresentative Churchillian myth of the national past.

For what was supposed to have been the 'people's war', there were *not*, to borrow from Donat in *The Young Mr Pitt*, 'plenty of people about'. Leaders were back in fashion in the cinema and they – eccentric archetypes, isolated among all but the finest of their fellows, and driven by paternalistic spirit – were now to recall the traditional ruling class to its true self and the public to its honour. As to where their paradigm might be found, there could be no doubt. 'Where', quavered Addington, 'are we to find such a man?' while the camera answered by panning the sheepfold, elms and churchyard of the Conservative English rural idyll before finding Nelson in public-spirited prayer.

Notes and References

1. P. Sorlin, *The Film in History* (Oxford, 1980) p. 80.
2. *The Times*, 2 July 1942.
3. Sorlin, *The Film in History* (op. cit.) p. 79.
4. Ibid., p. 19.
5. Ibid.

6. The film is discussed in Thomas J. Knock, 'History with Lightning: The forgotten film *Wilson* (1944)', in Peter C. Rollins (ed.), *Hollywood as Historian: American film in a cultural context* (Kentucky, 1983) pp. 88–108; Leonard J. Leff and Jerrold Simmons, '*Wilson*: Hollywood Propaganda for World Peace', *Historical Journal of Film, Radio and Television*, 3 (1983) 1, 3–18.

7. Karol Kulik, *Alexander Korda: The man who could work miracles* (London, 1975) p. 249.

8. Michael Korda, *Charmed Lives* (London, 1980) p. 154.

9. A. Aldgate, 'Ideological consensus in British feature films, 1935–47', in K. R. M. Short, *Feature Films as History* (London, 1981) pp. 94–103; Jeffrey Richards, *The Age of the Dream Palace* (1984).

10. N. Pronay, 'The political censorship of films in Britain between the wars', in N. Pronay and D. W. Spring, *Propaganda, Politics and Film, 1918–45* (London, 1982) pp. 98–125; J. Richards, 'The British Board of Film Censors', and J. C. Robertson, 'British Film Censorship goes to war', in *Historical Journal of Film, Radio and Television*, 1 & 2.

11. Richards, *The Age of the Dream Palace* (op. cit.) p. 265; Pronay, 'The political censorship of films . . .', in Pronay and Spring (op. cit.) p. 114.

12. Memorandum, 'List of Public and Private bodies consulting the Film Censorship', 19 November 1941 (PRO INF 1/178, CN 4, part 1).

13. R. B. Pugh to Professor Harlow, 3 April 1942 (INF 1/178).

14. Memorandum, 'Film Censorship: volume of work: increases over period of ten months (from Jan. 1941)' (INF 1/178).

15. Geoff Brown, *Launder and Gilliat* (London, 1977) pp. 104–5.

16. Herbert Butterfield, *The Whig Interpretation of History* (London, 1931) p.v.

17. Ibid., p. 7.

18. This was recognised in contemporary reviews: 'Gladstone is . . . apparently the villain of the piece', *Picturegoer and Film Weekly*, 22 March 1941.

19. I am grateful to Dr Tom Wildy for this material, which is on a BBC radiophone transcription for 6 December 1942 held at Caversham (R 34/693).

20. Particularly marked in British Movietone, Gaumont-British and Pathé.

21. Sir Geoffrey Butler, *The Tory Tradition* (London, 1957) p. 57.

22. Arthur Bryant, *The Years of Endurance* (London, 1942) p. ix.

23. Neville Chamberlain (ed. Arthur Bryant), *In Search of Peace* (London, 1938).

24. Bryant, *The Years of Endurance* (op. cit.) p. ix.

25. *News Chronicle*, 7 March 1941.

26. *Picturegoer and Film Weekly*, 22 March 1941.

27. *Daily Mail*, 4 July 1942.

28. Ibid., 7 March 1941.

29. *The Times*, 5 March 1941.

30. Ibid., 2 July 1942.

31. *Picturegoer*, 19 September 1942.

7

Cinematic Support for the Anglo-American Détente, 1939–43

K. R. M. Short

The question of whether Great Britain was a democracy was a question of some importance in the period between 1937 and 1945. In retrospect it might appear a curious sort of question to be asking whilst the world was aflame, but it was there by the very nature of the relationship between Great Britain and the United States, both historically and at that particularly crucial period. As part of the inflated self-estimation of the United States, the average man and woman in the street – the so-called John and Jane Doe of George Gallup's ever-questing polls – believed that America was 'the land of the free and the home of the brave'; about 'England' (meaning Great Britain) they were not so sure. After all, England had been the tyrannical power against which American democracy had rebelled one hundred and fifty years earlier. Had England really changed? England was still being portrayed as an Imperialist Power subjugating the Poor Irish (a view particularly strong amongst the police forces of Boston, Chicago and New York). Moreover England was also imprisoning the courageous brown little Mr Ghandi – the loincloth-clad George Washington of his country who was peacefully fighting the power of the British Raj. Also any country which did not pay its world war one debts could not be trusted; indeed, only Finland could be trusted! Furthermore it was perfectly clear that any country with a king and queen, dukes, princes and the like could not be a democracy. England, therefore, could not be regarded as a 'land of the free' even if its inhabitants were demonstrating their bravery in the face of the Nazi threat.

These perceptions lay behind the answers to Gallup's questions and, as opinions, they had a relevance because the possibility of

America's second intervention in European wars in one generation partly rested upon American public opinion. If John and Jane Doe could not be convinced that England was worth fighting for, there would be no intervention on her behalf. And this time there would be no British propaganda flowing from Wellington House to seduce America into war, since Congress and the Fourth Estate was on full alert against such a campaign as had been launched between 1914 and 1917. Thus the British Embassy in Washington was carefully advising the Foreign Office to keep its hands off American public opinion. In March 1937 Ambassador Lindsay informed Foreign Secretary Anthony Eden that, in the end, 'Anglo-American relations are foolproof, and they are only in danger when you try to improve them.' Lindsay was quoting one of the 'cleverest American writers on foreign policy, a man whose friendship for England was so discriminating as virtually to disappear' and Lindsay's advice was that the only way to reach American opinion was through emotional appeals. He claimed that in recent years Americans had been moved by the late King George's broadcasts to his empire, Mr Baldwin's speech in the Commons on the abdication crisis, the Stratford Shakespeare Company, James Hilton's novel *Goodbye, Mr Chips*, Noël Coward's *Cavalcade* (made into a film by Fox in 1933), 'the successes of Great Britain' and the 'calmness and dignity of her people'.[1]

This assessment was undoubtedly optimistic and characteristically naïve, as the very things which Lindsay saw as Britain's strength could be seen in American eyes as its weakness, for the images he was so taken with were the very same images which potentially reinforced traditional Yankee views of the land of John Bull. *Goodbye, Mr Chips* and *Cavalcade* went to great lengths in order to illustrate that Britain still suffered from hereditary class divisions. Although, in the former, the greengrocer's son and the heir to a title both go during the first world war to the private Brookfield School (founded, of course, as audiences in 1939 were visually informed in the film version, in 1492 – the year Columbus discovered America), the heir becomes an officer and the greengrocer's son his enlisted batman. In the American experience Horatio Alger had every poor but worthy boy succeeding, whereas inherited wealth brought only ruin. And as for broadcasting to the empire, in American eyes empire meant India, it meant Ireland, it meant imperialism – something which all good Americans rejected because they had themselves fought their way out of the British Empire and had only recently made the Philippine Islands a commonwealth in preparation for independence. Abdication crises were about monarchy and, moreover, caused because the English would not accept an American as their queen – well, yes, she had been twice divorced. The 'woman I love' might have been romantic, but it could never have happened in America. Where Lindsay was correct was that some Americans did like Shakespeare, but a significantly smaller number than those who were forced to read it in those college and university courses in which the Bard figured so largely.

Generally supportive of Lindsay's view was a letter in January 1939 by William Elmslie to Angus Fletcher of the British Library of Information in New York.[2] The Library was Britain's only peacetime 'propaganda' organisation in the United States and had to register as such with the American government. Elmslie, who had worked for the British Mission in the first world war, wrote:

Dear Fletcher,
Here's a story – semi-suburban movie house, last night *Drums*, next to be *Heart of the North* (Canadian North West Mounties), Dickens' *Christmas Carol*, next *The Citadel*, next *Dawn Patrol*, in other words about a month of continuous British stories.[3]

The moral is DEEDS, not WORDS – put in stories of glamorous and glorious characters in action, all sympathetic to American idealism – let trained diplomats do their job, with their usual modesty, silence and skill, but it's my guess that all other *deliberate* attempts to influence opinion do more harm than good – and this goes for all visiting celebrities, [and] international broadcasts (except purely ceremonial Happy New Year sorts of stuff . . .)

Lindsay's reference to the Hollywood production of *Cavalcade* suggests that he and Elmslie would have agreed that the best way to capture American public opinion was via its emotions; and the most effective route was via the cinema.[4] The main problem was whether Hollywood would continue to make films with British themes. This was a problem because, as a British Library of Information report of January 1939 indicated, British films found it difficult to compete with American films 'in country places, and especially in the west, because British accents, whether genteel or dialect, are not easily understood'.[5] Nevertheless the three most successful films being shown in New York at that moment were *Pygmalion* (1938, Pascal; directors A. Asquith and Leslie Howard), *The Lady Vanishes* (1938,

GB; dir. A. Hitchcock) and *The Beachcomber* (1938, UK title *Vessel of Wrath*; Mayflower, dir. E. Pommer).

Although 'deeds' could indeed be communicated via the cinema, circumstances seemed to suggest that 'words' were also required. Interestingly Angus Fletcher prepared a memorandum for the Foreign Office on the future use of propaganda in the United States in time of war, but omitted any reference to films.[6] In a note on this report C. F. A. Warner of the Foreign Office News Department was surprised at this omission, since he considered films very important. He accordingly recommended that any future Ministry of Information 'should see that there is an ample supply of the right sort of film available for the States and ample facilities for American film companies, especially the news film companies'.[7]

The potential usefulness, however, of films like those commissioned by Sidney Bernstein (special advisor to the MoI's films division) from the GPO Film Unit in the autumn of 1940 could not be realised until a deal had been struck by Bernstein through Warner Brothers for MoI information shorts, such as *London Can Take It* (1940) and *Christmas Under Fire* (1941), to be handled commercially via Hollywood's Motion Picture Committee for National Defence. This deal was extended to include eight feature films. Because the MoI wanted this propaganda to pay its own way, 30 per cent of the profits thus went to the renters while it pocketed the remainder, less the costs of distribution. Thereafter it became a matter of how best to tell the story. *The Lion Has Wings* (1939) had been distributed successfully via Alexander Korda's corporate links with United Artists, an exercise which was also to sustain his production in 1940 of *Lady Hamilton* (distributed in the USA for reasons best known to the Hays Office as *That Hamilton Woman!*). The first wartime feature-length film to be commissioned by the MoI specifically for the North American market was *The 49th Parallel* (1942), produced and directed by Michael Powell with an Academy Award-winning original screenplay by Emeric Pressburger. Released in America as *The Invader*, the film concerned an 'invasion' of Canada by Germans from a sunken U-boat attempting to escape into the neutral United States. Long speeches were also employed to remind North American audiences that the war could quite easily cross the Atlantic Ocean. *The 49th Parallel* (the boundary between the USA and Canada from the Great Lakes westward) received honourable mention in the *New York Times'* list of ten best films for 1942, a list which significantly included Noël Coward's *In Which We Serve* (best remembered by the censors for its salty words – which in turn may have contributed to its Academy Award for best foreign film) and the second Powell/Pressburger film, *One of Our Aircraft is Missing* (1942).[8] These last two films, however, were films of courage and deeds, not of words; they were not films which by their very nature could meaningfully link the two democracies ideologically.

There is no doubt that in *Christmas Under Fire*, released early in the previous year of 1941, the approach was to effectively combine words with deeds. The deeds of Britain's resolve during the blitz were clearly portrayed, although the Germans chose not to send the expected raids on Christmas Eve 1940. Significantly Quentin Reynolds, correspondent for *Collier's Weekly Magazine* and the film's commentator, moved beyond the realm of *London Can Take It* to criticise the American government strongly for not doing more to help Britain, while stressing that Britain had taken 'the torch of liberty and had not dropped it': the Statue of Liberty was not the only guardian of freedom. The political dimensions of *Christmas Under Fire* were clear even if the main thrust was emotional, with its use of Christmas, religion and children to fulfil the pledge of Reynolds, together with the film's producer Harry Watt, 'not to leave a dry eye in the house'.[9]

The effort to minimise the political and social differences that existed between the two nations is particularly well illustrated in the film *Atlantic Charter* (1942). The idea of the film was Churchill's, who, with his customary sense of history, wanted more than merely a record of his historic meeting with Roosevelt at Placentia Bay, Newfoundland, in 1941; he wanted a monument in celluloid. Filmed by British Movietone, the commentary was written (gratis) by Arthur Bryant and narrated by Robert Harris. MoI documentation makes it quite clear that the film was originally intended 'solely for the purpose of a historical record to be presented to the President and that it would not be used commercially', although in fact the film was released in October 1942 by the MoI for non-theatrical distribution.[10] The message is clear as the commentary describes Churchill's visit to Roosevelt aboard the *USS Augusta*: 'Churchill hands to the first representative of the American people a letter from the King of England. The ancient breach between the two free peoples of the North Atlantic is forgotten forever in an hour pregnant with the future of human liberty.' The film went for the lowest common denominator: that is to say, it chose to overlook as far as possible the major differences which separated the two countries far more seriously than a 'common language'. Whatever its value from the standpoint of the converted – and Roosevelt was an anglophile by upbringing – it was ill-equipped to deal with the highly critical elements within America's political spectrum. An alternative, and perhaps more potentially rewarding, approach was to proclaim that British society and politics were, under the stimulus of war, making tremendous advances towards achieving a democratic system as broadly based and as practically conceived as that of the United States.

Those who chose to look critically at British society and then to mark its rapid progress towards the democratic utopia were in the company of Alexander Korda who, in *The Lion Has Wings*, not only considered how marvellous Britain was in comparison to the Fascist nations but also looked at the 'bad old days' in Britain before the National Government. Stressing how marvellous Britain was becoming naturally made it appear that the country about to emerge was a cause worthy of the present sacrifice, even if the old nation might not have been. The great problem was going to be defining precisely what *was* the real Britain. Indeed the selling of the new Britain became an important dimension of wartime cinema, particularly to American audiences in the early days of the war. As the conflict progressed, the MoI assumed an ever-increasing interest in defining for the British people what the real America was, and obviously not the Hollywood version of America. It was crucial that the answer be found before the man in the street had to enter his pub filled with American GIs.

If selling Britain to the American public came under the heading of public service, then it should have been no surprise that MGM took the lead in applying itself to the Anglo-American problem. MGM had invested in its British productions with a view to producing high-budget films for the American market which, under the recent Quota Act, would be equal to three quota films for the British market. Behind that partly economic decision lay the efforts of executive producer Sidney Franklin, whose pronounced anglophilia was occasionally embarrassing even for his English colleagues at Culver City, California. Three major films had come from MGM British in the two years before the war with its restricted production to British market films. *A Yank at Oxford* (1938), a starring vehicle for Robert Taylor, and a film version of A. J. Cronin's cautionary tale of British medicine, *The Citadel*, appeared in 1938. The following year saw the release of *Goodbye, Mr Chips*, directed by Sam Wood, which earned Robert Donat an Academy Award as best actor. From the safety of Culver City MGM pressed ahead with *Waterloo Bridge* (1940), an unexceptional first world war melodrama starring Robert Taylor and Vivien Leigh: he the officer missing in action and she the ballerina that he loved and married, who then falls into prostitution when she is rejected by his family. There was not much propaganda mileage, but lots of London fog. Franklin also brought director Victor Saville from London to Hollywood and set him to work on *The Mortal Storm*, also released in 1940. This was the strongest anti-Nazi statement made from the security of the Pacific coast thus far and, although the film did not use the word 'Jew', it dramatised the persecution of 'non-Aryans' by the Nazis. Franklin then pushed forward four more English-theme films scheduled for release in 1942. With Roosevelt's policy moving ever closer to an alliance with Britain, clearly set out in the Atlantic Charter of August 1941, the studio appeared to be moving with the times. There must however have been some wavering of resolve when the Senate Committee on Propaganda in the Movies set up shop in Washington the very next month. Yet production continued, the Japanese attacked Pearl Harbor, America entered the war and the Anglo-American connection was cemented – imperfectly, but the join was nonetheless made.

Four films at MGM represented a useful commitment to the Anglo-American side of the war effort. *Random Harvest* (1942) was a melodrama about an aristocratic-born captain-of-industry Guards officer type who loses his memory on the western front during the first world war, only to find it later through the superb ministrations of Greer Garson. The only contribution made to blunting American prejudices was to stress the egalitarian nature of the hero, played by Ronald Colman. *Journey for Margaret* (1942) was, according to the British Film Institute's *Monthly Film Bulletin*, 'the most moving and human film'.[11] Five-year-old Margaret O'Brien was introduced to movie audiences as a traumatised London orphan who wore a spent incendiary bomb around her neck. Margaret and her brother are rescued from the dangers of London and whisked away to the safety of neutral America, a fate suffered by children of major international corporations like Eastman Kodak. The film was about the evacuation of children from British cities, which was a subject approached earlier by MoI documentaries. *Mrs Miniver* (1942) was of course the blockbuster of the day, about which much has already been written concerning its contribution to the war effort. The fourth film from the laurel wreath of the Roaring Lion was the Mickey Rooney parody of *A Yank at Oxford*, *A Yank at Eton* (1942).

Normally our insight into the contemporary reception of films is limited to the professional reviewers. However, by the time these films were released, America was at war and an America at war needed an Office of War Information (OWI). Hollywood was to be included and by March 1942 there was a Hollywood office for both the domestic and the overseas branches of OWI. Staffed by committed New Deal internationalists, these offices immediately began to assess the contribution made by films – features, shorts, cartoons and newsreels – to the war effort, and their reports provide some fascinating contemporary evaluations. *Journey for Margaret* was praised as an example of to 'what splendid purpose films can be used to further the understanding of war' whereas the OWI reviewer seriously doubted that Oscar-winning *Mrs Miniver* (Sidney Franklin's proudest achievement, according to Kevin Brownlow) would 'sell Americans on British democracy'. *A Yank at Eton*, voted by the *New York Times* as one of the year's ten worst films (along with Jack Benny's *To Be or Not To Be*) was 'poisonous from start to finish'. *Random Harvest* was not only 'irrelevant to the war effort', but the scene at tea on the terrace of Westminster of the House of Commons gave the impression that the House 'was a fancy club of snobs, rather than being a great democratic assembly'. The scene had been staged without a single identifiable Labour Party member; nor could there be heard a single Yorkshire, Lancashire or Scottish accent.

Back in August 1941 Sidney Bernstein had a three-hour meeting with Louis B. Mayer of MGM concerning the latter's intention to make the story of Mrs Miniver into a film. A couple of weeks later, on Labor Day, Bernstein had vetted an early script to ensure that the 'details were authentically English'. He returned to the USA for the film's première at the Radio City Music Hall in June 1942. By the end of the summer *Mrs Miniver* had been seen by a million and a half Americans, but although it proved a tremendous box-office success, it was not a hit at the British Embassy in Washington. Bernstein does not seem to have accepted seriously the embassy's claim that the film presented 'a shocking and distorted picture of Britain'; after all, his home in Coppings, with its 175 acres, does not seem to represent an essentially different life-style from that of Clem Miniver's Hollywood home in Kent. Bernstein's response was to test the popular impact in America of *Miniver*, together with two other films,

Eagle Squadron and *This Above All*, rather than question the film's authenticity or lack of it. By October George Gallup delivered a free survey indicating that those Americans who had seen the films were 17 per cent more favourable towards Britain in their sympathies than those who had not. Gallup considered this result 'remarkable'.[12]

Hollywood's New Dealers were convinced that they alone understood the current state of democracy in Britain. Furthermore those most in danger of distorting British society for American audiences happened to be British expatriots like MGM's Claudine West and her fellow writers James Hilton, R. C. 'Bob' Sherriff and Arthur Wimperis, who had collaborated along with Nazi refugee George Froeschel on *Mrs Miniver*. Sherriff was not a permanent member of the Hollywood community, but arrived in 1940 to write the script for *Lady Hamilton* (1941), remaining long enough to do the script for *This Above All* (1942) which Darryl F. Zanuck was producing at Twentieth Century Fox.

Zanuck, one of the most outspoken studio heads, was deeply involved in the industry's response to the claims that it was propagandising the nation in favour of war. Writing in July 1941 to Lowell Mellett, personal assistant to Roosevelt, he asked, 'why not think about the moral side of the question of whether or not we should actively join with England to crush Hitler on the grounds that it is right for us to do so? Everyone, even though he be an ardent Lindbergite, must recognise the undeniable fact that Hitler is a vicious aggressor.'[13] This opinion was put in the most forceful way in Fox's *Man Hunt* (1941), directed by Fritz Lang; the film also offered positive comments on the English character. John Ford's *How Green Was My Valley* (1941) was a marvellously warm drama of a Welsh coalmining community which had the potential effect of opening American eyes to part of the reality of contemporary British life. Zanuck had also moved to link his own personal commitment to supporting Britain's fight against Germany with increasing public interest in Americans flying with the RAF. Thus in 1941 he put director Henry King on the job with a headliner cast of Tyrone Power, Betty Grable, John Sutton and the ubiquitous Reginald Gardner. *A Yank in the RAF* (1941) was written by Zanuck (under the pen name of Melville Crossman) and operated on a tried and true formula of a 'brash young man' (Tyrone Power) who becomes a ferry pilot to Britain but who lacks any real commitment to anything except himself, contrasting with the serious RAF pilot who is also in love with the singing and dancing Betty Grable. Power has a 'conversion experience' and was scheduled to die as a consequence, but for the unofficial request of the MoI via Sidney Bernstein that he be allowed to live.[14] Zanuck also released *Confirm or Deny* in 1941 with Don Ameche and Joan Bennett, a film with the same storyline but with the hero, 'Yank' Mitchell, as an American news agency chief and the beautiful Joan Bennett as a Ministry of Information teletype operator. The subject of Yanks fighting for Britain in the RAF while their country remained neutral was quickly adopted by other studios, leading to the release of *International Squadron* (Warner Bros., 1941) starring Ronald Reagan, *Flying Fortress* (Warner Bros. GB, 1942), Walter Wanger's *Eagle Squadron* (Universal, 1942) with Robert Stack and a large section of the Hollywood English community including Nigel Bruce, Gladys Cooper and Peter Lawford, and Warner Brothers again with James Cagney in *Captains of the Clouds* (1942). Interestingly enough there exists correspondence in Washington between John Grierson and Lowell Mellett in which Grierson is lobbying on behalf of Canadian interests to have Cagney as the star, which one would have thought inevitable.

Zanuck also had a distinctly offbeat film based on the best-selling novel of Eric Knight entitled *This Above All*, made into a film in 1942 starring Joan Fontaine and Tyrone Power and directed by Anatole Litvak. Knight had been born in Yorkshire in 1897 but emigrated to the United States at the age of fifteen. He did, however, return to Britain to fight in the first world war. Surviving the horrors of the western front, he returned to America and became a newspaperman and movie critic for the Philadelphia *Public Ledger*. Publishing his first novel, *Today We Live*, in 1937, he maintained a deep interest in his mother country despite his having in the meantime taken up American citizenship. His major concern was with the contrasts between American democracy and society and contemporary Britain, a not unnatural interest for a working-class Yorkshire boy who, as Horatio Alger had promised, made good in America.

Through Knight's writings on film the British documentary filmmaker Paul Rotha got to know Knight in 1937 and this led to a correspondence which, over the next few years, ran to thousands of pages of single-spaced letters. Knight's interest in British society and the threat to its continuation in late 1939 led to what Rotha called 'a piece of personal soul searching' which produced the novel *This Above All*, which appeared in 1941, the year after Alice Duer Miller's famous poem *The White Cliffs*.[15] Both authors, with their differing style, effect and perspective, sought to focus American attention on Britain's needs while conceding that the island kingdom was far from perfect. Harpers published *This Above All* in the United States (Cassell in Great Britain) and the novel went to the top of the best-seller lists without the assistance of being a book-of-the-month selection. *The Times Literary Supplement*, under the title 'Defeatist Hero', stated:

> Many people are going to be angry with Mr. Knight, but they must still admit, however grudgingly, that he has written one of the outstanding novels of the war – a novel so full of realism and reforming fire that it has already had much success in the United States. Nothing escapes the lash of his tongue – the social system, the old school tie, the Church; nor is there anything new in it. One need not turn to a novel for the truth of some of these things, but one questions the wisdom of writing them down in this way just now . . . He has written a challenging book, which in itself is a tribute to the continued liberty of thought and speech that makes its appearance possible.[16]

From the lips of the film's hero, Clive Briggs, came a catalogue of what was wrong with Britain, and a cast of characters proved it with their opinions, including Prudence, the beautiful aristocrat with a social conscience who joined the enlisted ranks of the WAAF. Clive began as a Dunkirk hero who deserted his regiment after leaving hospital, and the story ends with Clive's fatal injuries sustained while rescuing a family in the blitz as he returned to his regiment. Pru is carrying his unborn child and looking towards the day when the war would end and an egalitarian society would emerge. In the novel Pru stands in a raid following Clive's death in a London hospital and declares to her unborn child:

> Without a father – like your father. But you're going to have a better England to live in: because we were both right. Both right! We have to fight now for what I believe in. And after this we'll have to fight for what he believed in. We'll win this war because – because we can stick it. And then, God help us, we're going to win the peace too. You won't have it like him. You'll live in a better England than he did, because you deserve it! Everyone deserves it.[17]

Zanuck's choice of Bob Sherriff to write the screenplay was fortunate, for he had a reputation (apparently well disguised) for keeping to the book; the exception was *Lady Hamilton*, which had to be written from scratch at great speed while the film was being shot. Sherriff had solved the moral problem of the fictitious scene in *Lady Hamilton* of Nelson's father condemning his son for the illicit relationship, along with Emma's unhappy end. Sherriff again had to face Hays Office limitations with Knight's novel. Thus a steamy haystack scene in *This Above All* is suggestive to the knowing but is actually chaste on screen; and there was naturally no hint of a premarital pregnancy. With this exception, the movie is remarkably faithful to Knight's intentions and only the criticism of the Church of England is toned down, probably deliberately. Also, as in the case of Tyrone Power's previous excursion into Anglo-American relations, *A Yank in the RAF*, his character does not die on screen, although he is perilously close to doing so.

The reviewer for the BFI's *Monthly Film Bulletin* complained only of an un-English railway platform, an overelaborate 'small' country pub (where they had separate rooms, naturally), a comical drum major of the WAAF band and a couple of bad cuts. Joan Fontaine, as Pru, was superb and the 'strong and moving story' was 'expertly handled' by director Litvak. Remarkably, the reviewer summed up the message of the film thus: 'It is Pru who ultimately restores his faith in human nature and the ideals for which we are fighting this war.' Thus, for the reviewer, all of Clive's ranting about English society and the gentle non-threatening egalitarianism of Pru (as distinct from the aristocratic pretensions of her gentry relatives established early in the film) is resolved by the triumph over the radical working-class view. The film was acceptable to the British Board of Film Censors because Clive repented of his desertion, behaved heroically during the blitz scene and, in the final shot, the heavily bandaged Tyrone Power calls for total resistance to the enemy regardless of the cost. Yet despite the comfortable misinterpretation available, the message of the film was in fact the same as that of the book: *Clive was not converted, it was Pru*. Clive was prepared to fight for what Britain currently represented, but only to save it for post-war reformation. This was a comment on British society not markedly dissimilar from that of Alice Duer Miller when she concluded in *The White Cliffs*:

> I am American bred,
> I have seen much to hate here – much to forgive,

But in a world where England is finished and dead,
I do not wish to live.

Eric Knight's impact on audiences did not end with *This Above All*
for, like Anatole Litvak, he was soon to join Frank Capra's *Why We
Fight* team. This was a useful acquisition since, when he joined the
team in April 1942, Knight was already familiar with the techniques
of the British documentary movement; he was, furthermore,
passionately committed to American ideals. It was Knight, with
Anthony Veiller, who wrote the first two films of the series, as well
as *Know Your Ally – Britain* (1943); unfortunate delays in the
production of the series meant that millions of men went through
their basic training without seeing the films, although doubtless
most saw them later in military theatres. Knight's influence in
examining British society and its survival for the GIs went still
further, for he was also the author of the American army's *A Short
Guide to Great Britain*, which was apparently written in conjunction
with *The Battle of Britain*. The film's comically illustrated accompanying booklet doubtless had a greater impact on American servicemen
heading for Britain.[18] This is not to say that film was unappreciated:
Hollywood executive John Balderston urged the OWI to put the film
on general release because he felt so strongly about the 'danger to
the whole war involved in anti-British feeling' and because 'it
happens to be . . . the most effective and powerful film on this
subject. I think the public would go for it and that it would have the
same effect on public opinion here about England that *Mrs Miniver*
did.'[19]

Knight's approach to both film and guide book is very different
from that adopted in his novel *This Above All*. In the novel he
explored Britain's problems with a view to providing an honest – as
honest as he could make it – view of the nation's failings without any
myopia about America's shortcomings; they do not, however, form
part of his story. The novel pursued the idea that national unity
before a common enemy presented a great opportunity for national
progress socially, economically and politically. When it came to *Know
Your Ally – Britain* Knight stressed national courage (which was the
message of Clive Briggs at Dunkirk and in the blitz) while presenting
a basic contention that Britain was a democracy. In the *Short Guide*
Knight told his readers, particularly the Irish-Americans, that now
was not the time to fight old wars, that the British were reserved not
unfriendly, that they shouldn't boast or show off but, most
importantly, that Britain was the cradle of democracy. Knight

summed it up by saying that 'the important thing to remember is that within this apparently old-fashioned framework the British enjoy a practical working twentieth century democracy which is in some ways even more flexible and sensitive to the will of the people than our own'. The booklet is a fascinating, if not brilliant, exposé of Britain and its people, including a glossary of terms and the excellent advice to avoid commenting on the British government or politics, telling the British that America won the last war or mentioning war debts, and NEVER to criticise the king or queen *or* the beer.

The problem of Americans on British soil called for even greater information efforts and the MoI and the OWI collaborated on *A Letter From Ulster* (Crown Film Unit, 1943) to prove how well looked after the recently arrived American troops were in Northern Ireland. The cultural shock encountered by American servicemen in Britain could only have been mildly cushioned by the *Short Guide to Great Britain* and so a second joint production, *Welcome to Britain* (Strand, 1943), was conceived as a cinematic introduction by Burgess Meredith to pub manners, currency and the need to stay away from prostitutes, the last point being put in the most subtle of intelligible ways. The great problem, however, involved the realisation that Britain did not as yet have a race problem and this aspect tended to dominate the film, with explicit statements being made concerning the importance of the Negro soldier to the war effort.

The English were clearly going to have difficulties in understanding Americans, and the segregation of the American army into black and white units would be a particular problem. The Women's Voluntary Service had to set up separate clubs for the Americans, with the black troops being served in the curiously-named Silver Birch Clubs. How were the British going to fathom their allies who were, as it was soon said, 'overpaid, oversexed and Over Here'? The problem had been recognised early and in the summer of 1941 special summer schools had been run for schoolteachers across Britain, preparing them for putting American studies into the curriculum. Books on America, such as George W. Southgate's *The United States* (Dent, 1942) and Maurice Colbourne's *America and Britain: A Mutual Introduction* (Dent, 1943), began to inform the British people about their transatlantic allies at the same time as D. W. Brogan's *The English People* (Hamish Hamilton, 1943) kept the dialogue going. MoI documentary films had been crossing the Atlantic steadily and not only found their way into the British Library of Information in New York for 16mm distribution but also into commercial cinema release via the American Motion Picture

Industry's now renamed War Activities Committee. These films were normally edited for American distribution, as was Thorold Dickinson's *The Next of Kin* (Ealing, 1942; US title *Raid on France*), and American commentary was especially added for *Target for Tonight* (1941). Such films were also extensively gleaned for illustrative footage for other projects, for example by Capra's team for *The Battle of Britain*.

The British army also recognised the problem of understanding the Americans as being peculiarly, or particularly, one it would have to face. Thus the Army Bureau of Current Affairs published *Meet the Americans*.[20] The booklet recognised that 'there's a bit of prejudice on both sides, a colossal ignorance of each other's attitudes and characteristics – but there's also a willingness to get together'. Extolling the need for goodwill, respect and patience, British troops were also urged to respect American achievement, in particular combustion engines and refrigerators:

> Peoples as foreign to each other as the Americans and ourselves have a lot to learn before we reach understanding. The first necessity is to be informed about each other, to replace the film version and the story book version by the real facts. We shall get the facts one way and one way only – by seeking them in a spirit of genuine interest.

Yet how was this understanding to take place, and did the cinema have a role to play?

The MoI continued to use the device of American newsmen to narrate films for the American market. One film designed to record the American contribution to the war effort was *America Moves Up* (1941). Directed by Ralph Elton for the Crown Film Unit, it was to be the first of a series of on-the-spot reports of Americans on 'Front Line Camera'. CBS newsman Bob Trout was the star of the fourteen-minute film, which was begun just before the American entry into the war and had its première in April 1942 as the first GIs began to land in Northern Ireland. The theme, which was illustrated by such events as the men of the Jones Machine Tool Works in America putting a case of 'White House' brand evaporated milk along with machinery being shipped to Britain on Lend-Lease, was that 'Long before the Japanese attacked Pearl Harbor, Americans were at their posts in Britain, pioneers in the fight for humanity against the aggressor nations.'[21] The American connection was also evident in

War and Order (1940), *Words for Battle* (1941) and *Listen to Britain* (1942).

While these films were partly made to tell Americans about the British contribution to the war, the MoI was increasingly concerned to tell Britons about America, using both commercial distribution and the 16mm non-commercial world of the factories and church halls. *Collier's Magazine* correspondent Quentin Reynolds returned to the screen to represent the pre-Pearl Harbor American position in the 1942 feature docudrama *The Big Blockade* (released in January), produced by Michael Balcon's Ealing Studio for the MoI. Reynolds was fairly well known to British audiences already from his part in *Britain Can Take It* (1940) and *Christmas Under Fire* (1941) and his voice had become even more familiar through his two Sunday evening 'Postscript' programmes of the summer of 1941, 'Dear Doctor' and 'Dear Mr S.' *The Big Blockade*, a star-studded film dramatising the work of the Ministry of Economic Warfare and its 'blockade of the Axis powers', may have had its desired educational and morale-building effect, but it may also have provided large numbers of people with the opportunity to go for a smoke. Perhaps the most interesting section of the film was that of a meeting in the Ministry of Economic Warfare which featured the showing of a Nazi newsreel depicting U-boat victories in the Atlantic. When faced with the question of what would happen if Uncle Sam decided to leave Britain 'to stew in our own juice' – would England be 'sunk'? – Reynolds replied:

> Oh believe me Gentlemen, America is with you heart and soul. Our Atlantic fleet is at sea. We have taken on the job of policing the Western Atlantic and we are going to see to it that vital cargoes reach Britain. The battle of the Atlantic is a tough proposition alright, but it's just as tough for the Germans, and Britain and America are out to make it tougher for them every day.

While Reynolds spoke, audiences saw what passed for the American fleet in the North Atlantic; the next scene was the Royal Navy's re-enactment of the sinking of a highly co-operative U-boat.

The vast majority of MoI films that dealt with the war did so quite happily without reference to the American allies and no real effort was made to educate the population as to the complexity of American society when, after all, teaching people how to cope with bombing and shortages dominated informational shorts. When it was necessary the Yanks did of course sneak into such information films as *We Sail at Midnight* (1943) and *San Demetrio, London* (1943) because it was from American ports that the life-sustaining convoys sailed, carrying essential materials produced by American factories. *We Sail at Midnight* showed rather more of American industry and the fashion in which the US army's tank-building machine tools could be diverted to the needs of 'Churchill' tank production in Britain. A year previously *Coastal Command* (1942) showed the defence of Britain's shores by its airforces, including the Royal Australian Air Force, and made the point that there were American-built aircraft like the Lockheed Hudson and PBY Catalina playing an important role, as well as US Army Air Corps squadrons operating out of Iceland. Former Hollywood star Bessie Love, who had emigrated to London in 1935 following a divorce, made a short documentary for Spectator Short Films in 1942 with Basil Radford and BBC announcer Leslie Mitchell, called *London Scrapbook*. This film was concerned with how London had taken it and was now getting on with the war with a sense of humour – just the message the Americans needed to have, particularly with its emphasis upon the stringency of rationing acted out by Miss Love at a butcher's shop. This theme was later exclusively dealt with in *Rationing in Britain* (1944) which was shown only in North America.

While the MoI was concerned with continuing to project the real Britain onto American screens, American efforts had not ceased to do the same thing from the vantage point of Hollywood.

The Hollywood branch of the OWI was certain that it knew the facts and attempted to guide Hollywood producers concerning the 'truth'. As with horses, however, you could lead the producers to the truth but you could not make them film it. The type of approach to British society typified by *Random Harvest* and *Mrs Miniver* was what Hollywood knew best and, so far as it was concerned, represented the 'real' England. Foremost in this group were members of the English community who, led by Cedric Hardwicke, assembled in *Forever and a Day* (RKO, 1943); 'one of the most brilliant casts of modern times', wrote James Agate, 'to bolster up one of the poorest pictures'.[22] The history of a house on London's outskirts from 1804 to the blitz paid its profits to war charities and terrified the OWI's Hollywood people for its reinforcement of the traditional English image. Even so, all OWI efforts to block production of the film failed.

The projection of British society by Hollywood was one side of the story of the wartime Anglo-American relationship, but what did the Americans learn from it? And what did the British learn from seeing themselves through the eyes of the Hollywood lens? In fact the number of films from America which dealt with British themes were few and far between, as one might expect, and the constant stream of filmland America continued to dominate the British cinema. If this, after all, was the image of America which Americans wanted to project, then why bother to change it?

There was however considerably more interest on this side of the Atlantic in dealing seriously with the long-term Anglo-American relationship, but it emerged in a significant way only as the war was coming to an end. There were earlier treatments, such as *The Big Blockade*, already mentioned in another context, which was released at about the same time as Warner Brothers GB's *Flying Fortress* (1942). This film, made at Teddington Studios, was built on the same formula as *A Yank in the RAF* and its ilk. One of the Americans involved in the Atlantic Ferry Service is a professional pilot whose licence is revoked when he is involved in a fatal crash, and another is a rich and spoiled playboy who was really responsible for the accident. Both make good in the RAF fighting Nazis. Hollywood's OWI reviewer, Marjorie Thorson, could not tell if the screenplay was written by Englishmen with a low opinion of Americans or by Americans who did not realise the disservice they 'are doing their country by such a portrayal of American fighting men on the screen'. She guessed from the faulty American slang that it was the former.[23] A rather more positive approach was evident in Warner Brothers GB's *Atlantic Ferry* (1941; US title *Sons of the Sea*). Directed by Walter Forde and starring Michael Redgrave, the screenplay saw the hand of Emeric Pressburger. The *Monthly Film Bulletin* suggested that the film was good propaganda 'especially at the moment [June 1941], and should be seen with enthusiasm, both here and in America'.[24] In August of the same year British National released *Penn of Pennsylvania* (1941; US title *The Courageous Mr Penn*), supposed to have been inspired by President Roosevelt's inaugural address, which opened the film before it retreated back to the late seventeenth century. The *New Statesman* lamented: 'it is a pity that a historical theme which links together the souls of Britain and America should have been handled so heavily and tediously'.[25]

At the time when these two Anglo-American theme films were being put into production a radically different film on the same subject was being planned by Eric Knight and Paul Rotha. This was to be a documentary which would tell the unvarnished truth about America in the same fashion as Knight's attempt to tell the truth about the England he had left in *This Above All*.[26] Although there were a large number of American documentary films available, when MoI representatives (including Tom Baird) looked at them they found that the films had been made to 'criticise America and warn Americans about unsatisfactory conditions in their own country'. This clearly would not fit into the MoI's established policy of 'showing the best of America to Britain'. It was finally decided not to use or re-edit American documentaries but to make its own, modelled on the exemplary *Minnesota Document* produced in 1942 by the University of Minnesota's Visual Education Service. The MoI project was to be a two-reel non-theatrical release produced by Paul Rotha, with the majority of the film material being supplied by Thomas Baird from New York. The first script was available by early July 1942 and was described as being 60 per cent Yvonne Fletcher's and 40 per cent Eric Knight's. The latter, by now hard at work on the *Why We Fight* series, was largely responsible for the initial treatment of *America, The Land and Its People* being such an honest portrait, warts and all. Whereas Baird and the British Information Service in New York were committed to 'showing the best', Knight wanted to be patently honest, particularly when dealing with America's racial problem concerning the Negroes. The importance of the film was underlined by a letter of 27 June which stressed that the MoI should spare no pains since the film 'may have an important role to play in the reception areas for the American Expeditionary Forces'. Arthur Elton wanted Ed Murrow, the London CBS correspondent, to do the narration, even though he had reservations about the script. What Elton was asking for was a 'neutral sympathetic observer' and he doubted if anyone in Rotha's circle would have the 'right touch'. It was essential for the film to avoid any possible charges of New Deal propaganda in the same way as films about Britain had to avoid portraying its 'welfare state' as supporting the New Deal!

While the sanitised view of America was gaining support in New York and London amongst key MoI personnel, Knight was writing to Rotha encouraging him to stand firm: 'Show what you *know* is real of America and its people, and if you show it clearly enough no verbiage will be needed to foster the natural interest and liking the British people have for this country.' Knight, whose earlier offer of help to the British Information Service had been ignored, was not prepared to pull punches. The script continued to attract criticism, especially from Sidney Bernstein, who strongly objected to what he considered to be 'politically inept if not actually dangerous at this time'. By the autumn of 1943, with the country filling up with GIs, Arthur Elton still did not have a film, although there was at least a budget and a contract with Rotha. The non-commercial audience of two and a half million people would just have to wait.

To cover this gap in the MoI programme the OWI's new films *Jeep* and *Oswego* were shown in January 1944 in those areas which billeted the largest number of American troops. *Swedes in America* and *Cowboy* were distributed that spring. Editing problems delayed progress on *America, The Land and Its People* but finally a preview of 3000 feet of material (5 reels) took place on 8 February 1944 for MoI and OWI representatives. The project now seemed doomed to slip into the control of the OWI's London people, who seemed to want a two-reeler of 20 minutes 'to end all films on the USA'. In despair Elton asked Jack Beddington if he might finish the film as a travelogue or 'throw it away': 'BUT FOR GOD'S SAKE, NO MORE SHOOTING'. Frank Darvall of the MoI's American Division rewrote the script, which was accepted by the OWI, except that the Paul Bunyan language 'that "impossible" was not in the American vocabulary' was replaced by the sterile: 'We feel that one of the criticisms in England of America and Americans has been their big-scale talk . . .'. Work continued and finally, on 23 February 1945, with barely eight weeks of the European war left, the show copy was delivered. The film was released in March but, in Paul Rotha's words, 'was a pale shadow of its original conception'. As it stands the film had an honesty about it which wears well even today. It has black families in poverty, the sign 'For Colored Only' in the shop window, white poverty, Ford assembly lines, cops and traffic jams and Negro university students. One can argue about the balance but not about the effort.[27] As for Knight himself, he wrote one more film, *Know Your Ally – Britain*, which was in production by the end of May 1942, before his untimely death in a plane crash off the coast of Dutch Guiana in January 1943.

In retrospect what is amazing is the extent to which Hollywood committed itself to pro-British propaganda between 1939 and 1942, bearing in mind that many of the films released in 1942 had gone into production before Pearl Harbor. Had the senators investigating Hollywood for propaganda actually seen these films they would have had all the evidence they needed to prove the charge. The OWI really had very little to offer Hollywood except unacceptable advice.

The MoI's films, on the other hand, did a competent job – with the help of Hollywood distribution – of getting the British message onto American screens from 1940 onwards.

The MoI was less successful in preparing the British people for the GI invasion and occupation and *America, The Land and Its People* did not appear until after the Americans had gone. It proved to be as difficult for the British to encapsulate the Americans as a nation (particularly with its 'ignored' poverty and racial problems) on film as it was for the Americans to create a filmic view of the British that would prove acceptable to critics on either side of the Atlantic. When the Yanks did go home they invariably remembered their time in Britain with a romantic nostalgia appropriate to Hollywood *à la* Walter Scott, whereas British memories tended to be more selective. For most Britons America remained a mystery, except for those culture-shocked war brides who had to put to the test Margaret Mead's views on American courtship.[28]

Notes and References

I should like to express my thanks to Jeffrey Richards, Sue Harper and I. C. Jarvie for commenting on an earlier draft of this paper, and to Steve Perry, Film Department of the Imperial War Museum, who put a print of *America: The Land and Its People* at my disposal.

1. Lindsay to Eden, 22 March 1937 (PRO FO 414/274).
2. Elmslie to Fletcher, 12 January 1939 (FO 395/656).
3. *Dawn Patrol* was Warner Brothers' 1938 remake of their 1938 production using much the same footage. Produced by Hal B. Wallis, this 103-minute feature starred Errol Flynn and Basil Rathbone and featured David Niven and a large section of the Hollywood English community. The plot centred on not only the heroism of English pilots but also the failure of the British government to give them airworthy planes, thus leading to heavy losses – hardly a theme to instil confidence in contemporary attitudes concerning Britain's air preparedness for another war. *A Christmas Carol* (1938) came from MGM, was naturally well-mounted and featured the reformation of the 'capitalist' Scrooge amidst the horrors of Dickensian London. The third film mentioned in this letter, *The Drum* (1938), was released in the USA as *Drums* and was Alexander Korda's London Films' story of the British army's assistance to an Indian prince in resisting his 'usurping uncle'. *Heart of the North* (Warner Bros./First National, 1938) was a cliché-ridden Technicolor epic of the Mounties and surely one of the worst pictures of the year.
4. From the American viewpoint see Pare Lorentz's review of *Cavalcade*

for *Vanity Fair* (March, 1933) reprinted in *Lorentz on Film: Movies 1927–41* (New York, 1975) p. 105. Lorentz notes that Coward 'wrote shrewd patriotic spectacle, and if there is anything which moves the ordinary American to uncontrollable tears, it is the plight – the constant plight of dear old England . . . William Cameron Menzies [assistant director for the war scenes] made the war scenes as impressive, even though one could not help but remember that the brave laddies who relieved Mafeking were engaging in one of the most inglorious wars England ever waged.'

5.   Report of the British Library of Information, 18 January 1939 (FO 395/656).

6.   Memorandum by Angus Fletcher, 6 February 1939 (FO 395/656).

7.   Note by Charles Warner on the above (FO 395/656).

8.   *New York Times*, 27 December 1942.

9.   Actually, in an interview with the author, Watt's phrase was 'not a dry seat in the house'.

10.   INF 6/333.

11.   *Monthly Film Bulletin*, October 1943.

12.   Caroline Moorhead, *Sidney Bernstein: A Biography* (London, 1984) pp. 133–42.

13.   Washington National Record Centre (WNRC), Suitland, RG 208, 1433, Entry 264: Zanuck.

14.   Mel Gussow, *Zanuck: Don't say Yes until I finish talking* (London, 1971) pp. 103 ff. The power of the example (perhaps linked with flyers in the RAF having a chance with Betty Grable) led to the film being banned in the Irish Republic.

15.   K. R. M. Short, 'The White Cliffs of Dover: promoting the Anglo-American alliance in World War Two', in *Historical Journal of Film, Radio and Television*, 2 (1982) 1.

16.   *The Times Literary Supplement*, 15 November 1941.

17.   Eric Knight, *This Above All* (London, 1941) p. 473.

18.   The copy of *A Short Guide* held by the Library of Congress was received on 3 August 1943; an earlier edition entitled *Britain* for all members of the American Expeditionary Forces in Great Britain seems to have appeared as early as February. Other guides which provide important insights into the Anglo-American relationship (the official Allied view) include the *Pocket Guide to Northern Ireland* (1942), *A Pocket Guide to India* (1943) which warned that GIs were going to India at a time when relations between the Indians and British were tense and that the American forces should 'exercise scrupulous care to avoid the slightest participation in India's political problems, or even the appearance of so doing', and *A Pocket Guide to Egypt* (1943) which compared the British role there with the American desire to maintain troops 'as we do in the Panama Canal zone'. The US Army Service Forces' Special Services Division also produced a large set of pocket guides to various counties where American forces were stationed.

19.   Balderston to Lowell Mellet, 8 February and 16 March 1943 (WNRC, RG 264). Kenneth MacGowan of Twentieth Century Fox wrote to

OWI chief Elmer Davis in exactly the same vein on 10 April 1943. *The Battle of Britain* was not in fact shown on general commercial release on the grounds that it showed nothing new; it had all been seen in the newsreels. The film had got caught up in the controversy concerning the general release of the *Why We Fight* series which is discussed at length in David Culbert, 'Social Engineering for a Democratic Society at War', in K. R. M. Short (ed.), *Film and Radio Propaganda in World War II* (London, 1983) and K. R. M. Short, 'Prelude to War: The Office of War Information, the War Activities Committee and the US Army, 1942–3', in K. Fledelius and G. Jagshitz (eds), *Studies in Film and History* IV (Copenhagen and Vienna, 1986).

20.   ABCA Bulletin, No. 22, 18 July 1942.
21.   INF 6/343. This film is wrongly dated in F. Thorpe and N. Pronay, *British Official Films in the Second World War: A Descriptive Catalogue* (Oxford, 1980). This catalogue (and its introduction by Pronay) is essential to the researcher.
23.   Participants in *Forever and a Day*: Written by Charles Bennett, C. S. Forester, Lawrence Hazard, Michael Hogan, W. P. Lipscomb, Alice Duer Miller, John Van Druten, Alan Campbell, Peter Godfrey, S. M. Herzig, Christopher Isherwood, Gene Lockhart, R. C. Sherriff, Claudine West, Norman Corwin, Jack Hartfield, James Hilton, Emmet Lavery, Frederick Lonsdale, Donald Ogden Stewart, Keith Winter; Photographed by Robert de Grasse, Lee Garmes, Russell Metty, Nicholas Masuraca; Music by Anthony Collins; Produced by Rene Clair, Edmund Goulding, Cedric Hardwicke, Frank Lloyd, Victor Saville, Robert Stevenson, Herbert Wilcox; Cast: Anna Neagle, Ray Milland, Claude Rains, C. Aubrey Smith, Dame May Whitty, Gene Lockhart, Ray Bolger, Edmund Gwenn, Charles Coburn, Ian Hunter, Jessie Mathews, Charles Laughton, Montague Love, Cedric Hardwicke, Reginald Owen, Buster Keaton, Wendy Barrie, Ida Lupino, Brian Aherne, Edward Everett Horton, June Duprez, Eric Blore, Merle Oberon, Una O'Connor, Nigel Bruce, Roland Young, Gladys Cooper, Robert Cummings, Richard Haydn, Elsa Lanchester, Sara Allgood, Robert Coote, Donald Crisp, Ruth Warwick, Kent Smith, Herbert Marshall, Victor McLaglen and many others in bit parts.
23.   WNRC, Suitland, RG 208/1435.
24.   *Monthly Film Bulletin*, 8 (1941) p. 81.
25.   *New Statesman*, 30 August 1941.
26.   Knight was particularly critical of the 'Mrs Minivers' who thought of Britain as circa 1912 or just simply as bad; nor did he think Goebbels could have done more damage to Anglo-American understanding than that done unwittingly by *A Yank at Eton* or *Johnny Doughboy*. See Eric Knight, *Portrait of a Flying Yorkshireman: Letters from Eric Knight in the United States to Paul Rotha in England* (London, 1952).
27.   Documentation regarding the making of *America, The Land and Its People* can be found in the PRO, INF 1/217. The file includes Rotha's unrelenting efforts to get paid for the film.
28.   M. Mead, *American Troops and the British community* (London, 1944).

8

Creative Tensions: *Desert Victory*, the Army Film Unit and Anglo-American Rivalry, 1943–5

Anthony Aldgate

Desert Victory was a considerable commercial and critical success. It was afforded a prestigious première at the Odeon, Leicester Square, on 5 March 1943, was put into three showcase venues for its West End run and was given a general release throughout Britain ten days later. It was first screened in New York on 31 March at the Twentieth Century Fox Building and by the end of April some 400 copies were in circulation across America. The film proved to be far and away the biggest box-office winner of all the 'official' British documentaries produced and released during the war, accruing receipts of £77 250 up to May 1944 alone as against total production costs of £5793.[1] And it received massive acclaim from the critics in both Britain and the United States, culminating in the award of an 'Oscar' from the Academy of Motion Picture Arts and Sciences for 'the most distinctive documentary achievement of 1943'.[2] Moreover *Desert Victory* has withstood the test of time well. It is celebrated in most standard histories of the British cinema and is frequently included in retrospective seasons of British films on television and in cinemas. The Services Kinema Corporation holds it in sufficient esteem to retain it, still, in its *Catalogue of Documentary and General Purpose Films*.[3] And even the more trenchant of contemporary analyses are compelled to acknowledge and spotlight the film's ideological significance in constructing 'a nationalist and populist position in relation to the conduct of World War II'.[4] In short, *Desert Victory* has been recognised generally – and rightly – as 'one of the outstanding documents of the war'.[5]

144

A great deal has been said, then, upon the matter of the film's obvious propagandist intentions and achievements. Little mention has been made, however, of the film's undoubted importance in certain other vital respects. The documentation on *Desert Victory* reveals much in regard to the working relationships within the Army Film Unit (AFU) which produced it and the problems which arose between the AFU and the Films Division at the Ministry of Information (MoI), but most of all it reveals the rivalry which developed between the 'official' agencies of film production in Britain and America.[6] The success that *Desert Victory* enjoyed clearly had an impact, for instance, upon the films being produced by service units in the United States. Some effects were undoubtedly beneficial, but the film also engendered a measure of jealousy, plain and simple, and ironically the AFU was to prove the ultimate loser when it came to the joint Anglo-American production of a follow-up, *Tunisian Victory*.[7] The popularity of the former militated against the AFU contribution to the latter. The occasion of an isolated British cinematographic success in the American market served only to preclude the opportunity for continued success there. It was not the first time this had happened and it was by no means to be the last.

Work commenced on *The Battle of Egypt* (as *Desert Victory* was initially to be called) concurrent to the campaign which began on 23 October 1942 when Allied forces went on to the offensive in order to reverse the setbacks they had suffered at Rommel's hands during the previous year. Captain Roy Boulting was well into production at Pinewood Studios when he was abruptly removed from the project: 'the reason given to me by Major Bryce was that as Commanding Officer of the Army Film Unit he should be responsible for making the film'.[8] Alex Bryce had already done two films for the AFU on the war in the desert (*The Siege of Tobruk* and *Tobruk*, both 1942) and clearly felt the subject fell well within his domain. As he was CO, Boulting felt he had no choice but to comply with the takeover, even though it meant losing control of a project which he very much cherished and in which he had invested a considerable amount of time and effort.

In the event, however, Bryce's draft construction for the film made little impression. Indeed it was received badly and criticised heavily. On 25 November 1942 Ronald Tritton of the public relations section at the War Office (PR 2) sent the draft to Jack Beddington, head of the MoI's Films Division, accompanied by a budget outline proposing £809 for a film of 2000 feet. Tritton explained that the draft had also been sent to the RAF Film Unit and to Ian Dalrymple at the Crown Film Unit. They were all being 'fully consulted' but 'cutting is going ahead fast and a rough assembly is expected within a few days'. He accordingly asked Beddington for his comments as quickly as possible.[9]

The comments followed thick and fast and invariably expressed disappointment at what was proposed. Arthur Calder Marshall, a production specialist, agreed with Beddington that the draft was 'very thin' and outlined his reservations in a long memorandum on 26 November. The draft, he felt, did not capture 'the scope of the actual operations' and he compared it with Churchill's Armistice Day speech to the Commons on 11 November when the desert campaign was explained:

> The Prime Minister divided his speech into three sections.
> 1. The time required for preparation. 2. The need of combination and concert. 3. The importance of surprise. I can think of no better text on which to base the film of these operations than the Prime Minister's speech itself.
>
> It would be tedious to compare the draft construction in detail with the Prime Minister's speech but I can show what I mean by a few simple examples. The Army Film Unit treatment begins with the retreat and deals in great detail with the operations between 2 July and the final attack. I appreciate that they intend to add further material when the full military details of the last phase of the battle of Egypt come in. But I am sure that it is a mistake to fix such attention firstly on the retreat and secondly on the holding operation preceding the October offensive and break through.
>
> The Prime Minister emphasises that even before the fall of Tobruk most of the six pounders we are now using were despatched from this country. The same applies to the more heavily armoured and more heavily gunned British tanks. In the AFU treatment there is no sense of this important historical development . . .[10]

In short, Churchill's account revealed 'a broadness of vision which is entirely lacking in the AFU treatment'. Calder Marshall felt that the deficiencies boiled down essentially to one thing: the AFU script proposed a defensive-minded film whereas he wanted an offensive-minded film which justly celebrated the 'historical British victory' that Churchill reported was being won in the desert and which suitably marked 'the end of the beginning'. Nor was he alone. The Films Division felt the same way and so too did a good many other folk.[11]

Bryce did not retain his control over the production for much longer. On his return from Egypt – where he commanded the No. 1 unit of the Army Film and Photographic Service (AFPS) which was attached to the Eighth Army and sending back front-line footage to the AFU at Pinewood – Major David MacDonald took charge of the film. Boulting was reinstated as director and supervising editor. A broader treatment was prepared, to everyone's liking. It was now envisaged that the film would run to 3500 feet, be budgeted at £2882 plus overheads and include, for the first time, some 800 feet of newsreel footage in addition to the first-hand material shot by the AFPS, and whatever else might be forthcoming from that quarter as the Eighth Army continued its victorious advance.[12]

The budget was agreed by the MoI Films Division on 27 January 1943 – though not without some typically pointed remarks to the effect that 'the agreement is not intended to relieve the War Office of their financial responsibility for the budget or for the control of expenditure by the Army Film Unit'.[13] But the War Office and AFU were quite prepared to put up with such admonitions so long as they could get on with their production. After all, they were still working in comparative harmony with the Films Division and everybody agreed that it was essential to finish the film as quickly as possible. As the Films Division pointed out: 'This film is wanted for our distribution programme and we should be glad if AFU would proceed with it at once.'[14]

One other facet of the AFU's willingness to accede to Films Division requests at this time manifested itself in the course of its obvious adherence to Calder Marshall's suggestions about building the film around Churchill's speech. Difficulties in meeting production deadlines were compounded as a result of this well-meant advice. There was little problem in getting hold of the Prime Minister's directive to General Alexander to destroy Rommel's forces, since that had been recited openly to the Commons – though what they received from 10 Downing Street, of course, was a typewritten copy of the handwritten original. But by the time the original instructions were made available the AFU proceeded to quietly forget about the matter, since they arrived so late and only after the film had been completed, printed up and distributed to 'all corners of the world and already shown in New York and

Moscow'.[15] There was also a problem when it came to including extracts from Churchill's speech made on a recent visit to the Eighth Army in Tripoli. The AFU wanted to end its film with material of Churchill on that occasion reviewing the troops in a victory parade and to put on the soundtrack some lines of his speech praising the men. It would make 'a grand ending' and 'put Churchill's share in the victory just right'. The AFU had the footage, but not the speech. Nor was there a decent BBC recording of what had been said that would suit their purposes. The production was already running beyond its original completion date of 15 February 1943 when the idea was hit upon of asking Churchill to re-record it especially for their purposes. Churchill consented and a recording session was hastily arranged.[16]

The film was finally completed by the end of February, with a commentary written by J. L. Hodson and music provided by William Alwyn. It was first shown to an invited audience at the War Office's tiny private cinema in Curzon Street House on 1 March 1943. Sir James Grigg, the War Minister, Major General F. Lawson, Head of Public Relations at the War Office, and Major Sir Leonard Woolley, the official historian, were all present along with the anxious film-makers MacDonald, Boulting and Hodson.[17] *Desert Victory* was immediately proclaimed a success. Beddington wrote to MacDonald expressing his 'very deep admiration and many thanks' to all concerned at the AFU for a film which projected 'a strong, virile, confident and victorious people – that is what I have always wanted to see in one of our pictures and I can assure you that it is worth many, many munitions of war'. To Hodson he added: 'The film is a first rate one and your commentary does more than anything else to make it so. I hope we shall have many more Victory films and as many more admirable commentaries from you.'[18] The fact that the film had ended up closer to 6000 feet and had overrun its budget was quickly forgotten as the praise mounted and the plaudits increased. Immediately after the film's general release on 15 March Lord Beaverbrook wrote to Sidney Bernstein at the MoI extending his congratulations for 'the extraordinary fine record which has been made of the Eighth Army' and full of confidence that 'the film, I know, will have an immense success throughout the country'.[19]

So indeed it did. But ironically it was from this point, as *Desert Victory* began to gather an unprecedented degree of popular, critical and commercial success, that the AFU started to experience intractable problems with the film. In the first place Churchill saw the film just prior to its general release and suggested two alterations: that footage of the march past by the 52nd Division be inserted at the film's climax, and that a line or two be added to the commentary pointing out that New Zealand troops were seen on parade. But because the film was due for imminent release, some powerful arguments were needed to dissuade the Prime Minister. On his first point it was argued that such a change would require re-recording the music which had already been cut carefully to cover the existing film; on the second it was noted that shots of the New Zealanders came after the commentary had finished and when the film was ending with Churchill's own words. It was thought that 'perhaps he had not noticed this because of the considerable bathos there would have been in introducing a very short statement by the commentator after the stirring words spoken by the PM'. In other words, Churchill's point would have resulted in an anti-climax.[20]

Churchill was momentarily convinced and the film was allowed to proceed on release. But he was far from finished with *Desert Victory*. Within a month he had sat through the film again, this time accompanied by its director Roy Boulting, and had viewed in addition some four reels of uncut material. Boulting recounted the outcome of the meeting to Jack Beddington on 13 April 1942. Churchill wanted to see a considerable amount of unused material, including newsreel footage, added to the existing last reel of *Desert Victory*. Once again a cogent and convincing response was required, and Boulting lived up to the occasion, pointing out that such changes could not be effected for some time since the tracks for the film were by now in the United States, where they were being dubbed into foreign-language versions for distribution abroad. The Prime Minister relented and 'expressed a wish that any work being undertaken in America should not be interfered with'. Churchill was thus assuaged, although the repercussions of that meeting were to haunt the MoI Films Division and the AFU for a very long time to come.[21]

Churchill was not the only source of bother. The AFU was soon to be hoist on the petard of its success. Much of the publicity, for example, surrounding *Desert Victory* had made great play out of the number of casualties suffered by the Army Film and Photographic Service in the course of its duties. This was not the AFU's doing[22] but the film critics had duly repeated the casualty figures in the midst of their effusive comment and, on occasion, had dutifully embellished them. Figures as high as 40 per cent of AFPS personnel – either killed, wounded or taken prisoner – were cited in some accounts.[23] And these casualties were supposedly suffered whilst accumulating material for *Desert Victory* alone. The result was that no less a person than the Minister of Information himself, Brendan Bracken, was prompted to investigate the matter with a view to writing to next of kin. Fred Lawson of PR 2 heard about the idea and sensibly tried to scotch it. He wrote:

> I think this project had better be dropped because though two officers and four sergeants have been killed in the whole of the operation, actually the only photographer killed in the battle of Egypt was a stills photographer. The figures which have been given of the casualties in the Army Film and Photographic Unit were the figures of their total casualties in action and have never been given out as being specially incurred in the battle of Alamein.
>
> These men have taken every sort of risk and their casualties throughout the whole show have been 25% of the unit but in this particular battle they were fairly lucky.
>
> Can we, therefore, leave this alone?

The minister obliged and dropped the subject.[24] It proved more difficult, however, to deal with complaints to Bracken that though Indian troops had taken part in the desert campaign there was nothing to be seen of them in action during the course of *Desert Victory*. In this instance urgent telegrams were hastily despatched to MoI film officers in India suggesting that the film be carefully studied before any public showing. It was essential to avoid giving offence, and so Jack Beddington had no objection if they wished to insert footage of Indian troops in action.[25]

The point was, of course, that *Desert Victory* was turning out to be immensely popular. It had attracted a considerable amount of attention and had been given a very high profile. A good many people began to wonder why they had not figured more prominently in either its story or its success. Beddington, for example, wanted to know what contribution the Crown Film Unit had made to the production. Ian Dalrymple, former head of production, replied that Crown had provided the services of its art department, construction department and electricians (for the studio sections), it had supplied the musical director and front commentator for the film (Jack

Holmes, who replaced Dalrymple as Crown's head) and it had supplied library footage for other sequences. For his part, Dalrymple claimed to have read Bryce's script and MacDonald's treatment and to have seen and commented upon the MacDonald-Boulting version of the film. His 'chief contribution', he believed, was in making MacDonald 'aware of the situation in which Boulting had been pointedly and specifically excluded from the production'. And yet for all that, Dalrymple added wryly, 'Crown wasn't credited at all.' This was, he continued, 'a pity' if only as 'a gesture to the studio personnel'.[26]

In fairness it should be noted that Boulting and MacDonald did not receive individual credits on *Desert Victory* either, and it was they after all who had been largely responsible for its completion. J. L. Hodson, for one, very much regretted that. He recorded in his diary: 'I don't feel very comfortable that the only names given a screen credit are William Alwyn's and mine. The men who've done the major work are David MacDonald and Roy Boulting.'[27] Yet Dalrymple clearly resented that Crown had not been given a mention and, on at least one occasion, showed his 'visible jealousy' over the popular success which the film enjoyed, which far outstripped anything afforded to his outfit's productions.[28] Such feelings doubtless go a long way towards explaining why, between mid-March and mid-May 1943 when he resigned, Dalrymple did his utmost to ensure that Crown would secure production control of any follow-up film project to *Desert Victory*.

In the event the sequel was also lost to the Army Film Unit and, once again, Major Hugh Stewart and Captain Roy Boulting took charge of the production. But the AFU was in turn to lose control of the film, which was finally released as a joint Anglo-American production, *Tunisian Victory*.[29] Here again to a large extent the AFU was to prove the victim of its own success over *Desert Victory*, though in this instance it was wounded American pride that it was up against. *Desert Victory* was heavily promoted in the United States from the outset. Even before the film had been released in Britain Beddington stated that he was 'very anxious for David MacDonald to get to America at the earliest possible moment to help in the exploitation of *Desert Victory*'. 'The Minister is entirely with us in this', he continued, and 'is doing all he can to help in this and other ways.'[30] As a result MacDonald was indeed present at the private screening in New York to address the Americans 'and answer questions on the campaign'.

'The film of the African campaign which Prime Minister Churchill sent to President Roosevelt' was shown to the Foreign Press Association at the Twentieth Century Fox Building on 31 March 1943. Everyone agreed it was a hit.[31] MacDonald then toured America with the film before returning home in May.

> David MacDonald . . . is now back, having shown the film in about 120 different places, and triumphed everywhere. David made a speech every time (although speech-making is new to him) and looks thinner for his ordeal. Some very highly-placed person in the USA has sent a message to our Government saying that the film has done more for us than any other piece of propaganda in America. In New York . . . the film started at 8 am and went on showing till 4 am next day. The queues waiting at 4 am continued to wait till the theatre opened again at 8 am next day.
>   In Hollywood he was told: 'You know, you've revolutionised war films with this picture. We shall have to revise our ideas.' President Roosevelt, I believe, said it was the best war film seen in the White House this war. Winston himself has said it is a 'work of art'.
>   One amusing crack. A woman who had seen it in a Middle West theatre said: 'It's a fine film. I wonder where they took it?'[32]

Obviously hyperbole played a big part in the selling of *Desert Victory* to America, as with any film hoping to succeed there. But it worked. The film made a tremendous impact, not least on the US Army Signal Corps and upon its most noted film director, Colonel Frank Capra, in particular.

The US Army Signal Corps had long been interested in all aspects of the British army's film activities. In May 1942, for example, Colonel Darryl F. Zanuck visited Britain as a 'special observer' and engaged in four informal conferences with the director of army cinematography, Paul Kimberley. Zanuck was mainly concerned with the production of training films – as was Kimberley – and with seeking to co-ordinate the training film programmes of both armies, a specialised area of concern. But it was soon agreed that 'there must be the closest collaboration regarding the production of films in battle zones, not only for training purposes but for newsreels, propaganda films, battle records, etc.'. It is moreover clear that

Zanuck was greatly impressed with what he saw of British army film production generally and that he was intent upon saying as much in his report to the general staff back in Washington.[33]

Furthermore it is evident that, at least throughout 1942, Britain had the edge over its American ally in many realms of film work within the armed forces, and was recognised as being markedly better. A US report of 13 August 1942, for example, noted that British aircraft recognition films 'possess a very high degree of technical quality'; their photography 'is very fine and so is the animation'; and concluded 'they are wider in scope and superior in production' to anything forthcoming from the American services.[34] Indeed the Americans continued to experience profound problems with such films for some time, even after they engaged the Walt Disney studios to produce them. A British inter-services committee saw some and decided that 'the commentaries seem needlessly complicated, dull and lifeless, compared to those of British films'. The diagrammatic work was considered to be 'technically excellent' but that too was criticised for making 'no use of cartoon exaggeration or humour to concentrate the eye on the outstanding characteristics of the aircraft'.[35]

The US authorities soon came to a similar conclusion and decided to abandon the series of films started by Disney for the army and navy. Production would cease, the films would be re-edited and new commentaries added.[36] Mistakes such as these were of course inevitable. American forces were still finding their feet in regard to certain specialised areas of production. They were relative newcomers, and it showed. It was therefore not uncommon for the US Army Pictorial Service to enlist British expertise in the setting up of training films. They borrowed British films for use with their own units and, in fact, simply adapted British films for their own purposes, substituting a few shots depicting American equipment here and there and adding an American commentary.[37] Such practices went on well into the early months of 1943.

But the comparative lack of experience and expertise was only part of the problem. It masked a more deep-rooted malaise. In the case of the aircraft recognition films, for instance, the fault did not lie with the Disney Studios but elsewhere, as with so much armed forces film production at this time. The real problem lay in the fact that film was simply not given a high ranking in the American army's list of war priorities.[38] Major G. F. Emmanuel of the British army staff in Washington said as much after visiting the Disney base in California, when he concluded that he could quite happily work there on any number of training films:

> I do not think that the persons concerned in the United States yet realise the possibilities of training films not only for their instructional but also for their interest value. As a result the American films are dull and stereotyped. The Walt Disney Studios could produce magnificent training films under the guidance of our own War Office.[39]

Frank Capra also felt he could work with Disney and indeed did so to great effect when, in 1942, his Signal Service Photographic Detachment set about the production of the *Why We Fight* series. This series was intended to render in film form a sequence of orientation lectures which had been delivered to the armed forces, though none too successfully, by the Army Bureau of Current Relations. It was planned in the spring of 1942, library material was amassed, scripts were drafted and animated inserts worked out during the summer. The concept of the whole series was fixed by September and production began in earnest thereafter. Owing to production difficulties the first of the series, *Prelude to War*, was not released to the forces until November 1942 but, like the rest of the films which followed from 1943 onwards, it became mandatory viewing for all US military personnel.

Prelude to War was well received in many influential quarters, both within the service community and beyond – so much so that in the spring of 1943 it was given an 'Oscar' for the best documentary of 1942. The War Activities Committee (WAC) considered the film for commercial release, which was finally granted from 27 May 1943. 'It was, relatively speaking, a box-office failure', one eminent commentator has observed,[40] but Capra revelled in the critical acclaim he was now receiving. Though he had already won three Academy Awards for feature film direction, in his autobiography Capra recorded his feeling that he 'personally had never cut the mustard with the theatrical films' as far as the critics were concerned. 'I did with the Army films', he added proudly. And when in 1944 the series earned the New York Critics' Award, it clearly meant a great deal to Capra.[41]

Prelude to War did not, however, have a trouble-free passage to commercial release in that spring of 1943. Several people, notably Lowell Mellett (a presidential assistant and chief of the Bureau of Motion Pictures, Domestic Branch, Office of War Information), doubted the wisdom of releasing the picture to the general public. Mellett thought the commentary 'an affront to the American people'; Senator Holman felt the film smacked of 'propaganda' and 'a fourth term for Roosevelt'. Acrimonious debate followed at the War Activities Committee: the army pressed for commercial release and got what it wanted, but the seeds of discontent with the series had assuredly been sown at the very outset.[42]

Moreover *Prelude to War* was released to the public just as *Desert Victory* was enjoying the full fruits of its American success, receiving both critical *and* popular acclaim. While Capra's series was just beginning to pick up momentum, the British AFU was already riding the crest of a wave. Comparisons were inevitable and they duly came from no less a source than 'our Army Brass', as Capra put it. Having at long last 'gotten into film', they now proceeded to question why their own 'Public Relations people' had not made 'pictures like *Desert Victory* about the American war effort'.[43] *Desert Victory* continued to be cited for some time as a film to emulate, not least by Robert Sherwood, director of the Overseas Branch of the OWI, who complained:

> All of the great documentary pictures were made by the British – *Desert Victory* and *Target for Tonight*, for example, are excellent pictures of the British war effort. And we, the greatest motion picture producing country in the world, were represented by films which indicated that we were taking no serious interest in the war and had no interest in anything but frivolity and luxury.[44]

By the summer of 1943, then, several factors doubtless conspired to compel Capra to keep at least one eye on the AFU's activities in Britain: the Signal Corps knew full well what its British counterpart was capable of. For all the undoubted achievements with *Prelude to War*, the *Why We Fight* series emerged only slowly and then under fire. Indeed the lukewarm public reception given to *Prelude to War* helped its OWI and WAC enemies ensure that the rest of the series would not be guaranteed a commercial release. *Desert Victory*, by contrast, was a proven success and was being actively touted as a model to follow, not least by American sources. Small wonder therefore that Capra jumped at the first opportunity to get in on the AFU's act.

The opportunity arose when the AFU ran into problems with the sequel to *Desert Victory*. Having finally wrested control of *Tunisian*

Victory from the Crown Film Unit's hands in May 1943, the AFU pressed hard to get the film completed as quickly as possible. Under its original title of *Africa Freed*, a rough cut was shown to interested parties in London in mid-July.[45] Among the audience were Major General Lord Burnham, director of public relations at the War Office, Sam Spewack of the OWI's London branch, and Colonel Tristram Tupper of the Public Relations Department of the US army, European Theatre of Operations. All three expressed profound reservations about the film, as Jack Beddington subsequently noted:

> Mr. Spewack has given considerable thought to the Tunisian film. General Burnham pointed out that not enough prominence was given to the American participation in the North African campaign and made at least two suggestions for remedying this. Lord Burnham's views were agreed by Colonel Tupper on behalf of the US Army. All present were in entire agreement.
>
> Since that showing, however, it has borne in on Mr. Spewack that Anglo-American friction is rising. He hears this from many sides, particularly the mercantile marine. He therefore feels it is more necessary than ever to safeguard ourselves against attacks by American isolationist newspapers and even more by that section of the American community which has not made up its mind . . . His anxiety is the same as mine – this was a joint operation and to present a heavily loaded film can do an enormous amount of harm. He does not believe that an introduction by the American Ambassador or a high ranking general would prevent newspaper attacks.[46]

In short the film should not be released for fear of alienating a sizable proportion of American opinion. It was a fair point and one worthy of careful consideration.

But why did *Africa Freed* fail to cover adequately the American contribution to the Tunisian campaign? Beddington hinted at the answer when he noted that Spewack 'accepts the fact that we asked for American film and didn't get it, we asked for a joint film with Capra and didn't get it, and that there is no blame attached to anybody'. This was undoubtedly diplomatic; blame rested largely on American shoulders. An Inter-Services Film Publicity Committee meeting on 6 April 1943 had decided, at Brendan Bracken's own behest, that though 'this film was about the British angle of a combined Anglo-American operation', the OWI should be approached 'once a full treatment had been prepared' and asked for 'full facilities and co-operation in the making of the film'.[47] The OWI was duly approached and a number of American personnel were released for the reconstructed scenes. But it was nowhere near enough; American support was half-hearted. By the end of April the MoI's Films Division was reiterating that 'we are very anxious to get this co-operation so that the part played by the Americans can be fully represented'.[48] By the end of May Beddington was anxious that 'US representation will be adequate'.[49]

The problem lay partly in the fact, as Films Division knew, that 'no library is maintained by the American forces in this country' and that all their film material was sent to Washington.[50] This clearly gave the AFU the excuse it needed to get on with the production in the hope of making do with a foreword to the film which would explain the course they had been forced to take. Major Hugh Stewart admitted as much over the telephone to Beddington on 20 July 1943:

We have all been aware that for some time there would be inadequate representation in 'Africa Freed' of the part played by the Americans in the Tunisian campaign. This is due entirely to lack of satisfactory film material of American troops in action . . . In order to clear ourselves of the unavoidable charge of intentional bias, I feel we must say somewhere that we were short of good American battle material.[51]

But it is also evident that the Americans themselves showed little interest in the project until the point at which it was nigh completed, when they could judge the fruits of the AFU's labours. Only then did they realise where their lack of interest had led them.

The film was finished by the end of August and immediately shelved. The Americans quickly sought to make amends for their sins. The Bureau of Public Relations in Washington agreed to send fine-grain duplicating prints of all their footage to London for the MoI's use and Frank Capra's team was hastily assembled and rushed over to England, arriving on 16 August.[52] A new joint production was finally agreed and, after considerable internal wrangling and innumerable difficulties, the film of *Tunisian Victory* was shown to the press in London and New York on 16 March 1944 – a year after the end of the campaign it covered.[53] The film was given a mixed reception, despite the banner headlines proclaiming:

'Never before has a film carried the main lead credit – The Governments of the United States and Great Britain present *Tunisian Victory*: An Official Record.'[54] Capra cites only a favourable review in his autobiography: 'While *Desert Victory* was a great picture, *Tunisian Victory* leaves it at the post.'[55] Ironically, though, two weeks before *Tunisian Victory* was shown in America its predecessor was given the ultimate Hollywood accolade – an 'Oscar', and one given at the expense of the hot favourite, *Battle of Russia* from the *Why We Fight* series.[56] Capra had good reason never to forget *Desert Victory*.

Nor indeed had the American film industry in general heard the last of the film. It subsequently turned out to be the source of a feud between the MoI and some American companies over the promotion and distribution of British 'official' films in the United States. The row was started inadvertently when the newly promoted Director of the Films Division at the British Information Services (BIS) in New York, Thomas Baird, wrote to the general sales manager at Twentieth Century Fox, who had distributed *Desert Victory* throughout America. Baird thanked Fox on behalf of the MoI and BIS for its salesmanship in gathering nearly 10 000 bookings and for helping 'to secure for this very important picture the popular success it has achieved'. The letter was forwarded to Spyros Skouras, Chairman of Fox, who, never one to miss a chance to blow his company's trumpet, passed it on to Brendan Bracken,[57] who was all for endorsing Baird's views: 'May I add my own thanks for the great success you have given us in distributing *Desert Victory*.'[58] But George Archibald, Baird's predecessor in New York, was invited to comment on Bracken's draft reply[59] and he had a very different story to tell. While recognising that Baird may have had 'good local reasons for writing his letter', he nonetheless felt that Fox had had 'to be pushed by us into doing even the job that they did'.[60] Bracken's comment was thus deleted, resulting in a short terse reply to Skouras's original fulsome letter.[61]

Twentieth Century Fox did not let the matter rest there. Before long the managing director wrote directly to Archibald. Again Baird's congratulatory remarks were included 'in view of the remarks you made concerning the way we handled this film in America'.[62] Archibald was unmoved and his response was barbed: 'How fortunate that we have both been so long in show business.'[63] On the same day, 18 April 1944, he wrote to Baird:

You know as well as I do how dissatisfied we were with 20th Century-Fox's handling of *Desert Victory* and, in particular, how Hal Horne lay down on the publicity and could have sabotaged it completely if we had not weighed in with our own resources plus Mack Miller, plus all our special screenings for columnists, radio commentators, etc.

But for the press and radio space we secured, Fox's sales organisation would not have done even the job that they did, and the job that they did isn't by any means as good as could have been . . . Also you know that the allocation of rentals as between Fox's first features and *Desert Victory* was grossly unfair to us. You will remember also that I employed the technique of taking Murray Silverstone out to lunch and told him of our dissatisfaction so that he in turn could tell it to Spyros Skouras.

In view of all this, I am completely at a loss to know why you should write in such glowing terms to Tom Connors. Surely it must have been in your mind that we were putting on a dissatisfaction act here and that you were cutting the ground from under our feet in giving them such a letter. If such a situation should ever arise again, which I think it won't, I hope you will check with us here in order to avoid crossing wires.[64]

The letter was signed 'Yours in sorrow'. It clearly took Baird by surprise. Nobody had informed him, after all, that the MoI in London was putting on a 'dissatisfaction act'. Furthermore, as he pointed out, there were indeed very good 'local reasons' for his complimenting Fox directly, though he had not anticipated his comments being used in the way they had been. For one thing Fox did secure 10 000 bookings for *Desert Victory*, despite their occasional lapses into lethargy. For another he now had *Tunisian Victory* to promote, and MGM were the agreed distributor. Films of this type were not easy to sell and it was altogether 'a far more difficult market'. While Fox 'did not do the best job in the world for us', he did feel it 'politic to hold up what they did do (no matter how it was done), as an example and incentive to other companies whom we might ask to distribute sometimes difficult films'. Finally, Baird implied, he had a bit of a retrieval job to perform. Archibald had started to criticise the US film companies for their distribution policies even before he left New York and his criticisms had not gone down well at all: 'several people remarked on this to me' and there was 'a great deal of whispering around the town'. Baird had simply sought to redeem the position of BIS by praising Fox's efforts in the promotion of British 'official' films. It was a sensible move.[65]

Archibald was mollified and he admitted that Fox may have been done 'a little injustice'. But he was convinced that the tough stand he had adopted was the right one. He was in fact inclined to regard the criticism of him 'as quite a useful factor in our general aim'. Business in the American cinemas was booming and that was why American companies were increasingly 'loath to give up profitable playing time' for the exhibition of official British films. The American film industry was, moreover, 'obviously feeling stronger in relation both to the United States and British governments'. 'The further away they get from the period when their monies were frozen here the less they feel that they have to play ball with us' and, in consequence, the American majors were more inclined than ever to sit back on their distribution contracts with the MoI, simply 'put our prints in their exchanges and await any exhibitor demand which might arise'. The only way to combat this, and to get 'such publicity, exploitation and selling effort as the films deserved and required', Archibald concluded, was to keep the Americans on their toes: 'I believe our best strategy with them is to keep them a little nervous if possible.'[66]

In truth however the time for this type of 'tough talk' had long gone. The MoI needed the American outlets far more than American exhibitors needed British 'official' films. Compromise and accommodation were now more in order, as Tom Baird recognised. He was after all on the spot and he knew how much Archibald's brusque approach had merely served to alienate certain influential sections of the American film industry. He cited an editorial by Sherwin Kane in the *Motion Picture Daily* on 13 March 1944:

We are reminded of a story that was being told and repeated around New York by emissaries of a branch of British government recently. It was their contention that a well known British war film was being neglected in this market by the company entrusted with its distribution because a producer affiliated with the company was identified with an American war picture which another company was distributing here. The neglect of the British picture, it was said, was deliberate because the company did not want it to get the comparable number of playdates which the American picture would receive and, thereby, embarrass its associated producer. It was not conceded by those making the charge that an American war picture was of more interest to the American public than a British one.

After the story had subsequently been repeated, an investigation was launched to ascertain the number of actual showings of each film:

While the American picture had received the greater number of playdates, the difference in number was too slight to support the charge being made. The next time we heard the story repeated we quoted the figures to the British official who conceded their accuracy. But rather than retract his charge, he stated that the showing on the British picture had been made tardily and was due in large measure to the 'rescue' efforts in special publicity and promotion which were undertaken, he said, by his office without the co-operation of the American distributor of the British documentary. That assertion can be disputed easily. What is significant is that the story and the charge couched within it died a natural death thereafter.

However, the British film industry, by its public charges and complaints against the American industry, and the expressions of active sympathy and interest of the British government in its film industry, has done more to help our industry gain the serious attention and, perhaps, the future assistance of our own government, than any other factor. In past years, Washington was not particularly interested in the industry's problems. But when the British industry and government, hand in hand, began world market exploration (if only verbally) our State Department began to sit up and take notice. If it listens long enough, it may learn what other governments have known about their film industries for long.

It would appear that our State Department was unable to regard the motion picture as a serious international force until the clamour out of London called its attention to British government policy on films.[67]

The AFU production of *Desert Victory* won many friends in the United States, and the popular success it enjoyed there did much to cement Anglo-American relations. Yet it is also a sad but true fact that, in some circles, it was the cause of much discord and rivalry.

Notes and References

1.   'Receipts from commercial distribution of films, summary of statement 18 prepared for evidence for the Public Accounts Committee in May 1944' (PRO INF 1/199); H. G. C. Welch to J. Beddington, 22 May 1943 (INF 1/223).

2.   See the microfiche on the film held at the BFI Library, London, for a collection of the critics' responses.

3.   See also 'Film Progress in the Services', in *Documentary News Letter (DNL)*, 4 (1943) 5, pp. 210–13; 'Army Film Unit Productions', *DNL*, 5 (1945) 50 p. 109; J. D. Forman, 'Army Experiments in Film Presentation', *DNL*, 6 (1946) 51, p. 6; 'The RAF Film Unit', *DNL*, 6 (1946) 52, p. 23. The Arts Enquiry, *The Factual Film* (London, 1947) also has much to say on the role of the AFU. My thanks to Jim Ballantyne at the British Universities Film and Video Council for providing me with a copy of the latest Services Kinema Corporation *Catalogue of Documentary and General Purpose Films*.

4.   Annette Kuhn, '*Desert Victory* and the People's War', in *Screen*, 22 (1981) 2, p. 68.

5.   See, for example, Ernest Betts, *The Film Business* (London, 1973) p. 187; Peter Rollins, 'Document and drama in *Desert Victory*', in *Film and History*, 4 (1974) 2, pp. 11–14; Elizabeth Sussex, *The Rise and fall of British documentary* (Berkeley, 1975) pp. 147, 160 & 174; Roger Manvell, *Films and the Second World War* (London, 1974), pp. 152–5; Erik Barnouw, *Documentary: A history of the non-fiction film* (New York, 1976) pp. 147–8; Ian Grant, *Cameramen at war* (Cambridge, 1980) pp. 17–18. More recently, *Desert Victory* was included in a Leslie Halliwell season of world war two films shown on Channel 4 in Britain, entitled 'The British at War', and broadcast on 15 November 1984.

6.   '*Desert Victory*', INF 1/221, is the major source of information on the film and is used extensively hereafter.

7.   See files on 'War in the Mediterranean – Africa Freed' (INF 1/223) and 'Tunisian Victory' (AFU 41, Imperial War Museum). My thanks to Clive Coultass, Anne Fleming, Kay Gladstone and Conrad Wood at the IWM for the generous help they provided at such short notice.

8.   Transcript of interview with Roy Boulting, *British Service Cameramen 1939–45*, Department of Sound Records, IWM, accession no. 004627/06, p. 21. Roy Boulting also kindly granted me an interview on 21 March 1986; his comments and insights were, as always, invaluable.

9.   R. Tritton to J. Beddington, 25 November 1942 (INF 1/221).

10.   A. Calder Marshall to Beddington, 26 November 1942 (INF 1/221). Churchill's speech can be found in *Hansard*, vol. 385, cols. 20–40, 11 November 1942.

11.   Roy Boulting believes that Bryce's version of the film was completed and shown to the MoI – 'they thought it to be rather less than adequate to memorialise an historic turning point in the war' – and that MacDonald was advised by Montgomery to 'take the film over': *British Service Cameramen* (op. cit.) p. 21.

12. 'Revised budget for Battle of Egypt', 4 January 1943, and covering note from Tritton to Beddington, 15 January 1943 (INF 1/221).

13. E. L. Mercier to Tritton, 27 January 1943 (INF 1/221).

14. The AFU's willingness to comply with Films Division requests extended, it seems, so far as to take note of a 'recently expressed objection' to the commentator they proposed to employ on the film, Joseph McLeod. See Mercier to Watson, 20 January 1943 (INF 1/221). In the event, of course, Geoffrey Wincott, Leo Genn, Frank Owen and J. B. Holmes were used to speak the commentary.

15. See J. M. Martin to A. Hodge, 25 March 1943; Beddington to S. Gates, 29 March 1943; Gates to Hodge, 30 March 1943 (INF 1/221). It was proposed and agreed, finally, that a facsimile copy of Churchill's handwritten instructions might be introduced into the non-theatrical version of the film, though it had not proved possible, as yet, to ascertain whether this actually happened.

16. See F. Lawson to B. Bracken, 13 February 1943; Hodge to J. H. Peck, 16 February 1943; Peck to Hodge, 17 February 1943 (INF 1/221). These documents suggest overwhelmingly that *Desert Victory* was released from the outset with the re-recorded voice of Churchill reading his Tripoli victory speech. Moreover, Roy Boulting is convinced this was the case. And Annette Kuhn has obviously seen a copy of the film 'with the voice of Churchill himself' at the relevant moment. See her '*Desert Victory* and the People's War', in *Screen*, 22 (1981) 2, p. 65. Since the copy of the film she saw was an American print and one knows full well that there was an almighty rush in 1943 to have the film shown in the United States as soon after its British release as possible, one might reasonably assume that all prints of *Desert Victory* bore Churchill's own words. Unfortunately this is not the case. The version shown on Channel 4 had Leo Genn rendering Churchill's speech, and I am reliably informed that the IWM print of the film contains the same. *Desert Victory* is also held by the Central Film Library and the National Film Archive in London, the Museum of Modern Art in New York and the National Archives and Records Service in Washington DC. Clearly it will only be possible to speculate on the reasons once all these prints have been checked. The files in the PRO do not provide the answer.

17. James Lansdale Hodson, *Home Front* (London, 1944) p. 305. This is a published record of Hodson's diary between 1942 and 1943. His subsequent volumes – *The Sea and the Sand, And Yet I Like America* (both London, 1945) – offer many lucid insights on the problems also experienced over *Tunisian Victory*, for which he was employed once again as writer, and upon his visit to America, where he was entertained by Frank Capra.

18. Beddington to Major D. MacDonald, 4 March 1943, and Beddington to J. L. Hodson, 10 March 1943 (INF 1/221).

19. Lord Beaverbrook to S. Bernstein, 16 March 1943. For the final costs of the film see also Tritton to Beddington, 1 March 1943 (INF 1/221).

20. Beddington to Gates, 15 March 1943 (INF 1/221).

21. Boulting to Beddington, 13 April 1943, with covering note to same

that read, significantly: 'Herewith the letter which is, perhaps necessary for the both of us'. (INF 1/221). As the record shows, for sometime thereafter the Films Division sought to retrieve the film from the United States, ostensibly for the purpose of fulfilling Churchill's wishes. Telegrams were exchanged as late as June 1943, but there is little reason to assume that they achieved the results which the Prime Minister desired.

22. Interestingly, Hodson recounts that after the film was first shown he felt compelled to telephone Sir James Grigg 'to suggest a title be thrown on the screen saying what casualties were involved in making the picture. He promised to turn it over in his mind. One can understand, of course, that everyone will say lives have been wasted but this is not so. Propaganda is a weapon of war and a powerful one. Moreover, the facts of what losses were incurred will impress both Russia and America, to say nothing of our people at home.': *Home Front* (op. cit.) p. 305. This did not happen in Britain, though such a title was clearly inserted for American consumption, as Hodson subsequently acknowledged: 'In America, we put in the film a title saying how many casualties were suffered in making it. We tried to get that done here, but the War Office didn't think it wise.' *The Sea and the Sand* (op. cit.) p. 75. Kuhn concurs about the American title by making the point about the print she saw that 'in the making of the film, four British army cameramen were killed, seven were wounded, and six were captured by the enemy': '*Desert Victory* and the People's War', in *Screen* (op. cit.) p. 54. Obviously a completely different stand was taken in regard to the American context.

23. See in particular Campbell Dixon, 'A great film about a great feat of arms', in *Daily Telegraph*, 8 March 1943. Of course the fact that Lord Burnham, a former proprietor of this paper, was Director of Public Relations at the War Office may have been instrumental in this case.

24. Lawson to Beddington, 27 March 1943, and the reply of 29 March 1943, with note to Lawson by Hodge, 30 March 1943 (INF 1/221).

25. Sir I. Fraser to Bracken, 30 April 1943, and Beddington to Gates, 3 May 1943 (INF 1/221). Fraser's letter of complaint arose out of a conversation with Sir Ramaswami Mudaliar, though it clearly drew support from ministry officials.

26. Dalrymple to Beddington, 9 June 1943 (INF 1/221). Dalrymple's letter of resignation, 10 May 1943, is partly reproduced in E. Sussex, *The rise and fall of British documentary*, p. 151.

27. Hodson, *Home Front* (op. cit.) p. 307.

28. Tritton noted as much in his diary. See Clive Coultass, '*Tunisian Victory* – a film too late?', in *Imperial War Museum Review*, 1 (1986).

29. Ibid. This is by far the best account of the problems encountered in the production of the film, ably supplemented by Hodson's published diaries.

30. Beddington to Brigadier W. A. S. Turner, 3 March 1943 (INF 1/221).

31. The tickets were distributed by Bernard Musnik, secretary-treasurer of the Lotos Club. See also the *Bulletin of the Foreign Press Association*, 223 (30 March 1943) in INF 1/221.

32. Hodson, *The Sea and the Sand* (op. cit.) p. 75.
33. See 6th and 7th monthly progress reports for the Army Council, April and May 1942 (Directorate of Army Kinematography (DAK), WO 165/96).
34. 10th monthly progress report, August 1942 (DAK, ibid.).
35. 15th monthly progress report, January 1943 (DAK, ibid.).
36. 17th monthly progress report, March 1943 (DAK, ibid.).
37. See the monthly progress reports from November 1942 to January 1943 (DAK, ibid.). The films utilised by the US Forces included such titles as *Care of Tyres* and *That's the Spirit*.
38. David Culbert puts part of the problem down to the 'diehard opposition' of officers and career men in the US army and concludes categorically that 'as a general proposition, for American soldiers, audiovisual instruction existed mostly on paper until the autumn of 1943. Not only were films not ready, but distribution and effective utilisation remained acute problem areas until that time.' Culbert, '*Why We Fight*: social engineering for a democratic society at war', in K. R. M. Short, *Film and radio propaganda in world war two* (London, 1983) pp. 178 & 183. Also, for the background to the series, see Karsten Fledelius et al. (eds), *Why We Fight – An American example of wartime orientation* (Copenhagen, 1974) and T. Cripps and D. Culbert, '*The Negro Soldier*: film propaganda in black and white', in *American Quarterly*, 31 (1979) 5, 616–41.
39. 12th monthly progress report, October 1942 (DAK, WO 165/96).
40. R. D. MacCann, *The People's Films* (New York, 1973). Since *Prelude to War* had not been shown publicly in 1942, some queried whether it was genuinely eligible for an Oscar that year. It was finally decided that its exhibition to US forces constituted a public showing of sorts.
41. Frank Capra, *The Name above the Title* (London, 1972) pp. 349–55.
42. Ibid., p. 349, and MacCann, *The People's Films* (op. cit.) pp. 129–31.
43. Capra, *The Name above the Title* (op. cit.) p. 351.
44. Quoted in MacCann, *The People's Films* (op. cit.) p. 140. The remark was made on the occasion of Sherwood's appearance before a Congressional hearing. The OWI's objection to the 'glamour' image of the war perpetrated by Hollywood is explored further by Alan M. Winkler, *The Politics of Propaganda: The Office of War Information, 1942–5* (New Haven, 1978) pp. 59–60.
45. 'War in the Mediterranean – Africa Freed' (INF 1/223). The completed film is held at the Imperial War Museum. The Department of Sound Records there also has a transcript of an interview with Colonel Hugh Stewart, *Army Film Unit Cameramen, 1939–45*, accession no. 004579/06.
46. Beddington, 'Notes of meeting with Mr. Spewack', 20 July 1943 (INF 1/223).
47. Minutes of the Inter-Services Film Publicity Committee, 6 April 1943 (INF 1/223).
48. M. Gordon to Gates, 30 April 1943 (INF 1/223).
49. Beddington to Major A. Newman, 21 May 1943 (INF 1/223).
50. Gates to Beddington, 5 May 1943 (INF 1/223).

51.   Stewart to Beddington and Bernstein, 20 July 1943 (INF 1/223). This was dictated over the phone. It was followed up by a letter of 21 July 1943 which included the text of the proposed foreword to the film, written by Boulting and Hodson, and was accompanied by a covering note to Beddington from Stewart that read 'I quite realise none of this is your fault but it had to be said. And it may be useful for you too.'

52.   G. Archibald to Beddington, 11 August 1943 (INF 1/223). Archibald of the BIS in New York relayed the gist of a message he had received from Colonel Curtis Mitchell at the Bureau of Public Relations, War Department, Washington.

53.   The negotiations over who should take charge of the film proved long and complicated even before a joint production was agreed. The British contingent then soon found a struggle on its hands to retain a decent measure of joint control. It was constantly necessary, as Hodson records, to do 'a little fighting to prevent our picture on the Tunisian campaign becoming disbalanced in favour of America': *The Sea and the Sand* (op. cit.) p. 117. The wheel had truly come full circle.

54.   In Britain, almost inevitably, there was considerable criticism of what *DNL* described as 'the fell hand of Capra's Hollywood'. 'The moral of the film, which is obvious enough, is lost in a lot of sentimental and incredibly well-meaning vapourings': *DNL*, 5 (1944) 2, p. 20. By comparison with the 'sober' documentary techniques employed on *Desert Victory*, the British critics largely disliked the introduction of the Burgess Meredith and Bernard Miles characters on the sound-track and the 'pie in the sky' message at the film's ending. Campbell Dixon in the *Daily Telegraph* on 20 March 1944 thought that, 'as a revelation of Allied power, it is terrific'. But he also found the film 'faulty', guilty of 'sins of omission', and concluded that it 'shows signs of having been edited largely for the American public'. Not surprisingly the film did better overall with the American critics, though Bosley Crowther in the *New York Times* felt that 'the most obvious encumbrance on this picture is the fact that it is woefully late'. He further noted: 'It opened here a week ago Thursday to a perceptibly lukewarm audience and, despite encouraging press notices, exhausted its first-run "draw" within a week.' *Tunisian Victory* was the first Anglo-American co-production; *The True Glory* was the last in 1945. Many felt this last film 'gave a convincing demonstration of how the Americans conquered Europe as well'. This nationalist animosity reached its peak with *Burma Victory* in 1945. It was an AFU production, under Roy Boulting and David MacDonald, and with no American input. The critics, led by Dixon, praised it wholeheartedly, gave thanks that there was no American interjection and that the AFU was now back on the true path to documentary, and roundly applauded the fact that *Burma Victory* would supplant *Objective Burma* at the cinema, where it had been given a première and from which it had been withdrawn after criticism that Errol Flynn misrepresented the true nature of the Burma campaign.

55.   Capra, *The Name above the Title* (op. cit.) p. 354.

56. The British Consul in Los Angeles, Eric Cleugh, accepted the award on behalf of the MoI and made a brief speech in thanks for the same. He was 'pretty certain that it [*The Battle of Russia*] would get the award'. His report on the awards ceremony noted also that 'there was no dinner this year' and while the event was 'quite entertaining' it 'lacked the excitement and confusion of previous years' (INF 1/221). The Oscar eventually found its way back to Beddington for presentation to the AFU.

57. Skouras to Bracken, 30 March 1944 (INF 1/221). Baird's letter to Connors was cabled to London, 28 March 1944. Skouras was visiting London at the time.

58. Bracken's handwritten draft, undated, is appended to Skouras's letter.

59. B. Sendall to Archibald, 31 March 1944 (INF 1/221).

60. Archibald to Sendall, 3 April 1944 (INF 1/221).

61. Bracken to Skouras, 3 April 1944, which finally read 'Many thanks for your letter of 30 March. I am certainly glad to see Mr Connors's cable to you about the success that *Desert Victory* has enjoyed.' (INF 1/221).

62. F. L. Hartley to Archibald, 13 April 1944 (INF 1/221).

63. Archibald to Hartley, 18 April 1944 (INF 1/221).

64. Archibald to Baird, 18 April 1944 (INF 1/221). Marked 'Private and Personal'.

65. Baird to Archibald, 27 April 1944 (INF 1/221). Also marked 'Private and Personal'.

66. Archibald to Baird, 11 May 1944 (INF 1/221). By now marked 'Private and Confidential'.

67. Sherwin Kane's editorial was enclosed in Baird to Archibald, 27 April 1944 (INF 1/221).

9

The Representation of Women in British Feature Films, 1939–45

Sue Harper

To wish for the fragrance of the rose, we must have an organisation capable of receiving pleasure from it, and must be persuaded that such lovely flowers as roses exist. To wish for the enjoyment of the higher pleasures of sympathy and communication between the sexes, heightened by that mutual grace and glow, that decorum and mutual respect, to which the feeling of perfect, unrestrained equality in the intercourse gives birth, a man must be able to have heard of such pleasures, be able to conceive them, and must have an organisation from nature or education, or both, capable of feeling delight from them when presented to him.

(W. Thompson, *An appeal on behalf of one-half of the human race. . .*, 1825)

I

In periods of acute social change and insecurity, popular cultural forms have a threefold function. They provide reassurance for marginal groups by according them a symbolic presence, they produce pleasure for the audience by temporarily resolving real tensions in their lives, and they clarify confusions about moral or social boundaries.[1] These three processes – persuasion, pleasure and ritual clarification – must be taken into account in any analysis of the fictional representation of subordinate groups. Of these, women constitute the largest – and arguably the most important. In world war two cinema, women's images were appropriated to serve an

168

extraordinarily wide variety of purposes. Endlessly polysemic, the female form could be employed to signify forbidden wilfulness (*The Wicked Lady*), ratified monogamy (*In Which We Serve*), innocent sensuality (*Lady Hamilton*), doomed feminism (*Thunder Rock*), proletarian doggedness (*Millions Like Us*) or aging support (*The Prime Minister*). But 'employed' by whom? By those in control of government agencies and film production companies – all of whom were male. There were comparatively few female workers in wartime *feature* film, as any attention to *Kine Weekly* records will show. Muriel Box, for example, had great difficulty finding a niche in wartime feature films,[2] while Betty Box's and Wendy Toye's directorial careers only developed after the war. It was part of the management philosophy of some studios (Ealing in particular) to encourage female employees to behave in a 'ladylike' manner,[3] which of course meant that sort of unobtrusiveness and decorum which is so rarely conducive to creativity. By and large, female technicians specialised in the traditionally 'feminine' areas of décor and costume design[4] and tended to be excluded from the camera and sound sections. At Gainsborough there was a significant female presence in the scriptwriting group, but this was an exception among the studios to which I shall return in due course.

Cinematic history in this period, therefore, in the case of women, cannot be written as a 'history from below'. A very wide range obtains of different types and codes of gender representation, but they are images over which women had minimal control. Coincidentally feature films also appeased female audiences, but they mainly carried information about the repertoire of male desire and power and the need to negotiate new roles for women in swiftly changing social conditions. Hence the absence or paucity of certain themes, such as female friendship or the pleasures of childlessness or celibacy.

II

Wartime imposed peculiar demands on the female population and radical realignments took place in two fields in particular, those of work experience and of sexual behaviour. Feature film dealt differently with these issues and their threefold functions – persuasion, pleasure, ritual clarification – related to each other in different ways. In the case of women's paid work, ever since the industrial revolution swift changes in demand for female labour have invariably caused a crisis, if not a redefinition, of patriarchal relations.[5] Gail Braybon has demonstrated that male workers in the first world war displayed extreme anxieties about the violation of the sanctity of their workplace and higher pay, and she has shown that strenuous official efforts were made to accord a more central ideological role to motherhood and traditional femininity.[6] In the second world war the war ministries also performed a balancing act between the pressures of industrial demands and the claims of conventional views about women. It was, as Mass Observation pointed out, the first war in which British women had partaken as enfranchised citizens.[7] A swift series of regulations ensured their involvement in the war effort, such as the National Service Act of 1941, the Registration of Employment Order of the same year and the Employment of Women Order of 1942. Thus by 1943 the government was exercising a considerable degree of compulsion over women. Such were the material changes in the employment structure that by 1943 47 per cent of the female industrial workforce was married, and one-third of these women had young children.[8] Optimism was expressed by the Ministry of Information that women would welcome their entry into the labour process for 'democratic' reasons.[9] A similarly positive view was expressed by J. B. Priestley, who claimed that working women with homes were suffering only minor inconveniences;[10] this was however compensated by the 'piquancy' of the sight of muscular female arms and 'handsome postwomen'.[11]

But such feelings were not shared by the population at large. The conscription of women produced considerable friction and hostility by mid-1942, even when not publicly admitted.[12] Industrial absenteeism by female workers was remarkably high and was not attributable solely to domestic reasons. While extreme difficulties were indeed experienced by women workers in areas of housewifery and childcare,[13] it is clear that many women were alienated from the industrial process: they found it fatiguing; they were discontented with hierarchical labour arrangements and supervision;[14] they found factory work socially 'degrading'.[15] As a preferred job, factory work ranked nowhere. Women wanted creative, secretarial or nursery work[16] and the extreme ill-feeling towards industry ensured that the factories, instead of being a social 'melting-pot' as the Ministry of Labour claimed, were places where very little social mixing in fact took place.[17]

There is considerable evidence of the hostile reactions of male industrial workers towards their female colleagues. These included sexual harassment, unfair treatment by the unions (especially the AEW) and general unhelpfulness.[18] Two things are clear: that there was a grave crisis in the morale of female industrial workers by late 1942, and that male workers actively resented the breaking of the old framework. Nevertheless it is possible to argue that, in the latter period of the war, the patriarchal principle was temporarily dislocated. When a wage form is reconstituted, and when it shifts from the notion of a 'family' wage with a male breadwinner to individually earned contributions, spaces can be opened up in which power relations within the family can be renegotiated. Women in this period may have lost their battle for equal pay, but their strikes arguably exposed the contradictions within entrenched male views. In its report 'Will the factory girls want to stay put or go home?' Mass Observation blandly concluded that most women wanted traditional arrangements to be reinstated after the war.[19] But this is not at all borne out by the files on which the report was based. A significant proportion of women, while loathing the nature of the labour for which they were conscripted, did welcome the degree of autonomy it produced. Moreover, having worked – and often fought – on equal terms, women were much less inclined to accept male domination unquestioningly. One ATS conscript suggested that 'it's absurd to think that this war is going on against tyranny and aggression, and yet this place [the army] is full of it'.[20]

Government attitudes towards women's work were unenlightened. There was a dispute in 1942 between the Ministry of Health and the Ministry of Labour over maternity leave. The former wished for an extension after birth to establish breast-feeding and maternal wellbeing but the latter insisted that such concessions would be a luxury in wartime, although the increase in the female workforce meant that some disruption of this type was inevitable.[21] The Ministry of Labour won its case and insisted that pregnant women could work late into pregnancy, crawling around on hands and knees when their condition made standing uncomfortable.[22] An enormous amount of public disquiet and debate ensued, in which the lack of government concern for mothers and its refusal to pay sick benefit was criticised by a range of public figures.[23] The government was moreover relatively harsh with female conscientious objectors and enforced rigorous methods of treatment.[24] The Ministry of Labour was also unsympathetic to factory workers' domestic problems (especially shopping)[25] and attempted to form a uniformed Domestic Service Corps in 1943 into which women could be conscripted.[26] There were a number of gross mismatches, particularly in industrial work, in which qualified and experienced workers were disadvantaged, with the result that there was a severe crisis of morale among volunteer workers and industrially placed Wrens.[27] The Ministry of Labour complained that women were 'not putting their backs into their business' and suggested that many more women were refusing war work because they were prostitutes and in a more profitable trade.[28]

There were some government attempts to mollify women. The National Association of Girls' Clubs was co-opted as a body likely to produce a desirable sense of community life and prevent the nervous breakdowns common among industrial workers.[29] Entertainment for factory workers was also provided, but a great deal of ministerial energy was spent in defusing the tension between ENSA (Entertainments National Service Association), which wanted 'populist' culture, and CEMA (Council for Education in Music and the Arts), which wanted to give the workers operatic arias and extracts from *Thunder Rock*.[30]

The reality, then, was that there was intense anxiety among women about conscripted labour, there was hostility from male workers and insensitive management from the Ministry of Labour. Yet how did this crisis in morale and self-definition appear in feature films? Patriarchy, of course, always provides grounds for a convergence between male workers and male bourgeois radicals or intellectuals. It is precisely such a convergence that we can see in the cinema in the case of the image of the female worker. The vast upheaval in the working lives of British women appeared in a very idiosyncratic way in films. There were very few features which took women's work as a central narrative motif, and those that did concentrated on civilian work or the services, even though the vast majority of conscripted women went into industry. Two Cities produced two films about the ATS: *The Gentle Sex* (released in April 1943) depicted a group of raw recruits who were not welded into a homogeneous group (as the men in *The Way Ahead* were) but who 'naturally' found their separate places and mates of the appropriate class and nationality while the epilogue lauded them as 'strange, wonderful, incalculable creatures';[31] *English Without Tears* (released in August 1944) presents a rich ATS girl who falls in love with her own butler, who had been elevated to the status of Major.[32] The transformation wrought in one individual by the WRNS is a crucial aspect of Korda's *Perfect Strangers*, but as it was released in September 1945, its topical relevance was limited.[33] The Women's Land Army (and 'handsome postwomen') played an important role in *A Canterbury Tale* (1944) and land girls also appeared in the musical *Up With The Lark* (1944), in which they unmasked a black marketeer.[34] None of these films gained more than modest popularity.

It would appear that most studios, therefore, if they addressed changes in women's work at all, chose to represent those types of work in which there was little or no crisis of morale. The work of the women's services and the Land Army, because they contained a wide range of differing activities, provided a greater number of narrative functions. The wartime cinema manifests a significant silence on the crisis in attitudes to female industrial work. There were two MoI-backed 'dramatic' shorts in 1940: *Call for Arms*, in which two chorus girls enter munitions, and *Her Father's Daughter*, in which the heroine does likewise. But these are too early to be of any real significance. *My Ain Folk* (Butchers, 1944) is a musical in which a factory girl falls in love with a wireless operator, but here her social role is of minimal importance.[35] Even Gainsborough's *Waterloo Road* (1945) is structured around Tilly's 'day off'; the audience sees nothing of her job and it is clumsily suggested that her serious malaise and alienation is the result of repressed desire and maternal instinct. The only film which can be said to address the issue of female conscription and industrial work is Launder and Gilliatt's *Millions Like Us*, appropriately released in September 1943 at the height of the crisis of confidence on the part of female workers.

While Launder was preparing for this film, he was the Honorary Secretary of the Screenwriters' Association (SWA), the work of which has been described elsewhere.[36] Launder had led a series of successful campaigns on behalf of film writers and claimed that as a group they were apolitical: 'just simple, progressive, benevolent anarchists'.[37] But he displayed a very sophisticated awareness of that group's interests. *Millions Like Us* was the result of two government overtures to the SWA. In 1940 the Ministry of Labour enquired about scriptwriters for its recruitment films[38] and in late 1941 the association was contracted as a voluntary workforce by the MoI. Launder emphasised that its role was 'to suggest or consider stories and ideas with the object of recommending to the Ministry suitable prospects for propaganda films. We believe the majority of writers will not look upon payment.'[39] Such a comment suggests that the intellectual initiative lay with the association secretary, although in 1977 Launder claimed that the ministry had in fact suggested the film.[40] In any case the breadth of the film's propaganda aims were narrowed by Launder and Gilliat, who wished to deal with the plight of the 'mobile woman', whereas the MoI wanted a more extensive documentary. The film was shot in actual factories and used serving soldiers as extras,[41] although it was produced by Ted Black, who had an unerring sense of popular taste, and it had a team which had excelled in non-documentary work: Jack Cox on camera, Louis Levy as musical director and John Bryan as art director.

As a result the film visually combines documentary and fictional modes and its narrative pace is varied, with a proliferation of short scenes. Its endorsement of patriarchal values has had some recent critical attention,[42] but what should also be addressed is the way in which the film repeatedly elides the discourses of patriarchy, class and culture. *Millions Like Us* presents traditional working-class forms of entertainment in a negative way. At the beginning of the war the Pierrots are presented as sort of living fossils, overly portentous with their phrase of 'no sense have they of ills to come'. The seaside funfair and dance hall produce only isolation and insult for the heroine (Celia). By contrast the wartime experience is presented as one which can weld different aspects of culture together into a coherent whole. The music hall song ('My wife won't let me') is immediately succeeded by the strains of Beethoven's Fifth as planes roar overhead, and it is clear that both types of music answer the case equally. Because she has been incorporated into a wartime community, Celia can now experience the dance hall as a place of pleasure rather than humiliation. An overhead shot of the hall shows an unruly mob of soldiers bursting in on the disconsolate unpartnered females, whereupon male boisterousness is tamed by the decorous procedures of the dance.

Millions Like Us insists that individual female happiness can only be secured within the normalising rituals of society, and this is frequently signalled by long crowd shots taken from above. The typicality of the heroine is stressed above all: 'I'm ordinary myself.' But in what does this typicality consist: what female characteristics are being elevated to the level of a stereotype? Celia is diffident and agreeable: 'I don't mind'; 'I suppose we might'; 'anytime you like, Fred'. Her body language – consistently lowered gaze, closed posture – speaks of demure primness. We are granted no access to her sexual feelings; one close-up of her bare feet during a telephone call from her husband shows the likelihood of chilblains rather than erotic potential. Her desires are for family life and her two fantasies are shown to be either of submission to men (with a ring as reward) or of suicide because of male unkindness. Only a female constructed in such a way can inspire the war effort. While the hero was dropping bombs on Germans, he was 'thinking of you all the time'.

The film attempts to make the lot of the female factory worker more attractive by showing pre-war conditions to be oppressive and by implying that industrial work was at least preferable to filling the 'cooks only' jobs offered by the services. The hostel, feared as a 'house of correction', proves to be humanely run by a motherly staff and the work process itself, though initially feared by Celia, enables her to produce objects 'correct to within a thousandth of an inch', a feat of which she is proud. But tedium and fatigue are absent from the factory. It is presented as a place where the familiar structures of class and gender-power comfortingly reassert themselves. The film does show the negative aspects of patriarchy in Celia's father – his petty tyranny, his pomposity, his domestic ham-fistedness, his 'fee-fi-fo-fum' – but these are carefully outweighed by the positive aspects of patriarchy, as represented by the overseer (Eric Portman). His authority is vested in experience, physical strength, honesty. Even the accusation that he is 'old-fashioned and morbidly suspicious' is converted into a virtue. His confidence comes from his awareness of being the flower of his generation and class. There is no female equivalent in the film: the Lancashire working-class girl is ignorant and malodorous. Indeed, the film throws its weight behind the overseer: his authority would be vitiated if he married an inferior, albeit a middle-class one who calls herself both 'loose' and 'tight'.

The film's publicity material suggested that it should be presented as an index of the new female experience,[43] but contemporary critics insisted that the real subject matter of the film was not women's work but family life, romantic love and the working class.[44] The film's claims to 'quality' were thought to reside in its delicacy and understatement,[45] and 'the general air of social security' was evoked by the Portman character, who was much praised.[46] The only evidence of audience response to the film comes from 1948, when a young female lower-middle-class clerk, though very impressed by the film, retold the story in such a way as to foreground the love

interest and render the factory work invisible.[47] Another young girl
praised the film for its star values,[48] while a male student preferred it
because of its working-class realism.[49] This sample is too small to
allow any firm conclusion, but I would suggest that the film's
significance resides in its successful attempt to displace industrial
anxiety and to reposition it in the context of emotional and familial
experience, where it can be resolved. Launder and Gilliat, artists
with a particular political and professional interest, produce a text in
which the heroine experiences anxiety, loss and grief – but they are
all for, or on behalf of, someone else.

It would appear that feature films dealt only selectively with
changes in female work experience. They attempted to win over that
part of the female audience which was unsure of its role in war work
by suggesting that the pleasures of love were the inevitable
accompaniment and reward. They also suggest, to a larger male and
female audience, that government mismanagement and male hostility were either absent or resolved. Of course such films implicitly
endorse certain models of female behaviour – obedience, indus-
triousness, uxoriousness – but the line between acceptable and
unacceptable female behaviour was drawn in a much more ambiguous and complex way in feature films dealing with women's
sexual attitudes.

III

The war disrupted conventional procedures in the area of sexual
behaviour as well as in others. However, evidence on matters of the
emotions and morality is notoriously difficult to quantify and such
material is often missing from files because of its sensitivity.[50] But
there is no doubt that sexual activity greatly increased during the
war and there was a distinct break with some taboos about adultery
or intercourse in public places.[51] There was also a temporary
liberalisation of moral attitudes, among women at least. J. B.
Priestley even suggested that the proximity of violent death had an
aphrodisiac effect upon the population at large.[52]

It has recently been suggested that the war provided a temporary
escape for women from the limitations of marriage[53] but that, in the
last analysis, the new freedom did not produce any radical redefinition of sexual love.[54] Be that as it may, women did engage in what

was called 'the great man-chase' with unprecedented vigour.[55] 'We played dangerously and talked dirty', claimed one ATS girl, 'we wanted to express our liberty and rebelliousness from the male-set archetypes of loving wife and mother that they had always tried to tie to us.'[56] Many servicewomen appropriated modes of behaviour hitherto reserved for males: 'naturally, the more men one can fasten to one's train, the more prestige one gains in the chase'.[57] The million and a half GIs who entered Britain after 1941 were enthusiastically welcomed by women.[58]

The female population much regretted the unfeminine clothes enforced by rationing. 'Utility' clothes (unembroidered, narrow-skirted and single-breasted) were unpopular with women, as was the banning after 1942 of the manufacture of heels more than two inches high.[59] Women compensated by a use of cosmetics which was much heavier than before the war and had a greater social 'spread'.[60] Thus women's appearance had altered radically, as had their behaviour. In a 1944 *Picture Post* survey of male taste about 'what is a pin-up girl?'[61] preferences were overwhelmingly in favour of a clean-cut, healthy outdoor type (quite different from the female images preferred by women). The male favourite was neither glamorous nor confident and, perched nude on a rather sharp rock, was seen by men as 'clean and decent' and 'worth fighting for'. Coincidentally she manifested a twisted, closed posture and lacked opulence.

There were, then, clear differences between male and female attitudes to sexual attractiveness and sexual morality. A Mass Observation directive in April 1944 on changes in sexual attitudes indicated that the majority of males regretted the liberalisation of morality but that the majority of women welcomed it, as indicative of the decline of double standards. Considerable disquiet was evinced in the latter years of the war about supposed female promiscuity. Mass Observation proposed that evacuation had deprived many young girls of salutary paternal authority,[62] and debates were structured around the desirability of restoring to females a proper sense of the duties of marriage.[63] The Archbishop of Canterbury intervened by urging Britons to 'reject wartime morality' of divorce and illegitimacy.[64] Indeed a 'moral panic' can be said to have been manifested in the behaviour of male servicemen and those in charge of controlling social institutions. The Markham Committee, with Edith Summerskill as its spokesman, was set up in 1942 to investigate intense rumours and allegations about the sexual conduct of servicewomen. Summerskill concluded that the gossip and accompanying moral strictures were promulgated by servicemen and were the result of male hostility to women's new freedom of action: 'a woman in uniform may arouse a special sense of hostility, conscious or unconscious, among certain people who would never give two thoughts to her conduct as a private citizen'.[65] An analogous situation obtained in the USA, and rumours about female laxity were so intense there as to lead to government suspicion that they were the result of fifth column activity.[66]

'Promiscuity' is, of course, simply a term applied to the unacceptable sexual behaviour of other people. It can rarely be used when there is any understanding of motives or emotional needs. The obsessive wartime concern about female 'licence' evinced by patriarchy in its various forms did not extend to male partners. The *emotional* livelihood of the nation could only be threatened by women. The 1942 Beveridge Report should be interpreted as an attempt to reinstate marriage as a career. It was implemented as government policy after a fivefold increase in the divorce rate.[67] The Ministry of Health only encouraged bodies which concurred with its own disquiet about the huge increase in illegitimacy.[68] It had close relations, for example, with the National Council for the Unmarried Mother and Her Child after 1942, and supported the council's views that it should be liberal towards the child but not the mother, that all unmarried mothers under its care should wear a ring and be called 'Mrs', and that 'the idea of home-making' should be an important part of propaganda.[69]

The government was also extremely solicitous about the overall decline in the birthrate, which had dropped sharply between 1939 and 1941. It began to seek means of encouraging women to produce the larger families which had been *de rigueur* in Victorian times,[70] and set up a Population Investigation Committee in 1943. The debates which followed reveal much about 'official' attitudes. The Medical Research Council robustly rejected 'ill-founded female talk about the hardships of childbearing'.[71] More liberal opinions were given little space. The Commons debate on 2 July 1943 was led by the Ministry of Health, which wanted 'more and better babies', while Edith Summerskill suggested that women had 'deliberately refused to produce the most valuable commodity in the world, the embryo worker'.[72] But most time and support was given to Sir R. Fremantle, himself a doctor on the Medical Research Council, who insisted that 'the virgin womb is sterilised by contraception'.[73] He continued: 'this war has given us a wrong turn. There is a great temptation because women have discovered the means of making money and of being better off than they were. That is not compatible with family life.'[74] Such remarks should dispel any illusion that population enquiries were 'neutral' or had women's interests at heart. Official concern was instrumental in sponsoring population surveys until well after the war.[75]

It is clear that those in positions of power felt impelled after 1942 to remind women with some rigour of their traditional duties, and of the snares of financial independence and sexual pleasure. It is in this context that we should interpret the major wartime furore on the issue of venereal disease and 'good-time girls'. The army was particularly obsessed with VD, although the ATS, for example, had a lower per capita incidence than the civilian population.[76] But the campaign was so intense as to produce psychosomatic VD symptoms among many female conscripts.[77] The spread of awareness of the disease was extensive.[78] The army standardised treatment at all its clinics, which entailed huge administrative problems.[79] What is particularly noteworthy, however, is that the Joint Committee on Venereal Diseases insisted that the blame for the spread of the disease should be placed at the door of the 'good-time girls' who, it was argued, were a greater source of infection than regular prostitutes.[80] Such girls, therefore, should be made to work 'where respectable women would not resent their presence'[81] and where they could be controlled and inspected for disease by being brought under the notorious Regulation 33 of the 1939 Defence of the Realm Act.[82]

Who, according to the authorities, were the 'good-time girls'? It would appear that those who caused such official anxiety were simply sexually active free agents. The government definition of 'young prostitute' (often synonymous with 'good-time girl') was to be interpreted 'as including all girls and young women whose mode of life is sexually immoral'.[83] Elsewhere they are defined as 'young people out of control'[84] who congregated around barracks 'in search of entertainment and excitement' and who had 'no moral background'.[85] All the available evidence indicates that the government panicked because there was 'no effective check on their activities'[86] unless arrested and placed in 'safe' custody. Girls of up to the age of 23 could be sent to Borstal for sexual laxness.

As Lucy Bland and Frank Mort have indicated, the problem was that the 'good-time girl' was difficult to identify.[87] A great proportion of women wore heavy make-up and consorted with conscripted men. The official 'moral panic', therefore, could be defused by encouraging or permitting those art forms which showed clearly the 'distinguishing marks' of such women to a mass audience, and for this role the cinema was admirably suited. There were of course certain external controls on the representation of sexuality. The British Board of Film Censors was rather less rigorous than in the pre-war period but, although Colonel Hanna and Mrs Crouzet continued to display a predilection for innocuous films, they were far more vigilant about the inclusion of seamy material in historical texts than in modern scenarios. Any historical project was rejected by them during the war if it discredited either women or royalty, while anything which cleansed the past of its 'somewhat coarse and crude atmosphere' was praised.[88] Even so, *Boule de Suif* was rejected out of hand as liable to encourage vice.[89]

The BBFC's attitudes provide one way of accounting for the absence or paucity of reference to illegitimacy, promiscuity and disease as film topics. The attitude of other bodies to the representation of sexuality was varied. The MoI displayed no interest at all in the issue in its encomiums on feature film.[90] But the British Film Institute did throw its weight behind those worried about the deleterious effects of screen sexuality,[91] as did the 'quality' critics. James Laver noted in the immediate post-war period that 'the last time I went to the cinema, the couple in front of me did seem to be stimulated rather than appeased by the comparative liberality with which the producer had adorned his picture with cleavage'.[92] This type of attitude doubtless lay behind the frenzied critical assaults on the popular Gainsborough melodramas.[93] Establishment figures such as Claude Mullins added their voices to the debate. Mullins was chairman of the Magistrates' Association and the doyen of the Society for the Unmarried Mother and Her Child,[94] and he campaigned against the representation in films of behaviour inimical to family life. He made a direct causal correlation between the length of screen kissing (timed with a stopwatch) and 5000 cases of marital trouble. He concluded that such images were 'very dangerous. Many men select for courtship women who they think will give them these thrills. When married to them, they only too often find that they have married women who are rotten housekeepers and bad mothers.'[95]

There was, then, censorship of both a direct and an indirect, invisible kind, and they were both fuelled by the fear that audiences would lurch into uncritical mimesis of seamy film sensuality. This obviously affected the range and type of gender representation in proposed film projects. But other factors must also be taken into consideration. Given, for example, male and official anxiety about female 'promiscuity', why did so few such women appear as such in wartime feature films? Why was it not possible for a film like *Good Time Girl* to be made until 1947? (In any case, the uncontrolled 'young person' in question was seen to have a taste for expensive frocks rather than fornication.)

It is evident that war films with contemporary settings which took female desire as an explicit narrative motif tended to defuse the issue in a variety of ways. *Talk About Jacqueline* (Excelsior, 1942) is a comedy in which the heroine takes the blame for her sister's murky reputation, and *Bees in Paradise* (Gainsborough, 1942) is also a comedy in which Arthur Askey lands on a remote island ruled by beautiful predatory girls whose law is that husbands must commit suicide immediately after the honeymoon. Sydney Box's 1944 *On Approval* makes a comedy out of a trial marriage between a duke and a rapacious female.[96] Box also produced *29 Arcadia Avenue* in 1945 for laughs. Here the absurdities of bourgeois moral 'respectability' were rehearsed, much to the outrage of J. Arthur Rank.[97] The musical was another form in which potentially explosive material was defused, as in Gainsborough's *Miss London* (1943) which dealt, via song and dance, with the vagaries of an 'escort agency' for lonely officers.

Gainsborough made a different narrative feature of 'fun-loving girls' in three 1944 films: *They Were Sisters*, *Waterloo Road* and *2000 Women*. *They Were Sisters* contains an errant sister (Anne Crawford) who prefers tangos to family life, but she gets her just deserts by falling unrequitedly in love when she leaves her husband and child to follow her lover to an African wasteland. The remaining – infertile – sister (Phyllis Calvert) wins the care of both her sisters' children, and is thus rewarded for her monogamous behaviour by having her fertility magically 'restored'. Such a stylistic arrangement – the evils of promiscuity cancelled out by motherhood – also obtained in *Waterloo Road*, where the generous heart of motherhood cancels out the previous overgenerous use of the body. Deny childbirth to women, argues the doctor in the film, and 'repressed and rebellious nature runs amok'. In *2000 Women* the Jean Kent figure is the only one of the internees to suffer the discomforts of desire, but this is clearly labelled as deviant by the other female prisoners who, viewing one of her German paramours, observe that 'the rat is about to enter the trap baited with the oldest cheese in the world'. To regain her patriotic status the 'good-time girl' agrees to perform a strip-tease to keep the German guards busy: 'no man ever leaves before the last veil drops'. She is summarily dispatched and, in a scene of delirious awkwardness, a novice nun (Patricia Roc) is required to take her place behind the ostrich plumes. The 'purity' of the agent clearly neutralises the 'pollution' of the act.

So, in film narratives which straightforwardly represent the sexual excesses of females, the dangers are either defused by comedy and music or else the female community in the film 'naturally' upholds the values of chastity and motherhood. Yet illegitimate motherhood, as Sue Aspinall rightly remarks, plays no role in wartime films.[98] Only ABPC's *Banana Ridge* (1941) uses it as an important aspect of the narrative, but this is after all a Ben Travers farce. Not until Gainsborough's 1947 *When the Bough Breaks* is illegitimacy a central motif, and the heroine's respectability is ensured by her 'husband's' bigamy.

Another important cause of wartime anxiety after 1942, the enthusiastic 'fraternisation' of British women with American troops, appears in feature films in a curious form. Two films appeared towards the end of the war which presented Anglo-American sexual relations in terms of a necessary alliance between the effete scions of aristocratic stock and vigorous US males: *Welcome Mr Washington* (British National, 1944) dealt with the lady of the manor who falls in love with an American sergeant and *I Live in Grosvenor Square* (ABPC, 1945) presents Anna Neagle as a duke's daughter in a similar predicament with a sergeant from Flagstaff (!), Arizona. The publicity material suggested that the latter film be sold not as 'propaganda but a love story that crosses the Atlantic'.[99] Critics were, however, clear about the film's ideological status. *Time* praised it as 'the most pro-American film ever made outside the US',[100] whereas British critics reviled the film's complicity with American values.[101] Both films imply that this particular class fraction in Britain needed wholesome American penetration. Neither appear in any list of high box-office ratings.

The only other appearance of Americans in British features is noteworthy. In a number of films they appear not as rapacious consumers of virtuous British females but as *women* – submissive, helpful, smart – who succour British men. *The Foreman Went to France* (Ealing, 1942) has an American girl who mitigates the dourness of the engineer hero. *Candlelight in Algeria* (British

Aviation, 1943) centres on an American girl who helps a British agent, and *Give Me the Stars* (British National, 1944) shows how an American girl cures her Scottish grandfather of alcoholism. The only exception to this pattern of class and gender displacement is Sergeant Bob Johnson in *A Canterbury Tale*, but as his heart is safely engaged elsewhere, so also are his loins, and his relations with the heroine are thus unselfconscious and comradely. Powell and Pressburger were in any case developing a coherent argument at that time about élite groups and culture, and Johnson is part of that debate. Americans in British wartime features are 'over here', but they are neither overpaid nor oversexed.

The more general issue of adultery appears very rarely in films with contemporary settings. Early in the war *A Window in London* (G and S Films, 1939) contains an unfaithful wife who is killed by her husband, and adultery is a minor element in *They Were Sisters*. Otherwise the topic is only dealt with in the immediate post-war period by the deployment of the metaphor of the 'Enoch Arden' theme: the return of a hero presumed dead or missing. Sydney Box's *The Years Between* (1946) deals with an MP who is presumed dead and whose wife assumes his role in parliament. *Piccadilly Incident* (ABPC, 1946) features a 'drowned' Wren who returns to find her husband has solaced himself with another wife. An American film of the same year, RKO's *Tomorrow is Forever*, had the same theme. All three films appeared in the *Kine Weekly* report of box-office winners for 1946. The popularity of the motif clearly had to do with the reality of marital readjustments at the time, enabling audiences to rehearse a number of responses: they could admit fears that those who returned would be permanently changed and find no welcome home; they could experience the desire that the dead might revive and return home in a stranger's guise; or they could enjoy the provision of an alibi for having loved strangers.

These are, however, texts of the immediate post-war period in which the fiction resolved quasi-adulterous acts. The only wartime film text to foreground adultery as a contemporary problem was of course *Brief Encounter*, which came out in the same month as *The Wicked Lady*, namely December 1945. *Brief Encounter* does place female desire at its centre and, although it claims to be set in the immediate pre-war period, the film has a topical poignancy due to the way it locates death and the tension between excitement and security. Madeleine Mason has commented valuably that the energy of the married female protagonist is turned destructively inwards because the sensual and the maternal are 'impossibly' combined in one figure. She notes that a crucial scene takes place by the war memorial: Laura (Celia Johnson) has run away from a possible extra-marital consummation with Alec (Trevor Howard), and rests there. A policeman interrogates her, calling her 'Miss'. That, and the image of the soldier on the monument, combine to make Laura 'feel like a criminal'. Thereafter she has to deny her sexual impulses and devote her energies to her family.[102] The film was a critical but not a box-office success.

IV

So far I have considered those images of female sexual behaviour which are undisguised by metaphor or historical setting entailing the analysis of representations which may be termed 'tangential', that is, films which display a displacement, exaggeration, conceal-ment or falsification of contemporary anxieties and events. I should now like to suggest that, in other wartime films, unlicensed female behaviour also appeared in three forms of narrative 'disguise': amnesia, cross-class liaison and erotic metaphor or metonymy. Female pleasure could also be addressed profitably by two further forms of narrative coding, namely 'gypsyness' and historicity.

If one analyses a broad range of themes in British films of the period, only two motifs can be said to obtain across all genres and all studios. The first of these is the theme of amnesia. In a range of eleven films of the period this is a central narrative device.[103] The phenomenon ceases abruptly after the war: *Woman to Woman* and *Caravan* are the last of the type to appear in 1946, and they are of a different tenor. The victim of amnesia is a female in only two of these eleven and both of these, *The Girl Who Forgot* and *The Spider*, were made in 1939. The remainder feature males whose memory is restored during the course of the film.

How should we interpret the significance of this repeated motif? Freud suggests that repeated or excessive forgetfulness requires a far-reaching explanation and insists that it has to do with repressed or obsessive fears. In the act of forgetting, the feared element can be transformed or eliminated by the unconscious.[104] Although care should be taken to avoid too literal a Freudian interpretation of texts, it is possible to argue that the 'amnesia' films of the war period all express or address a male psychic trauma: the terrifying spectacle of female desire. The lost memories of the male protagonists of *The Twilight Hour* and *The World Owes Me a Living* function as a method of re-enlisting females into traditional supportive roles and of confirming the males' heroic past. The only exception to this pattern is *Caravan*, which is however post-war and made at Gainsborough by a production team which was extremely astute in appealing to its target female audience. The male amnesiac hero of *Caravan* forgets a past world of chaste love and awakens into a new one which contains female expressivity and his own dependence. Unlike *Caravan* the wartime 'amnesia' films do not highlight male vulnerability; nor is there any evidence that they appealed to a female or to a mass audience. None appear in *Kine Weekly* box-office reports, whereas films like *Caravan* and *Lady Hamilton*, which conferred an outright eroticism onto the wounded male, were very profitable.

The only other wartime narrative motif with a similar studio and genre 'spread' is the theme of cross-class marriage. A range of seven British-made films all take as the *raison d'être* of their central narrative the love between different class fractions – and they all express disapproval.[105] In *Kipps* and *Fingers*, for example, such relationships are displayed as exploitative and dangerous. It is clearly the sexual element which is under debate, since a film like *Medal for the General* (1944) dealt with a successful cross-class emotional transaction between an old general and a group of young East End evacuees. If the element of class hostility in these seven films were to be interpreted literally, the films would be seen as running counter to the prevailing official ideology of ratified community and mutual support so evident in *In Which We Serve* or *The Way Ahead*. But the 'disapproval' element in such films as *Tilly of Bloomsbury* or *There's No Future In It* should instead be interpreted as a hostility towards 'illegitimate', unratified relationships. In short such texts express, or appeal to, male anxiety about female promiscuity.

Both these patterns of narrative 'disguise' encapsulate, in a coded form, negative attitudes towards female conduct. Indeed the device of disguise itself, as an aid to adventure or salvation, appears to be a female prerogative in wartime films. In *Tomorrow We Live* (1942), *Escape to Danger* (1943), *Yellow Canary* (1943) and *Waltz Time* (1945) it is the heroine who conceals her identity, thereby giving rise to suspicions about her duplicity. But a third prominent feature, and one which permits a positive celebration of female sexual behaviour, is that of sexual metaphor. Forbidden images of pleasure often appear covertly in popular narrative forms. The highwayman activities of Barbara (Margaret Lockwood) in *The Wicked Lady* are instigated by her desire to regain the brooch left to her by her mother. In a markedly long insert she cradles the jewel in her hand, an image which is contrasted with one later in the film when Caroline (Patricia Roc) *displays* the jewel in an unfeeling manner on the flat of her hand. This jewel, which we are repeatedly told is a ruby (redolent of blood and warmth), functions as a metaphor for the female body in the same way as the secret passage in the same film. This passage gives private access to the forbidden world of criminal excitement, but initially the key is held by a puritan servant from whom it must be wrested.

The use of jewels with sexual resonance can also be seen in the earrings in *Madonna of the Seven Moons* and in the black pearl in the 1946 *Bedelia*. Significantly, wedding or engagement rings never appear as talismanic sexual objects in this way. Another symbol which has some currency is that of piano playing. In *The Seventh Veil* and *Love Story* some critics have suggested that the heroine's musical genius is of secondary importance when compared to the real 'message' of the films, the necessity of submission to male power.[106] Although both heroines are sick and dying (one is in the grip of a neurotic paralysis; the other has a fatal heart disease), they choose to continue playing. Their musical performance permits the expression of autonomy and both films should be interpreted as texts which, on one level, celebrate female creativity and energy in the face of insuperable difficulties. The heroines do not become 'real people' only by finding true love, but mainly by finding situations in which they can take pleasure in their own talents.

All the above examples are located in melodrama. Other genres, however, also produce sexually 'charged' metaphors. In *I Know Where I'm Going* the castle has a labyrinthine structure and a sunny courtyard which are forbidden terrain for the laird, who is afraid to break the cultural taboo. Powell and Pressburger were in fact in the process of developing an argument about the necessary relationship between erotic and political power and they suggest here, and in such later films as *Black Narcissus*, that any group which outlaws or devalues sexual pleasure is fallible. It is in this light that we should interpret the 'glue' cast by Culpepper into the girls' hair in *A Canterbury Tale*: like the priests in Blake's poem, Culpepper defiles the fairest joys and is thus consigned to the category of an ailing puritanism.

Clearly metaphors which covertly celebrate (or at least sympathe-
tically address) female sexuality are not found in films committed to
realism. Gainsborough's was a low-budget expressionism; Powell
and Pressburger's was a flamboyantly continental one. But a more
coherent exploration of female desire is located within the context of
two narrative themes of the war and immediate post-war years:
'gypsyness' and eroticised history.

The gypsy or itinerant theme in British literary culture – from
Lytton and Burrow in the nineteenth century to Nora Lofts and
Lady E. F. Smith in the 1940s – provided a means of addressing the
issue of marginality in a particularly suggestive way. Gypsies in
fiction are a declassed group and are able to signal an exotic,
eccentric, predominantly sexual energy. In world war two a group
of novelists produced historical texts which combined three groups
– gypsies, the aristocracy and sexually aggressive women – who
were inclined to excess and pollution. In such novels the pleasures
of the forbidden could be rehearsed and groups on the boundary of
society could be demystified and ultimately rendered safe. Such
texts demanded complex negotiations from their readers in terms of
literary and moral values. And they were extremely successful with
women readers.[107]

R. J. Minney, who was in charge of film production at Gainsborough from 1942 to late 1946, was instrumental in selecting these
novels for film adaptation.[108] The gypsy, itinerant or marginal
elements are strongly stressed in *The Man in Grey* (1943), *Madonna of
the Seven Moons* (1944), *Caravan* (1946), *The Magic Bow* (1946) and *Jassy*
(1947). Important changes, however, take place when gypsies no
longer present an exotic wisdom but a more explicit threat. The
Caravan script has them rifle a corpse, whereas the book insists on
their cultural purity. Pertwee, the scriptwriter of *Madonna*, has the
virgin heroine raped by a gypsy instead of her husband.[109] Even so,
the motif still gives rise to the expression of a vigorous female
heterosexual desire. *Madonna*, one of the most profitable and
popular films of the period,[110] sees the heroine split between frigid
bourgeois monogamy and an illicit passion of a gypsy or peasant
colour. Her entry into this more pleasurable second world is
signalled by the donning of lush gypsy clothes and savage adorn-
ments, which usher her into a realm of wildness and free movement. Gainsborough's astute publicity department used the clothes
of this film, and of *Caravan*, as an important selling point.[111] In both
films the heroine dies – but not as an atonement for her sins. Rather

the films imply, in a High Romantic formulation, that real life itself has become an anti-climax once the fantasy has been totally fulfilled. Such films suggest, as in *The Magic Bow*, that a true artist or a true epicure of the senses must be freed from social constraints. They also suggest, as in *The Man in Grey* and *Jassy*, that there is a special intuitive knowledge or second sight which is a female gift. 'Gypsyness' signals, by dress and lifestyle, that a mode of perception which is on the margins of acceptability provides intense pleasures as well as intense dangers.

History in world war two film was used in a variety of ways. Some films, such as *Major Barbara*, cannot easily be translated into modern terms. Some, such as Ealing's *Pink String and Sealing Wax*, firmly consign all females into the categories of deviants or virgins. Others, such as the historical epics *The Young Mr Pitt*, *The Prime Minister* and *Henry V*, deploy women straightforwardly as the bearers of cultural heritage. But in certain others the disguise of history permits the critical interrogation of traditional sexual roles. The Gainsborough costume cycle, particularly the phenomenally successful *The Wicked Lady*, presents history as a source of sensual pleasure; it underplayed historical authenticity as such and instead presented the past as a cornucopia of objects with uncertain meaning but available beauty.[112] As Maurice Carter commented: 'provided you could perform money-wise, and get the sets there on time, they were reasonably happy . . . your instinctive reaction was to make the thing as rich as possible'.[113] The past was not presented in *mise-en-scène* terms as closed and scholarly. The audience is put in the position of perceiving different historical components as being of equal cultural value.

Lady Hamilton was made in Hollywood by a British team and many accounts suggest that the film had strong backing from the British government. R. C. Sherriff, the film's scriptwriter, noted that Korda was required to make the film in order to persuade neutral countries (especially America) to support the British war position.[114] At the time the film was being made, in early 1941, America had yet to enter the war, while morale in Britain was low. The film itself was Churchill's favourite. He is rumoured to have written speeches for it, he showed it regularly to foreign dignitaries and he was, of course, a personal friend of Korda.[115] It was subject to investigation by a US Senate committee in September 1941 for the undue distortion of historical facts for British propaganda purposes.[116] Both Korda and Victor Savile were named in those proceedings as probable British agents. Korda was due to be subpoenaed to appear, but America's entry into the war defused the issue altogether.[117]

Lady Hamilton, then, had an impressive range of official British support. Duff Cooper had suggested to Olivier that it was a good way to commence his patriotic duties,[118] and the film crew had a common feeling that they were making a patriotic gesture.[119] The film was a popular success, in spite of bad critical reviews.[120] It was a very different type of film from *The Wicked Lady*, which in no sense could be interpreted as a propaganda vehicle, and since it was made in America it had different problems with the machine of censorship. The Hays Office forced the scriptwriters to make Nelson ashamed of his mistress and approved the device of a flashback through the eyes of a dissolute and ruined Emma.[121] But the film's structure underplayed the political element and emphasised the sexual, a technique Korda had deployed to great effect in *The Private Life of Henry VIII* and *Catherine the Great*. His wartime experience with *The Lion Has Wings* had also taught him a good deal about audience resistance to explicit propaganda.[122] In *Lady Hamilton* the figure of Emma is used as a means of consolidating a liberal argument about culture and class. The film allots a privileged role to sight and touch and brings the audience into direct contact with the artefacts of high culture, suggesting that there is a connection between female beauty and the pleasures of art. In an important scene Emma is compared to a Greek statue which has been 'raised from the mud', changing hands every year until it finds its rightful place in the hands of a true erotic connoisseur. On one level this suggests that a woman's value is relative to the worth placed on her by the men who 'own' her; on another the scene contains a refutation of the notion of virginity and female chastity. The film argues that the more variously and passionately a woman is loved, the greater is her significance. She is not besmirched or lessened by sexual exchange. Throughout Emma is presented as one whose naïvety and generosity of spirit throw into relief the pettiness and prurience of her detractors.

Lady Hamilton also examines the erotic 'charge' of political leadership in ways not encountered elsewhere. It investigates the manner in which sexual dominance and submission can feed into political events. Emma's heart is won on seeing Nelson's damaged eye and arm; his body paradoxically bears the signs of both vulnerability and power. Just as literary heroes such as Heathcliff, Mr Rochester and even Othello are feminised by their wounds or griefs, so is the desire of women for them aroused.[123] The fact that Nelson is 'damaged' – just as Emma is – fuels the dynamics of the affair and permits Emma a definition of marriage. Her husband complains that there are three kinds of husband: those born to be deceived, those ignorant of deception and those who no longer care. Emma retorts that there is a fourth kind: those who can afford to buy women in the marketplace, who have a cold heart and who therefore deserve all they get. Moreover the film's radical sexual politics are fed by its class politics. Nelson is presented as the condensation and consummation of popular tradition, and a crucial role of Emma's is to bind him to the people (at whom, after all, the film was aimed).

Korda, then, was in a unique position. He was able to marshall various types of official support and he was able to combine his instinct for popular success with a broad and sometimes radical liberalism which was rarely noted in his own time.[124] *Lady Hamilton* and the Gainsborough historical melodramas were in fact the only films of the period which were able to address and celebrate female pleasure. One could, I suppose, provide the ritual caveat that the definition and production of pleasure may further contribute to women's oppression, but one must avoid falling into that type of 'miserabilism' which afflicts some schools of feminist analysis. It is possible to be a feminist historian of culture while at the same time dreading the onset of a coercive puritan moralism.

V

A fuller account of the problems of the representation of women in world war two than has been possible here would need to consider the broad spectrum of film production and take proper account of two comedy series, the Old Mother Riley films and those of Gert and Daisy. Middle-aged women (or their facsimiles) in these films wreak havoc with stereotypes and, in an anarchic manner, call attention to the random nature of the conventions of body language. By way of comparison, the role which women played in the George Formby comedies of the period might be critically analysed.

Another, more important issue which requires extensive coverage is the social function of women in those films which were accorded the *imprimatur* of official support. Women in such films generally play a predictably supportive role. In Ealing's *The Next of*

Kin (1942) the original sin is committed by a female dancer who is first seen on stage dwarfed by a gigantic grotesque silhouette of a woman. Here she functions both as Pandora and Circe, and serves as an awful warning to the other female inhabitants of the film. In MoI-backed films, such as *The Way Ahead*, women exist in order to be left behind; they provide a secure backcloth for the military action. The nation's morality and culture is entrusted into their hands for safekeeping. *The Way to the Stars*, in its championing of wartime procreation, directly accords with the government position on the issue. *In Which We Serve*, which had such strong support from Mountbatten that Noël Coward was able even to overcome MoI reservations,[125] also insists that the female role in wartime is to comfort and sustain. But the classes are interestingly contrasted: the wife of Captain Kinross appears alone in her wedding photograph, wears masculine tweeds and a restrained manner and, in a moving speech, toasts her one serious sexual rival, *HMS Torrin*. No such resonance exists in the toast at the working-class home. There Shorty's wife shares the confined space with her family (all of whom are on the wedding photograph) while she herself is pretty, frilly and a little silly. It is implied that just as the two types of women complement one another, so also do the officers and men of the ship. They have different functions, but both are necessary to the smooth running of the ship of society. In short, films with a degree of official approval tended not to question traditional sexual values and they of course identified masculinity with the fighting instinct.

Another important determinant of gender representation is the production context and studio style. Although one must distinguish carefully between films and directors, and although one must periodise any historical account of a studio, it is nonetheless possible to delineate an overall pattern or tendency. Ealing, for example, had a large administrative staff and a small creative élite which followed the paternalist leadership of Balcon. Rigorous intellectual control was exercised and little autonomy was granted to the separate production units.[126] There is little room in the Ealing wartime output for a language of subjectivity. Rather, the discourses of class and sexual power are frequently elided. Ealing attempted to appeal to the lower-middle class – a group with a fragile sense of its own status – and the studio simplified the problems which that class was undergoing. But a precarious social group tends to perceive life in terms of a struggle rather than a settlement and it will prefer texts which help it resolve that struggle.

Wartime films at Ealing do not address important contemporary shifts in gender division or cultural competence and, since they are generally of a realist tendency, display a marked consonance between the different languages of décor, costume, script and music. It was not until the post-war period, with *The Captive Heart* and *The Loves of Joanna Godden*, that the studio foregrounded women at all. True, they play a role in *Went the Day Well?* and the postmistress and the lady of the manor do display bravery and self-sacrifice. But these are both women 'of a certain age' and therefore, in the studio's terms, safely neutral. The younger women are either pusillanimous or adenoidal. *Pink String and Sealing Wax* (1945) is the only Ealing film to take visual pleasure in a woman's appearance, even though the spectacle is formed by a combination of Googie Withers' beauty and suffering, especially in the prolonged final sequence. A production context which insists on overall intellectual control, consonance between textual languages and a concentration on one particular class fraction is unlikely to give rise to films which address gender or even problematic sexual convention.

The work of Powell and Pressburger is quite a different case. When The Archers was set up in 1942 under the Rank umbrella of Independent Producers Ltd, it had the effect of releasing them from legal and business matters and stringent financial constraints. The Powell and Pressburger films made under Rank develop a consistent argument about the construction of a conservative strategy for dealing with reform. They all posit the existence of an élite group with an aristocracy of perception, and within this group women play a very important role. *The Life and Death of Colonel Blimp*, for example, is an elegy to an older way of life when rituals, symbols and the personal life had more resonance. The use of the same actress for the three leading female characters indicates the desired existence of *das Ewig-Weibliche*, but with an overlay of courtly love. In the 1946 *A Matter of Life and Death* the supreme piece of 'evidence' is the girl's tear in the heart of the rose and her readiness to step onto the staircase. But this should not be read as proof of The Archers' sexist perfidy. The nuances and complexities of the woman's role in high Conservative philosophy should not be underestimated: romantic love, in Powell and Pressburger films of the war, is the highest possible expression of subjectivity, and 'chivalric' relationships can exist in a range of forms. Their films take a reverent, individualistic, chivalrous view of women. Anyone in their films who dissents from this view comes to grief: Culpepper the glue man; the tedious rich fiancé in *I Know Where I'm Going*.

The most profitable British studio of the war years was Gainsborough, which specialised in costume and modern melodramas aimed at a female audience. Until Sydney Box took over as production head in late 1946,[127] the films were made at Shepherds Bush under the aegis of Ted Black, the Ostrers and R. J. Minney, whose régime was characterised by careful pre-shooting costs and tight commodity control. Black even forbade personal telephone calls and kept writing paper at a premium.[128] The studio management paid little attention to bad reviews[129] but set great store by market size and the predictability of the product.[130] Most of the machinery was obsolete,[131] while technicians were left to their own devices in the camera and sound sections, and there was minimal interference in the area of art direction and costume design. Management and labour were kept separate,[132] although the scriptwriters did have a special relationship with the former.[133] Even so, between 1942 and 1946 Gainsborough was a place where low-budget expressionist work in the visual field could take place.

Gainsborough's management philosophy produced the conditions for a strong generic cycle. Tight economic control, a strong hierarchical organisation, a privileged intellectual élite, an insistence that production values appear in visual terms – all these combined with an unerring instinct for popular female taste. Yet one cannot broach the issue of gender and popular film without attention to audience research. There are, of course, problems with the agents who filter wartime responses to us. The middle-class interpreters of working-class behaviour were liable to misread audience reactions, and a peevishness in the face of historical contingency marks the work of hapless Mass Observation observers attempting to categorise such *données* as 'I can't talk to you now, ducks, I've got no teeth – look!'[134] Important researchers like Mayer held élitist views about popular culture: he evoked Petronius in his distaste for the 'decadence' of Gainsborough.[135] A fear of the moral effect of mass art motivates many academic studies and doubtless colours their results.[136] Moss and Box had a naïve belief in statistics which masked their sloppiness when distinguishing between audiences and genres,[137] whereas Bernstein and the 1943 *Kine Weekly* survey on taste do not distinguish adequately between classes.[138]

Bearing all these problems in mind, however, although there was little gender difference in humour,[139] there were appreciable differences in the area of historical and war films.[140] A Mass Observation directive of 1943 about favourite films showed that *Blimp* figured largely as a male favourite but that few men liked *The Man in Grey* (only 4 out of 104) and even then because they thought it was 'good taste', 'real history' and enshrined sexual inequality.[141] In Mayer's survey men liked Phyllis Calvert because of her pure diction,[142] disliked the salaciousness of Gainsborough histories[143] and rejected Stewart Granger's flamboyance. One commented: 'I sincerely dislike *showing off* in films.'[144] Even schoolboys were discomfited by the bawdiness of *The Wicked Lady* and ignored the costumes and settings which made it so popular with female audiences of all ages.[145]

Female responses differed markedly. In the 1943 Mass Observation directive *The Man in Grey* was favoured by six times as many women as men, who praised it for its acting and dramatic qualities, its décor and costume.[146] Mayer's survey also shows that the Gainsborough clothes were an important reason for their popularity with women,[147] as was the sexual charisma of James Mason.[148] Female audiences frequently attested to the emotional 'sincerity' of such films as *Madonna*,[149] while Mayer demonstrates that women selected from historical films symbols of self-identification and male dominance.[150] The films clearly aided a ritual excision and expression of deep-seated female fears, and invariably schoolgirls modelled their body language on them,[151] while the sight of Margaret Lockwood made them 'speechless with longing'.[152] In a Birmingham survey 67 per cent of schoolgirls admitted imitating Lockwood's appearance,[153] thus endorsing Ted Black's instinct that she had 'something with which every girl in the suburbs could identify herself'.[154] Lockwood's enormous popularity waned by 1947; her energy and *hubris* had only a wartime popularity, and her command of the popularity charts was assumed by Anna Neagle, an actress with a much more 'ladylike' aura.[155]

VI

At the outset I distinguished three functions of popular texts: persuasion, pleasure and ritual clarification. British wartime films articulated these different roles in a highly complex manner. The two most significant changes in women's lives during the war were dealt with unevenly by the film industry. The crisis of morale among conscripted women industrial workers and the corresponding male anxiety saw the cinema deal with such issues only indirectly, if at all. The only film to address the problems surrounding women's work, *Millions Like Us*, worked hard to render them invisible. Moreover, with the radical change which took place in female sexual attitudes and the accompanying official 'moral panic', films with government backing had traditional sexual politics. Others used a variety of textual disguises – amnesia, class transference, comedy – as a means of defusing anxiety about women's sexuality. There *was* room within British cinema for the celebration of female pleasure, but it was achieved through covert metaphorical means or via the motifs of gypsyness or history. We can assume that certain types of production context (and not necessarily 'liberal' ones) will give rise to mixed and contradictory texts which can be read positively and indeed were by the female audiences of the period. Historical films in world war two appear to have been the only form which permitted the expression of the female audience's fears about the boundaries of pleasure and moral power.

Class 'substitution' is a common feature in literary and cinematic culture. One class can frequently substitute for another, symbolically speaking, in a text, and an author (or director) can speak on behalf of a class which is not his own. Admittedly, in rare cases, the phenomenon of gender substitution can also be said to exist. Men *can* produce texts which encourage the female reader or audience to address their own potentiality and sexual pleasure – and such texts, which are the result of a rare coincidence of elements, cannot be dismissed as repressive. Although during the war women were largely excluded from the film-making process by a combination of industrial structure, official policy and cultural conditioning, the male progenitors of such films as *The Wicked Lady* or *Lady Hamilton* should be regarded as female 'substitutes', even though they were doubtless motivated partially by cupidity and acquisitiveness.

It is not perhaps too whimsical to imagine that, in some future land where the female principle has gained its proper space and power, medals will be struck to commemorate the artistic achievements of such cultural cross-dressers. In advance of that date, due recognition should be afforded to those wartime artists who produced popular texts which ushered women into the realm of pleasure and self-determination. Such artists may not, alas, have been women. But they were the next best thing.

Notes and References

1. See, for example, Mary Douglas, *Purity and Danger* (London, 1966) and *Implicit Meanings* (London, 1975).
2. Muriel Box, *Odd Woman Out* (London, 1974) pp. 162–78.
3. Interview with Mrs P. Porter in the author's unpublished MA thesis, Polytechnic of Central London, 1982.
4. Sue Harper, 'Art Direction and Costume Design', in S. Aspinall and R. Murphy (eds), *Gainsborough Melodrama* (London, 1983).
5. See, for example, Angela John (ed.), *Unequal Opportunities* (Oxford, 1985); Jane Lewis (ed.), *Labour and Love* (London, 1985); E. Garmarnikow (ed.), *Gender, Class and Work* (London, 1983); Barbara Taylor, *Eve and the New Jerusalem* (London, 1983).
6. Gail Braybon, *Women Workers in the First World War* (London, 1981).
7. Mass Observation (MO), *War begins at home* (London, 1940) p. 5.
8. Penny Summerfield, *Women workers in the Second World War* (London, 1984) pp. 29–31, 62.
9. Ian McLaine, *Ministry of morale* (London, 1979) p. 154.
10. J. B. Priestley, *British women go to war* (London, 1944) p. 37.
11. Ibid., pp. 24, 49.
12. MO, *People in production* (London, 1942) pp. 102, 158–9, 161–2. See also MO's *An Appeal to women* (No. 615, March 1940), *The registration of women* (No. 663, April 1941), *Women and the war effort* (December 1940), *Class and sex differences in morale* (No. 139, May 1940). *A report on female attitudes to compulsion* (No. 919, October 1941) is particularly interesting since it reveals that the majority were against female conscription and were worried about their families. Service life was preferred to munitions in most cases.
13. MO, *People in production* (op. cit.) pp. 180–8; Denise Riley, 'Pronatalism and working mothers', in *History Workshop* 11 (1982); MO, *Day Nurseries* (No. 276, 1941–2).
14. MO, *People in production* (op. cit.) p. 128.
15. Ibid., pp. 151–6, 164–5.
16. Ibid, p. 145.
17. Summerfield, *Women workers* (op. cit.) pp. 55–7. See also I. Holden, *The Night Shift* (London, 1941).
18. Summerfield, *Women workers* (op. cit.) pp. 153–63; MO, *People in production* (op. cit.) pp. 88–9; J. Costello, *Sex, Love and War* (London, 1985) pp. 201–4, 209–10, 363–4; H. Smith, 'The problem of "Equal Pay for Equal Work" in World War II', in *Journal of Modern History*, 53 (1981) 4. Ninety-five per cent of women were in favour of equal pay for equal work; the male percentage was much less. See A. Calder and D. Sheridan (eds), *Speak for yourself: a mass observation anthology* (London, 1984) pp. 183–4.
19. MO 2059, March 1944.
20. Quoted in MO 530, December 1940.
21. Exchange of memoranda between the Ministries of Labour and Health, November–December 1940. PRO, MH (Ministry of Health) 55/1569.

22. Ministry of Labour to Ministry of Health, 24 January 1941 (ibid.).
23. *Daily Herald*, 1 May 1942; *The Times*, 14 March 1942 and 23 March 1942; *Manchester Guardian*, 20 June 1942.
24. PRO LAB 6/183.
25. Memorandum from Minister of Production to Ministry of Labour, 19 December 1942, and report on conference on absenteeism and shopping problems, 8 April 1941 (LAB 26/61).
26. Ministry of Labour memorandum, 2 July 1943 (LAB 25/188).
27. Minutes of evidence to Committee on Women's Services, Welfare and Amenities, 29 May 1942 (LAB 26/63).
28. Undated Ministry of Labour memorandum (probably 1942) (LAB 26/63).
29. Memoranda of 5 October 1941 and 22 September 1945 (LAB 26/26).
30. Minutes of Ministry of Labour conference on concerts in munitions factories, 3 March 1941 (LAB 26/35). See also Ivor Brown, 'This entertainment problem', in *New Statesman*, 7 December 1940 and 12 December 1940.
31. The film had very good reviews. See *The Sunday Times*, 11 April 1943, *Manchester Guardian*, 27 July 1943 and *Observer*, 11 April 1943. All stressed the film's 'authenticity' and 'female angle'. See also J. P. Mayer, *British cinemas and their audiences* (London, 1948) pp. 185, 226, and *Sociology of film* (London, 1946) p. 231.
32. This film had some very bad reviews. See *The Sunday Times*, 30 July 1944 and *New Statesman*, 5 August 1944. The publicity material in the BFI Library predictably concentrated on the class element.
33. It was, however, presented in the publicity material (held in BFI Library) and by critics as having some topicality. See *Evening Standard*, 1 September 1945, *Daily Telegraph*, 3 September 1945, *The Times*, 21 August 1945 and *Observer*, 2 September 1945.
34. This was a star vehicle for Ethel Revnell and Gracie West – 'one an active and the other a passive nit-wit'. See *Monthly Film Bulletin*, September 1943 and *Kine Weekly*, 25 November 1943.
35. The publicity material in the BFI Library suggests that the film be 'sold' via song sheets and the headline 'A song that averted a strike'.
36. Sue Harper, 'The boundaries of hegemony: scriptwriting at Gainsborough in World War II', in F. Barker (ed.), *The politics of theory* (Essex, 1983).
37. Launder to the Screenwriters' Guild, June 1947. This letter was formerly in the files of the Society of Authors which, I am informed, have now been sold.
38. Ministry of Labour to SWA, 1940 (ibid.).
39. Launder to Secretary of Society of Authors, 5 January 1942 (ibid.).
40. Geoff Brown, *Launder and Gilliat* (London, 1977) p. 108.
41. Ibid.
42. Christine Gledhill and Gillian Swanson, 'Gender and sexuality in second world war films – a feminist approach', in G. Hurd (ed.), *National Fictions* (London, 1984); Sue Aspinall, 'Women, realism and reality in British films, 1943–53', in J. Curran and V. Porter (eds), *British Cinema History* (London, 1983); Andrew Higson,

'Britain's outstanding contribution to the film', in Charles Barr (ed.), *All our yesterdays* (London, 1986).

43. Publicity material in BFI Library.
44. *Observer*, 3 October 1943; *New Statesman*, 16 October 1943; *Evening Standard*, 2 October 1943; *Manchester Guardian*, 28 December 1943.
45. *Sunday Times*, 10 October 1943.
46. Ibid.
47. J. P. Mayer, *British cinemas* (op. cit.) p. 169.
48. Ibid., p. 177.
49. Ibid., p. 192.
50. For example, much material on illegitimacy and venereal disease is not available for readers in the Ministry of Health files at the PRO.
51. Costello, *Sex, Love and War* (op. cit.) pp. 316, 29, 14; Raymond Minns, *Bombers and mash: the domestic front 1939–45* (London, 1980) pp. 178–9; A. Calder, *The People's War: Britain 1939–45* (London, 1971) p. 362.
52. Priestley, *British women go to war* (op. cit.) p. 55.
53. Calder and Sheridan, *Speak for yourself* (op. cit.) p. 166.
54. Aspinall in Curran and Porter (op. cit.) p. 286.
55. Calder and Sheridan, *Speak for yourself* (op. cit.) p. 133.
56. Costello *Sex, Love and War* (op. cit.) p. 87.
57. Calder and Sheridan, *Speak for yourself* (op. cit.) p. 134. Cf. p. 194.
58. Costello, *Sex, Love and War* (op. cit.) pp. 311–31; MO, *The Americans* (No. 2222, March 1945).
59. MO, *Changes in clothing habits* (No. 728, June 1941); J. Robinson, *Fashion in the 40s* (London, 1980) p. 25; N. Longmate, *How we lived then* (London, 1971) pp. 250–2.
60. Longmate, *How we lived then* (op. cit.) p. 276.
61. *Picture Post*, 23 September 1944. See also Calder and Sheridan, *Speak for yourself* (op. cit.) p. 145.
62. MO, *Sex, morality and the birthrate* (No. 2206, February 1945). See also MO, *Women in pubs* (No. 1611, February 1943).
63. MO, *What makes a marriage successful?* (No. 1963, November 1943); MO, *Why people marry* (No. 2055, January 1944); MO, *The opposite sex and wartime difficulties* (No. 1210, April 1942); and MO, *Sex, morality and the birthrate* (op. cit.).
64. Costello, *Sex, Love and War* (op. cit.) p. 356.
65. Ibid., p. 82.
66. Ibid., p. 86.
67. In 1939 one in a hundred marriages ended in divorce. In 1945 the figure was five in a hundred.
68. Costello, *Sex, Love and War* (op. cit.) p. 276; Calder, *The People's War* (op. cit.) p. 361; Minns, *Bombers and mash* (op. cit.) pp. 181–2. One third of all births were illegitimate between 1939 and 1945. There were 28 160 illegitimate births in 1938, 64 743 in 1945.
69. MH 55/1506.
70. J. Weeks, *Sex, politics and society: the regulation of sexuality since 1800* (London, 1981) pp. 232–3.
71. Memorandum from the Medical Research Council, October 1943 (MH 58/407).

72. *Hansard*, Vol. 391, No. 90, p. 596.
73. Ibid., pp. 604–5.
74. Ibid., p. 608. See also Ann Scott James, 'Why women don't have babies', in *Picture Post*, 15 November 1943.
75. MO, *Britain and her birthrate* (London, 1945); Len England, 'A British sex survey', in *International Journal of Sexology*, February 1950.
76. Costello, *Sex, Love and War* (op. cit.) p. 82.
77. Ibid., p. 81.
78. MO, *The campaign against VD* (No. 1670, April 1943); MO, *Attitudes to VD* (No. 1573, June 1943).
79. MH 55/1337.
80. Memorandum from the joint committee, 20 July 1943 (MH 55/2325).
81. Ibid.
82. Ibid. See also Costello, *Sex, Love and War* (op. cit.) pp. 329–30.
83. Memorandum from the Home Office and Scottish Home Department on the rehabilitation of young prostitutes, August 1943 (MH 55/2325).
84. Home Office to Ministry of Health, October 1943 (MH 55/2325).
85. Memorandum on joint committee on VD to Ministry of Health, October 1943 (MH 55/2325).
86. Ibid.
87. Lucy Bland & Frank Mort, 'Look out for the good-time girl', in *Formations of Nation and People* (London, 1984) p. 142.
88. BBFC scenario reports, 4 July 1941.
89. Ibid., 18 December 1942.
90. Programme for film propaganda, 1940 (INF 1/867).
91. BFI, *Annual report for 1944*, p. 7; BFI, *Children and the cinema* (London, 1947) p. 9.
92. J. Laver, in *Screen and audience* (undated, but 1946) pp. 33–6.
93. *Chronicle*, 19 November 1945; *The Sunday Times*, 18 November 1945; *Daily Mail*, 16 November 1945; *The Sunday Times*, 17 December 1945; *Dispatch*, 16 November 1945.
94. Reference to Mullins in minutes of committee of management, 10 September 1947 (MH 55/1506).
95. Claude Mullins, 'Marriage à la mode', in *Screen and audience*, undated, p. 37.
96. Muriel Box, *Odd woman out* (London, 1974) pp. 164–5.
97. Ibid., pp. 176–7.
98. Aspinall in Curran and Porter (op. cit.) p. 282.
99. Publicity material held in BFI Library.
100. *Time*, 18 March 1946.
101. *Daily Telegraph*, 24 July 1945; *Daily Herald*, 21 July 1945; *Spectator*, 27 July 1945.
102. Madeleine Mason, unpublished MA dissertation, Polytechnic of Central London, 1984.
103. *Shadowed Eyes* (Savoy, 1939), in which an amnesiac eye surgeon operates on a lawyer who convicted him; *Ten Days in Paris* (Irving Asher productions, 1939), in which an amnesiac working as a chauffeur is mistaken as a spy; *The Girl Who Forgot* (Butchers, 1939), in which a criminal poses as an amnesiac girl's mother; *The Spider*

(Admiral, 1939), which sees a murder attempt on an amnesiac actress; *Dangerous Moonlight* (RKO, 1941), in which a Polish pianist loses his memory after the Battle of Britain; *I'll Walk Beside You* (Butchers, 1943), in which an amnesiac naval officer returns home to find his fiancée engaged; *Twilight Hour* (British National, 1944), in which a noble's amnesiac gardener is really a rich major; *The World Owes Me A Living* (British National, 1945), in which an amnesiac commando regains memory of his own heroism; *Flight from Folly* (Warner Bros./First National, 1945), in which a showgirl cures a playwright of amnesia. In 1946 there was only *Woman to Woman* and *Caravan*.

104.   Freud, *The psychopathology of everyday life* (Penguin, 1966) pp. 37–81.

105.   *Tilly of Bloomsbury* (RKO, 1940), in which a noblewoman objects to her son's love for a boarding-house keeper; *Room for Two* (Hurley, 1940), in which a playboy flirts with a maid; *Fingers* (Warner Bros./First National, 1940), in which an East End 'fence' falls in love with an upper-class girl but finally returns to a sweetheart of his own class; *Kipps* (Twentieth Century Fox, 1941), in which an enriched grocer falls in love out of his own class; *Asking for Trouble* (British National, 1942), in which a bookie poses as a big-game hunter to attract a general's daughter; *There's No Future In It* (Strand Films, 1943), in which a girl's father objects to her love for a bomber pilot; *Strawberry Road* (British National, 1945), in which a farmer weds a showgirl who ruins him.

106.   Aspinall in Curran and Porter (op. cit.) p. 275; Pam Cook, 'Melodrama and the women's picture', in S. Aspinall and R. Murphy (eds), *Gainsborough Melodrama* (London, 1983) p. 24.

107.   'History with frills: the "costume" novel in world war two', in *Red Letters*, 14 (1983).

108.   N. Lee, *Log of a film director* (London, 1949) pp. 34–5; R. J. Minney, *Talking of films* (London, 1947) pp. 4, 35, 43.

109.   Marjorie Lawrence, *Madonna of the Seven Moons* (London, 1931) p. 131.

110.   *Kine Weekly*, 19 April 1945 and 20 December 1945. The film cost £125 000 and its initial profits were £320 000.

111.   The *Madonna* publicity material in the BFI Library proposes a costume competition and the *Caravan* publicity takes the form of a large poster of Granger, frilled, earringed and lipsticked. It is suggested that all usherettes wear gypsy costume.

112.   This is more fully argued in 'Art direction and costume design', in Aspinall and Murphy, *Gainsborough Melodrama* (op. cit.) and in Harper, 'What's in a costume?', in *Monthly Film Bulletin*, October 1985.

113.   Interview with Maurice Carter, cited in Aspinall and Murphy, *Gainsborough Melodrama* (op. cit.) pp. 58–9.

114.   R. C. Sherriff, *No leading lady: an autobiography* (London, 1968) p. 321.

115.   E. Betts, *The film business*, p. 152; M. Korda, *Charmed lives* (London,

1980) pp. 147–9, 155–6; K. Kulik, *Alexander Korda: the man who could work miracles*, pp. 249, 254–6.

116.   US Senate, 77th Congress, 1st session. Senate resolution 152 (9–26 September 1941). Senate library vol. 684.

117.   Korda, *Charmed lives* (op. cit.) pp. 153–5; Kulik (op. cit.) pp. 251–3.

118.   L. Olivier, *Confessions of an actor* (London, 1982) p. 91.

119.   L. Hirsch, *Laurence Olivier* (Boston, 1979) p. 55; Kulik, *Alexander Korda* (op. cit.) p. 246.

120.   The film appeared high on *Kine Weekly*'s best-seller list. It had good reviews from the trade papers (*Kine Weekly*, 12 June 1941; *Today's Cinema*, 11 June 1941) but poor reviews from the following: *Monthly Film Bulletin*, 18, No. 91, p. 85; *Spectator*, 8 August 1941; *Observer*, 3 August 1941; *Sight and Sound*, Autumn 1941, p. 54.

121.   R. C. Sherriff, 'Writing for the films', in *Uncommon pleasures* (London, 1949) p. 22.

122.   There is extensive material on this film in the Mass Observation archive.

123.   I often did beguile her of her tears
When I did speak of some distressful stroke
That my youth had suffered . . .
She loved me for the dangers I had passed,
And I loved her that she did pity them.
                    Othello, Act I, scene 3

124.   One of the few examples is Michael Wasey, 'The influence of Alexander Korda, inspirer of intelligent films', in *Millgate Monthly*, April 1936. This was a Co-operative Society journal and quite left wing.

125.   A. Aldgate and J. Richards, *Britain Can Take It* (Oxford, 1985) pp. 198–9.

126.   J. Ellis, 'Made in Ealing', in *Screen*, 16, No. 1, p. 94; V. Porter, 'The context of creativity: Ealing studios and Hammer films', in Curran and Porter (op. cit.) p. 183; Charles Barr, *Ealing studios* (London, 1977) pp. 6, 44; Sue Harper, 'History in film: two British studios 1942–7', in D. W. Ellwood (ed.), *Studies in history, film and society* (Copenhagen, 1985).

127.   Harper, 'What's in a costume?', in *Monthly Film Bulletin* (op. cit.).

128.   On the costing of *The Bad Lord Byron* and *The Man in Grey* see *Daily Herald*, 2 March 1948, and *Kine Weekly*, 19 April 1945. See also Alan Woods, *Mr Rank* (London, 1952) p. 147.

129.   *Kine Weekly*, 19 April 1945; Minney, *Talking of films* (op. cit.) p. 16.

130.   *Kine Weekly*, 19 April 1945; Minney, *Talking of films*, p. 77.

131.   B. Woodhouse, *From script to screen* (London, 1947) pp. 63–4, and interviews with Bill Salter and Denis Mason in Aspinall and Murphy, *Gainsborough Melodrama* (op. cit.).

132.   Ibid., and interview with Maurice Carter in ibid.

133.   Salter interview, ibid.

134.   MO, *London Town Survey*, Box 15.

135.   Mayer, *British cinemas* (op. cit.) p. 8.

136.   B. Kesterton, 'The social and emotional effects of the recreational

film on adolescents of 13 and 14 years of age in the West Bromwich area', in *British Journal of Educational Psychology*, 19 (1949).

137. K. Box, *The Cinema and the public* (London, 1946) in MO 2429; L. Moss and K. Box, *Wartime survey: the cinema audience* (London, 1943) in MO 1871.

138. *Kine Weekly*, 14 January 1943; *Bernstein Film Questionnaire* (op. cit.) p. 9.

139. As evinced in the Mass Observation material on *Let George Do It*.

140. MO, *Report on film themes*, 17 March 1940.

141. In November 1943 it was asked: 'What films have you liked best in the past year? Please list order of liking.' The question was not a priority, but the last of six, which should be taken into account. The sample was 104 men and 18 women. MO archivists are unable to account for this imbalance.

142. Mayer, *British cinemas* (op. cit.) p. 41.

143. Ibid., p. 49.

144. Ibid., p. 192.

145. Kesterton, in *British Journal of Educational Psychology* (op. cit.) p. 72.

146. Mayer, *British cinemas* (op. cit.) p. 26.

147. Ibid., pp. 8, 22, 184; J. P. Mayer, *Sociology of film* (London, 1946) pp. 183, 216. On sets, see Mayer, *British cinemas* (op. cit.) pp. 189, 214, 234.

148. Mayer, *British cinemas* (op. cit.) p. 73.

149. Mayer, *Sociology of film* (op. cit.) pp. 92, 161, 166, 169, 174, 179.

150. Ibid., pp. 201–2, 213, 217.

151. W. D. Wall and W. A. Simpson, 'The Film Choices of Adolescents', in *British Journal of Educational Psychology*, June 1949, pp. 121–36.

152. Kesterton, in *British Journal of Educational Psychology* (op. cit.) p. 99.

153. Ibid., pp. 257–8.

154. Woods, *Mr Rank* (op. cit.).

155. *Kine Weekly* report of 1947 box-office favourites.

Index